This book was written for Christians.
If you are not one, go to Appendix A
now!

Authors Note: If you are reading this book as an eBook on a device that is connected to the internet, the URLs are "hot." Click on a URL in this book and the internet will take you to that website. The next page is a hot URL that takes you to my website for a quick way to get a brief overview of this book.

SpiritualAmbush.org

The

SPIRITUAL AMBUSH

Facing Spiritual Challenges in the Workplace

James M. Croushorn, D.P.A., M.P.A., M.S.W.

Spiritual Jungle Publishing
Tallahassee, Florida

Cover Design by Bonnie Mutchler
(https://bonniemutchlercovers.wordpress.com)
Author's Review: Outstanding! Bonnie was very professional, responsive, artistic, and affordable. She is 5 stars!

The image of Papyri P52 is used by permission of the Reylands Library, University of Manchester, England. Copyright of The University of Manchester. It appears on page 82 of this book.

The publishers of the Biblical Archaeology Review (BAR) have generously given permission to use the text of the sidebar from the BAR on page 65 of the March/April 2015 (Vol 41 No 2). It appears on page 82 of this book.

Scripture quotations marked NIV are taken from:

NIV.✚

THE HOLY BIBLE, NEW INTERNATIONAL VERSION®, NIV®
Copyright © 1973, 1978, 1984, 2011 by Biblica, Inc.®
Used by Permission of Biblica, Inc.® All rights reserved worldwide. The NIV permission allows up to 500 verses. There are 387 verses included in this book from the NIV.

"Messianic Prophecies of the Old Testament"
Used by permission Holman *Illustrated Bible Dictionary* (pp. 112, 113, 114). (2003) Holman Bible Publishers. Nashville, TN. This copyrighted material appears in Appendix J beginning on page 265 of this book.

Excerpt(s), "The Parable of the First Supper," from *Decision Making and the Will of God: A Biblical Alternative to the Traditional View* by Garry Friesen, copyright © 1984, 1999, 2000

1st Printing (CS-Final-011916(6X9)22.docx) (200) 1/25/16

TABLE OF CONTENTS

Acknowledgements

Struggling with the issues presented by this book for my entire adult life would have been impossible without friends and family who are loving and tolerant. I've always lived Dr. Seuss' great insight about behavior: *"Be who you are and say what you feel, because those who mind don't matter, and those who matter don't mind."* There have been a lot of people in my life that matter who have had great patience and love and let me talk out my ideas, and talk and talk and talk. Many have pushed back and challenged my ideas, but in the end all of that helped me hone the words that I have written here.

At the age of 76 I am pleased to acknowledge people and organizations that have had significant influence on the ideas in this book and the production of this book.

Let me start with several organizations that made this book possible. Create Space and Kindle Direct Publish are Amazon companies. Create Space is a printing company: (https://www.createspace.com/Products/Book/). I was able to submit my manuscript as a PDF file to their on-line system and they were able to print a book at a very reasonable price. Their technical support was very professional and available 24/7. If I asked them to call me, my telephone rang in 2 seconds from the time I hit return. Kindle Direct Publishing (KDP) is an eBook creator and distributor: (https://kdp.amazon.com/help?topicId=A3R2IZDC42DJW6).
Create space sent my PDF file to KDP. KDP produced an eBook and placed it on Amazon. They also had extraordinary technical support. Another company that made this book possible was Microsoft. I subscribed to Office 365: (https://products.office.com/en-US/?legRedir=default&CorrelationId=4bb542a2-354b-4d32-a46f-23bd739f2891). Their Technical Support comes from the Philippines. The Techs are amazing. They speak excellent English and via a "screen share" helped me format the manuscript with powerful tools I did not know Word had.

Among people I credit are a bunch of Baptist pastors that include Rev. Thomas Manzell, Dr. Doug Dortch, Dr. Bill Shiell, Rev. Josh Hall, and none more important than Rev. Fran Buhler.

Chapter 5 came from interviews with Christian laymen/laywomen. These were first recorded in my book, "The Jungle: Spiritual Danger Areas in the World of Work," published in 2002. Among those I interviewed were Jim Barger, Ken Boutwell, Jim and Shirley Eikeland, Virgina Glass, Larry Gonzales, Amalia Kane-Crawford, Dr. Senyoni Musingo, Jack Nix, Howard Rhodes, Dr. Gene Sherron, Ellen Williams, Mark Wodka and Doug Woodlief.

A whole host of friends have been extremely helpful, none more than Dr. Dwight and Kay Anderson and Dr. Don and Ruth Ann Nast. This host includes many friends from my 37 years as a member of First Baptist Church of Tallahassee.

I am also indebted to Rabbi Jack Romberg of Temple Israel in Tallahassee, a Hebrew scholar with great integrity and commitment to discovering and sharing the truths of the Hebrew Bible. Four years of "Lunch and Learn with Rabbi Romberg" every Wednesday at noon, a class that includes members of the Temple Israel congregation and Christians from a number of Tallahassee churches, has been invaluable. Many have become great friends. They have helped me better understand the Hebrew Bible and my Jewish heritage.

A unique contribution came from Jordan Gabriel Mallory, M.Div. May 2014 from the George W. Truett Theological Seminary at Baylor University. Jordan did a "Theological Review" of the manuscript to identify statements and conclusions I present to help me determine the degree to which they were supported by scripture. I did not always apply his informed recommendations and take full responsibility for the "theology" found in this book.

In May of 2014, I attended the Blue Ridge Mountain Christian Writer's Conference at Ridgecrest, North Carolina. As part of the program I was able to have the first 30 pages of this manuscript submitted for a critique. The faculty member that did my critique was Dr. Dennis Hensley, Director of Taylor University's professional writing program (https://www.taylor.edu/employee/deptHead/dennis-hensley). He said I needed to add 50 pages and have the manuscript "professionally" edited. I subsequently contracted with Dr. Hensley to edit the manuscript. After two months I called Dr. Hensley and asked when he might return my edited manuscript. He said, "Well sir, it is taking me a lot longer than I had planned, but when I am finished you will be able to present it to any publisher as an edited manuscript." I am sure he felt he was working on a manuscript from his freshman writing class. I learned so much from his editing. Dr. Hensley's editing is reflected in this manuscript but I take full responsibility for the liberties in style and deviations from Dr. Hensley's work.

Survival would have been impossible for me during the past 47 years without my very patient, trusting and tolerant wife, Linda June Barron of Troy, Alabama. She has always been beautiful from the day I met her at Dawson Memorial Baptist Church in Birmingham in 1968. She has had a quiet and gentle manner that allowed me to be me. Her faith and relationship with God has always been an inspiration. This book would have never happened without her presence. Our children, Amy, an entrepreneur and website designer, and John, a ER doctor in Birmingham, and their families have been a great joy and support because of their competent and creative handling of life's challenges. It has been fun for me and Linda to watch their accomplishments.

And my greatest acknowledgement of influence is that of God Almighty, His Son and Holy Spirit. I have been slow to realize their presence and nudging in my life challenges, but now can recognize their influence in my daily life in real ways. I think I hear them saying, "Well, it is about time!"

Dedication

I have warmed by fires I have not built.
I have drunk from wells I have not dug.
(Author Unknown)

Thank you God for all of the spiritual warriors who have fought the good fight in the past so that the spiritual warriors of today may build on their courageous struggle.

Preface

Simon Sinek, a professor of communications at Columbia University and adjunct staff member of the RAND Corporation, wrote a book in 2011 titled, *Start with Why: How Great Leaders Inspire Everyone to Take Action.* His simple but powerful discovery is that those people that have great impact with their endeavors are those that focus on the "why" of what they do instead of the "how" or the "what." People from Steve Jobs to Martin Luther King connected with people because people related to the "why" they were doing what they were doing. In the hope that the reader will connect with the contents of this book. I want to tell you "why" it has been written.

A Christian layman needs to know and accept that his job, what he gets paid for by an employer, is just as legitimate a calling from God, as is that of a person to the ministry. The layman's job is not ministry. The layman's ministry to those in his workplace is different from his paid job and should never be done "on the clock."

The Church is rightfully focused on evangelism of the lost and service and support to believers and the never-believers. But the Church is failing to explicitly prepare the layman for what he faces on Monday morning. Beyond being taught how to evangelize the world, the Christian layman also needs preaching and teaching that will prepare him to deal with power encounters with the dark forces of Ephesians 6 that he faces in the workplace on Monday morning.

These reasons are scriptural and **why** I wrote *The Spiritual Ambush.*

Introduction

Below freezing. Uncomfortable. Lying prone on the ground, hidden from the full moon by the shadows of the underbrush at the tree line. Glad to be there with my rifle pointed at the dirt road 20 feet below and 30 yards out. There were nine of us in the ambush party. Silently waiting. Waiting and hoping the North Koreans would show up in our kill zone. The same North Koreans who had ambushed and killed six of our 2nd Infantry Division soldiers in the DMZ just three weeks earlier. [1]

The ambush is a deadly weapon of war. Efficient, effective and lethal, so much so, that after a defeat at the hands of the City of Ai, God told Joshua to use an ambush:

> *"Listen carefully. You are to set an ambush behind the city. Do not go very far from it. All of you be on the alert" (Joshua 8:4 NIV).*

I was involved in one real ambush in the Korean DMZ in 1966, and several dozen ambushes in training exercises at the U.S. Army Ranger School, Infantry Officer Candidate School, and the 20th Special Forces. I know when you are caught in a physical ambush the shock and surprise is absolutely breathtaking and disorienting.

From personal experience I can tell you, the same is true when you are caught in a spiritual ambush. The Army Ranger response to physical ambushes is used here as a metaphor for how Christians can confront spiritual ambushes in the workplace.

In a physical war the impact of an ambush can turn the tide of battle. A *spiritual* ambush can have the same impact on Christians when the dark forces of Ephesians 6 confront us. I believe this is why the Bible cautions Christians to be alert to enemy attacks even after they have donned their spiritual armor:

> ***Be alert** and of sober mind. Your enemy the devil prowls around like a roaring lion looking for someone to devour (1 Peter 5:8 NIV).*
>
> *And pray in the Spirit on all occasions with all kinds of prayers and requests. With this in mind, **be alert** and always keep on praying for all the Lord's people (Ephesians 6:18 NIV).*
>
> ***Be on your guard**; stand firm in the faith; be courageous; be strong (1 Corinthians 16:13 NIV).*

To me, scriptures caution us to be alert because an ambush requires action. All acts of faith require behavior. When a Christian learns to be alert for the "roaring lion" and then has a surprise encounter with him, the question becomes, "now what?"

The Christian has very strong resources for these situations. They are the presence of the Holy Spirit and their own holiness. I believe the presence of the Holy Spirit is directly related to the degree that we are holy. We are all called to be holy: *Consecrate yourselves and be holy, because I am holy* (Leviticus 11:44 NIV).

So how does the Christian become more holy (sanctified, righteous)? I have found that more holiness may occur as a result of two things. One is that we must read and know the Bible. Jerry Bridges, author of *The Pursuit of Holiness* has stated, "I don't know that reading the Bible will make one holy, but I have never known a holy person that did not read their Bible daily."[2] The second comes from my behaviorist orientation to emotional and spiritual development. Some of this is captured in Henri Nouwen's quote: "You don't think your way into a new kind of living. You live your way into a new kind of thinking."[3] I have found that I can move toward holiness by doing holy things, e.g., helping others in need, visiting and helping the sick, following Christian values in relations and interactions with others even when it goes against my own best interest. These acts of living my faith change my thinking and my spiritual orientation toward life. By doing them I become more holy.

Some Christians have told me they are not concerned about the "now what?" moments. They get right with God in their morning prayer time, and their holiness alone protects them throughout the day, just as Jesus' holiness protected him during the temptations in the wilderness.

If you are as holy as Jesus, you will be protected. If you are as holy as Jesus, you do not have to be concerned about ambushes by the roaring lion. However, on this side of heaven, Christians will never be 100% holy. Holiness is necessary, but not sufficient alone to win spiritual battles. We must prepare ourselves for the spiritual challenges, the "now what?" moments in our workplace, or in fact, anywhere.

I always wanted to write a book on the Christian in the world of work. I chose the workplace as the venue for my study because I, as other laymen, spend so much of my waking hours in the workplace, and the Church and its ministers have largely ignored what the layman faces on Monday morning. Many preachers, with no work experience away from the Church, have no clue as to what laymen face in the workplace. The work organizations that employ ministers are Christian. That is, for the most part the people that are in the minister's work organizations are Christian. This is not true for their lay members. Many of our pastors and churches focus only on evangelism of the "lost" world. This is the focus of the New Testament and should be the primary focus of the Church. However, at the same time Christians are being gobbled up by the dark forces of Ephesians 6 in the workplace Monday through Friday. The Church can do more to prepare and equip those Christians for what they face on Monday morning!

Every time I tried to write that book about the Christian in the world of work, it always came out, "just go be a good Christian." But through the years as an employee of universities, state governments, not-for-profit organizations and the military I have observed a lot of "good Christians" get in trouble in the workplace. They are blindsided, surprised, and unexpectedly engulfed in destructive "non-Christian" behavior. They are ambushed! In discussing my ideas with a friend he stated, "It really is a jungle out there!"

That reference to a jungle prompted a whole range of thoughts from my Army experience. Particularly from the Army's Ranger School. The Ranger School not only teaches you how to be a better soldier, but they teach you about the jungle they are going to put you in. A hostile jungle has many dangerous places for a soldier; i.e., roads, trails, mountain ridges, open areas and streams. These are dangerous because this is where the enemy sets up ambushes, because the enemy knows that soldiers like to take the "easy path" through the jungle.

It is often the "easy path" that Christians take in their work life that makes them vulnerable to "spiritual ambushes." To get a handle on these "spiritual ambushes," I interviewed Christians and asked them to tell me about the spiritual challenges they had faced in the workplace, how did they recognize them, and what did they do. This book is about what they told me and how I have applied my Ranger training to help Christians counter spiritual ambushes. Before you are introduced to my research in Chapter 5, you need to understand:

What is Spiritual Warfare?
What is a Spiritual Warrior?
What is the Spiritual Warrior's Global Positioning System?
What is the Spiritual Warrior's Battlefield?

Notes

1. On Haynes' first night at the Demilitarized Zone, North Korean forces launched a pre-dawn ambush on a 2ID patrol that killed six Americans and one South Korean soldier just a half-mile south of the heavily patrolled border. A seventh American was wounded, accessed August 10, 2015.
   http://www.stripes.com/news/pacific/veterans-return-to-south-korea-to-mark-2id-anniversary-1.355687.

2. From an email from Jerry Bridges, author of *The Pursuit of Holiness* (Colorado Springs: NavPress, 1985), on September 14, 2010: "As to the quote you attribute to me, I do not remember making it. It was probably an extemporaneous thought in the course of a message that was given. Feel free to use it either with or without crediting it to me. Cordially in Christ, Jerry Bridges"

3. Henri J. M. Nouwen, https://www.goodreads.com/quotes/179153-you-don-t-think-your-way-into-a-new-kind-of (Accessed November 6, 2015).

Chapter 1: What is Spiritual Warfare?

This chapter will help you identify what spiritual battle you are fighting and thus help you avoid some of the fog of war. You will learn that there are four categories of spiritual warfare, and within the Classical Model there are three types. This book will help the reader with Type 3, Counter-Terrorism Spiritual Warfare.

Introduction

You will not find the words "spiritual warfare" in the Bible. However, if we define "spiritual warfare" as "power encounters" between God and Satan, the Bible is saturated with spiritual warfare.[1]

"Spiritual warfare is a pastoral, theological term for describing the moral conflict of the Christian life. It is a metaphor for our lifelong struggle with our lies and other liars, our lust and other tempters, our sins and other evildoers, the present darkness that continually unsettles us."[2]

Categories of Spiritual Warfare

The engagement in spiritual warfare today falls into four categories:

1. Confronting evil and worldliness found in societal institutions (World System Model)[3]
2. Confronting the devil as a purposeful, intelligent, malevolent personal agent (Classical Model)[4]
3. Confronting demons that are in an unbeliever or oppressing a believer (Ground-Level Deliverance Model)[5]
4. Confronting territorial demons (Strategic-Level Deliverance Model)[6]

Each model is developed in a book edited by Beilby and Eddy, *Understanding Spiritual Warfare: Four Views* (see review in Appendix C, page 222). Proponents engaged in each ministry wrote an essay that was critiqued by the other three contributors.

In the World System Model, Satan is not presented as a standalone entity exercising discretion and independence from God, but only as evil and worldliness expressed in societal institutions. The Christian can counter these forces through intercessory prayer.

The Classical Model emphasizes that Satan is not some "metaphor for human darkness, reducible to psychological or sociocultural forces." He is a person, the malevolent personal agent described in Ephesians 6:10-22.

This is the model of spiritual warfare used most in this book, *The Spiritual Ambush*. I believe Satan is alive and well and very much active today. However, it is my experience that he does not reveal himself as a specific entity in manifestations in society, but that he often uses people and events to activate his will. It is those actions that cause "spiritual ambushes" of spiritual warriors. It is the intent of this book to equip the spiritual warrior with information to counter the surprise actions of Satan.

The Ground-Level Deliverance Model is the practice of deliverance ministry that involves breaking demonic influences in an individual. It occurs on a personal level. This model assumes that demons can possess, be inside, a non-Christian. Demons can oppress Christians but not possess them. Christians can be "demonized" when they wallow in sinful behavior.

The Strategic-Level Deliverance Model requires power confrontations with high-ranking principalities and powers, as Paul described in Ephesians 6:12. These demonic entities are assigned to geographical territories and social networks. They are also referred to as territorial spirits. Their assignment is to keep large numbers of humans, networked through cities or any other form of social institutions, in spiritual captivity. There are no incidences of Strategic-Level Deliverances in the New Testament. Some writers warn that we are on dangerous ground when we move too far from real situations of that day described in the Scriptures to extrapolate lessons for today.

Books on Spiritual Warfare

On October 23, 2013 there were 18,525 books listed under "spiritual warfare" on Amazon.com. I have developed a synopsis and critique for each of the top ten bestsellers in order to understand the broader discussion of spiritual warfare in the Christian community and to help the reader understand just how this book fits into that discussion (see Appendix B, page 173). (Note: on December 1, 2015 there were 26,091 spiritual warfare books listed on Amazon. Four of the top 10 sellers on 10/23/13 were still among the top ten on 11/1/15. Those four are *Spiritual Warfare: Christians, Demonization and Deliverance by* Karl Payne, *Spiritual Warfare by* Jerry Rankin, *Spiritual Warfare: Fighting Demons by* Scott Meade, and *The Invisible War: What every Believer Needs to Know About Satan, Demons, and Spiritual Warfare by* Chip Ingram.)

Ministers wrote nine of these books. (Note: In my opinion, one of the ten books, Meade, *Spiritual Warfare: Fighting Demons*, is fiction and will not be discussed further. See Appendix B, page 185, Bestseller #4). I have identified five key attributes of each book in Appendix B:

1. The Model of Deliverance
2. Authors' Position on Demon Possession
3. The Emphasis on Staying Alert
4. The Use of Isaiah 14:12 to Identify Characteristics of Satan
5. Missionary Experience of Author and/or Exposure to the Non-Western Worldview Where There is Syncretism ("the amalgamation or attempted amalgamation of different religions, cultures, or schools of thought," from the Oxford Dictionary).

1. The Model of Deliverance

Four of the authors advocate the Ground-Level Deliverance Model. Four of the authors advocate the Classical Model. One author, Sherman (Bestseller #5), advocates for all four models. Warner (Bestseller #9) advocates for ground-level and strategic-level deliverance.

2. Authors' Positions on Demon Possession

None of the nine authors believes that a demon can possess a Christian, but three believe that non-believers can be possessed, and their ministries are directed at excising the demon from the non-believer. Dr. Ed Murphy states,

> "Can a true believer be demonized? Note that I am speaking not of demon possession, but of demonization. Possession implies ownership and total control. Christians, even disobedient ones belong to God, not to Satan. Thus, Satan cannot control them totally. Demonization is a different matter, however. By demonization I mean that Satan, through his demons, exercises direct, partial control over an area or areas of the life of a Christian or non-Christian."[7]

In a recent book on spiritual warfare Borgman and Ventura makes the point that the "devil's influence on the Christian is primarily deceptive scheming and trickery, not indwelling and controlling."[8] In my opinion, recognizing that the devil can "influence" a Christian is more helpful than saying that they are "demonized."

3. The Emphasis on Staying Alert

Three authors speak to the importance of being alert for the "roaring lion" but do not tell you how being alert can help you in the battle, which is the main goal of *The Spiritual Ambush*. The books reviewed are all about the theology of spiritual warfare. In contrast, *The Spiritual Ambush* is about your behavior when you are "spiritually ambushed." The author is not a minister but an Army Ranger with 35 years of spiritual warfare experience as an employee of universities, state government, and the United States Army.

4. The Use of Isaiah 14:12 to Identify Characteristics of Satan

This is an important attribute to identify because, in my opinion, those authors that use this verse or use the word Lucifer to talk about Satan are outside the generally accepted interpretation of biblical scholarship. Biblical scholars have concluded that this verse is referring to the king of Babylon, not to Satan. The King James Version states, "How art thou fallen from heaven, O Lucifer, son of the morning! How art thou cut down to the ground, which didst weaken the nations!"

The Hebrew and English translations that are accepted as "good translations" render this verse as:

> *How art thou fallen from heaven, O day-star, son of the morning! How art thou cut down to the ground, that didst cast lots over the nations* (ASV).
>
> *How you have fallen from heaven, morning star, son of the dawn! You have been cast down to the earth, you who once laid low the nations* (NIV).

Six of the authors do not invoke the name of Lucifer or this verse in order to identify attributes of Satan. However, three do. It is my opinion that using Lucifer from this verse undermines their credibility in exegesis of other verses.

5. Missionary Experience of Author and/or Exposure to the Non-Western Worldview Where There is Syncretism

The Oxford Dictionary defines syncretism as "the amalgamation or attempted amalgamation of different religions, cultures, or schools of thought." Murphy warns that syncretism permeates the worldview of the non-western world. "Syncretism is not only warfare with evil supernaturalism; it is also warfare with the world." [9] After teaching and training Christian leaders in Africa, Murphy quoted an anonymous source: "The church of Africa is like a river a mile wide but only an inch deep."

Murphy stated, "I was compelled to teach over and over again from Joshua 24:14-23, where Joshua challenged God's people to make the decision whom they were going to serve, the true God or the no-gods (Gal. 4:8)."[9]

Four authors have experience as missionaries or teachers of missionaries. All point out how much more demonic activity there is in non-Western countries. Some of this comes from the differences in worldview. The Western worldview makes a distinction between the natural and the supernatural world. The non-Western worldview does not. It is the difference between a society that accepts an objective, scientific view of nature and one that sees the supernatural in all things. There are many stories from the mission field about manifestations of demons. I believe that the writers of these nine best selling books that have been involved in mission work in cultures that have "non-western" world views are more prone to see demons in people and events.

The World, the Flesh, and Satan

The authors of the books reviewed write in various ways about the three major threats the spiritual warrior faces: the world, the flesh, and Satan. The first time these three spiritual challenges were clustered together in a published document was in the 1564 Common Book of Prayer.[10]

Payne, an advocate of the Ground-Level Deliverance Model (See Appendix B, page 175, Bestseller #1) states, "The world, the flesh, and the devil are each real, and each represents one third of the spiritual warfare pie that Christians must learn to recognize and confront. Demonic or supernatural warfare represents only one third of the battle we face as soldiers of Christ."[11]

Much of these nine books concern demon possession, demon oppression, and deliverance from demons. Frangipane, an advocate of the Classical Model of spiritual warfare, states," ...many of our problems and oppressions are not demonic but fleshly in nature."[12] "We are not talking about 'spirit-possession.' I do not believe that a Christian can be possessed, for when a person is 'possessed' by a demon, that demon fills their spirit the way the Holy Spirit fills the spirit of a Christian. However, I believe Christians can be oppressed by demons, which can occupy unregenerate thought-systems, especially if those thoughts are defended by self-deception or false doctrines! The thought, 'I cannot have a demon because I am a Christian,' is simply untrue. A demon cannot have you in an eternal, possessive sense, but refusing to repent of your sympathetic thoughts toward evil can be a demon. Your rebellion toward God provides a place for the devil in your life."[13]

The *Spiritual Ambush* focuses on a very narrow element of the Classical Model of Deliverance how to focus on being alert and how to react on the spiritual battlefield when your alertness makes you aware of a surprise attack by the "dark forces" of Ephesians 6.

Sin: The Object of Spiritual Warfare

For the Christian, spiritual warfare is about sin. The roaring lion wants the Christian to do it. The Christian is fighting not to do it. That fact alone is not very helpful to the Christian engaged in the heat of the battle. To be successful in this war, the Christian needs to understand the battlefield and the devil's schemes.

Sin is not homogeneous. Sinners are not homogeneous. Spiritual warfare is not homogeneous. The more precisely we can parse each, the more effective we will be in conducting spiritual warfare. Let us fight the correct battle and not be distracted by the noise of war. Let us start with sin.

In the Beginning, there was no sin.

> *Then God said, "Let us make mankind in our image, in our likeness, so that they may rule over the fish in the sea and the birds in the sky, over the livestock and all the wild animals, and over all the creatures that move along the ground." So God created mankind in his own image, in the image of God he created them; male and female he created them* (Genesis 1:26 - 27 NIV).

God then put man in the Garden of Eden:

> *Now the LORD God had planted a garden in the east, in Eden; and there he put the man he had formed* (Genesis 2:8 NIV).

But God's presence was not constant for man:

> *Then the man and his wife heard the sound of the LORD God as he was walking in the garden in the cool of the day, and they hid from the LORD God among the trees of the garden* (Genesis 3:8 NIV).

Sin was man's doing. He exercised his own free will and chose to disobey God. Note that the idea of disobeying God was introduced to man by the serpent **when God was not present**.

Now the serpent was more crafty than any of the wild animals the LORD God had made. He said to the woman, "Did God really say, 'You must not eat from any tree in the garden' (Genesis 3:1 NIV).

When God discovered that man had sinned, God banished man from Eden.

So the LORD God banished him from the Garden of Eden to work the ground from which he had been taken. After he drove the man out, he placed on the east side of the Garden of Eden cherubim and a flaming sword flashing back and forth to guard the way to the tree of life (Genesis 3: 24-25 NIV).

This is not what God wanted! It is not what God planned! I asked my son John, "Would we still be in the Garden of Eden if man had not sinned (disobeyed God)?" He replied, "Probably, and there would probably only be two of us, and we would be wandering about naked." I think John is right.

It appears that all God ever wanted in a relationship with man was to have him in Eden so that he could visit him periodically in the evening.

The "fall" did not change man's character; it changed his location. Man does not have a character that is intrinsically sinful; after all, he was made in the image of God. God Himself announced His creation to be "very good". It is my opinion that the first sin did not distort or change the character of this wonderful creation made in God's image.

However, with this act to disobey God, we now have sin in the world. This is the first sin. This original sin resulted in the "fall of man." So, lets explore the character of people born today. (Children before the age of accountability are an exception.) Every man born into the world today is made in the image of God with free will but without the presence of God. He is made in that same godly image as Adam, which God found to be "good, very good." We are Adam!

God declared that the creation of man was good (Gen 1:31). Although made in God's image and being a "good creation," non-Christians (never-believers) live continually outside the presence of God. There is nothing the never-believer can do to make himself more away from God's presence.

To restate my point made above, Adam did not change when he left Eden. There is nothing in the Scripture that says that Adam's soul or character changed, or that something changed in him that made him not want to obey God. It was not his character that changed but his location. Man was moved from paradise to the real world, a very difficult real world.

Man East of Eden was the same man as he was when he was in Eden, except God did not visit him regularly. Once he left Eden, Adam was without God's presence. Original sin removed man from God's presence. Sin happens when God is not present. When God is not present, the never-believer is not compelled to sin any more than the Christian.

By Genesis 6, man - without God's presence and exercising his "free will" was "out of control:"

> *"The LORD saw how great the wickedness of the human race had become on the earth, and that every inclination of the thoughts of the human heart was only evil all the time. The LORD regretted that he had made human beings on the earth, and his heart was deeply troubled"* (Genesis 6:5-6 NIV).

God killed all but eight of the humans with the flood. God's first experiment with humankind failed! It turns my stomach to say that, because it is so contrary to the God I grew up with and was preached and taught about. When I read this statement to a friend, he asked, "Why would you say that?" I told my friend that I needed to say this because it is the truth revealed in the Bible. The spiritual warrior must be brutally honest about what he sees, hears, and does on the battlefield. Our behavior must be based on reality, not myths. The Christian must be free of myths, including myths about God.

These eight were Noah and his family.

> *"But Noah found favor in the eyes of the LORD."* (Genesis 6:8 NIV).

> *The LORD then said to Noah,* "Go into the Ark, you and your whole family, because I have found you righteous in this generation." (Genesis 7:1 NIV).

Noah and his family were the exception to the rule. They found grace and righteousness in spite of God's absence. How about that! It could be done East of Eden, but it didn't happen very often.

There is no indication in the Scripture that the Flood changed the character of man. Humankind after the flood had the same character as Adam and Eve after they were driven from Eden. Man was once again headed for a sin-filled world.

Types of Spiritual Warfare

This book, *The Spiritual Ambush*, fits into the Classical Model as described by Beilby and Eddy. The Bible tells us about three "types" of spiritual warfare within the Classical Model. I have named them Universal (Global) Spiritual Warfare, Personal (Internal) Spiritual Warfare, and Counter Terrorism (External) Spiritual Warfare.

Type 1: Universal Spiritual Warfare

There is spiritual warfare that is global and universal. This type of warfare has been going on between God and Satan since the beginning of time. It is the universal struggle of good with evil. It began in the Garden of Eden and resulted in "Original Sin" (Genesis 3). The devil won that battle! But God won the war with the death and resurrection of Jesus Christ:

> "*I have told you these things, so that in me you may have peace. In this world you will have trouble. But take heart! I have overcome the world*" (John 16:33 NIV).

I will call this spiritual warfare Type 1 Universal Spiritual Warfare. The universal battle of Type 1 Spiritual Warfare continues today. The battleground is the "lost souls" of humankind living outside the presence of God. It is not so much that men in this state belong to the devil. It is that they do not belong to God; they are not in God's presence. Man in this state still has a soul that is made in God's image, which explains the many kind and good acts of non-Christians.

Non-Christians do not belong to the devil. The devil does not live inside these souls. That is good enough for the devil. The devil wants God to leave man untouched, for he knows if man with his free will is left in the devil's presence, it is only a matter of time before man will choose behavior that will continue to keep man from God. So, the devil says to God, "Hands off." Warner quotes C.S. Lewis on this point: "There are two equal and opposite extremes into which our race can fall about the devils (demons). One is to disbelieve in their existence. The other is to believe, and to feel an excessive and unhealthy interest in them. They themselves are equally pleased by both errors and hail a materialist or a magician with the same delight."[14] Evangelism is the Christian's tool to compete for lost souls.

In the beginning, 100% of the people were God's people. After Genesis 3, 100% of the people were not God's people. They lived outside the presence of God. We continue to lose this war to the devil. The U.S. Census Bureau's PopClock Projection estimates that on July 1, 2006, the population of the Earth was 6,525,486,603. Of these 6.5 billion people, 33% were Christians (2,153,410,579). [15]

Although Christians are the largest religious group, an estimated 4.5 billion people are not Christian. It is interesting to note that 19% of the population is Muslim and growing, and 13 percent is Hindu and stable. The percentage of Christians is dropping. Only 14.5 million claim Judaism as their religion, which is less than one percent of the world's population.

In Type 1 Universal Spiritual Warfare, both the devil and sin are present. Both Christians and non-Christians are involved. This book will not help you with Type 1 Universal Spiritual Warfare, the battle for "lost souls." This book is not about evangelism. This book is not about Type 1 Universal Spiritual Warfare! *spiritual* *Sanctification*

Type 2: Personal (Internal) Spiritual Warfare

Type 2 Spiritual Warfare did not exist before Jesus and the Holy Spirit lived in and among man. God created the "old nature." It was man with his free will made in God's image. The old nature is not inherently sinful; it is inherently without God. This struggle is between our original nature and the part of the Christian that is with God. The devil is not a part of Type 2 Spiritual Warfare.

God won a major battle in this spiritual war by creating a process by which individuals could enter and stay in His presence by accepting Christ as their personal savior and allowing God (the Holy Spirit) to *live in* each individual. However, individual victory is not dependent on God but on the individual. There are no guarantees of success. This is the Christian's personal internal battle for holiness (sanctification). Dr. Murphy brings clarity to this struggle with two statements: "The flesh-life (the self-life) and the Christ-life are continually at war with each other. Thus, any attempt to live the abundant life in this world means spiritual warfare."[16] "When we talk of the Christian Life we are in the area of sanctification.[17] Paul defines Type 2 Spiritual Warfare:

> We know *that the law is spiritual;* but I am unspiritual, sold as a slave to sin. I do not understand what I do. For what I want to do I do not do, but what I hate I do. And if I do what I do not want to do, I agree that the law is good. As it is, it is no longer I myself who do it, but it is sin living in me. For I know that good itself does not dwell in me, that is, in my sinful nature. For I have the desire to do

what is good, but I cannot carry it out. For I do not do the good I want to do, but the evil I do not want to do—this I keep on doing. Now if I do what I do not want to do, it is no longer I who do it, but it is sin living in me that does it. So I find this law at work: Although I want to do good, evil is right there with me. For in my inner being I delight in God's law; but I see another law at work in me, waging war against the law of my mind and making me a prisoner of the law of sin at work within me. (Romans 7:14-23 NIV).

Peter states that the believer must lay aside all malice, all guile, hypocrisies, envies, and all evil speaking (I Peter 2:1). These attributes are from the natural inclination of the human flesh, not from the Devil. Our souls are encapsulated in a human body whose natural inclinations are not always Godly. God makes this body and its nature. It is natural and normal. Yet scripture challenges us to be disciplined to resist this nature when it leads us toward sin. This is characteristic of Type 2 battles.

I do not reject my humanness. In fact, I want to experience all that I am as the human that God created me to be. I want to experience all of the emotions, thoughts, and behavior capable of humans. Dr. Robert McMillan wrote a book, *I'm Human, Thank God!* He declares, "When we become Christians, we are not ever dehumanized."[18] However, life as a Christian is not without parameters:

"Therefore, I urge you, brothers and sisters, in view of God's mercy, to offer your bodies as a living sacrifice, holy and pleasing to God—this is your true and proper worship. Do not conform to the pattern of this world, but be transformed by the renewing of your mind. Then you will be able to test and approve what God's will is— his good, pleasing and perfect will" (Romans 12: 1-2 NIV).

These parameters need not dehumanize the Christian. Dr. McMillian goes on to say: "The first motivating factor in Christian growth should be that you may know the good, acceptable and complete will of God." This comes only by knowing the Bible. For emphasis, I will restate some of the conclusions stated above: Type 2 Personal Spiritual Warfare is the personal war that goes on inside the Christian. It is the internal war. The devil is not a part of this war, because the devil does not live inside the

Christian. The never-believers are not a part of this warfare, because they do not have the "new nature" that comes with conversion.

We Christians have the opportunity to have a closer, more pure relationship with God than did Adam and Eve. Their relationship was a physical one. They were in God's physical presence when He appeared to them. They knew of His presence when they heard His voice. This is the relationship that God wanted, a relationship with man who had free will and lived in the presence of evil.

After man failed God, after God threw man out of Eden, after Noah, after the flood, God chose the Jews to be His people. He started on the long, progressive revelation of Himself to mankind. His relationship with man was based on laws. Keep the laws of God, and you will know and experience God. God was an intolerant keeper of rules. God was not going to take a chance on free-will humans to reject Him or to disobey Him. If man disobeyed God, justice was swift:

> *"When they came to the threshing floor of Kidon, Uzzah reached out his hand to steady the ark, because the oxen stumbled. The LORD's anger burned against Uzzah, and he struck him down because he had put his hand on the ark. So he died there before God"* (1 Chronicles 13: 9-10 NIV).

As it turned out, the relationship with God via laws was not good enough for God. It was not the type of relationship he had with His creation in Eden. Like Adam, the Hebrews could not consistently live within the rules God set. Therefore, we Christians believe God devised a path back to His original concept of a personal relationship with His creations, one that was not dependent on laws, but on a relationship with a freewill man in the presence of evil. That path involved man's acceptance of His Son, Jesus. God also gave man a helper. That helper was the Holy Spirit, who would live inside of man.

This is God living inside of man. Man would have the experience of fellowship with God living in him constantly. This is even better than what Adam and Eve had. It is a 24/7 relationship with the real God, a personal relationship that does not have to wait for God to visit in the "cool of the evening." God is present in the Christian every moment, even when he is confronted by the devil. In Christ, the Christian's relationship is far more intense and real than what Adam and Eve had. Thanks be to God!

This Type 2 Internal Warfare can be won and God's people are winning it every day. Plain and simple, for this book, God's people are the

Christians. Even though Christians, Muslims, and Jews all share Abraham as the father of their religion, only the Christians are now God's people, because they have entered into the personal relationship with God that He now requires. That relationship requires belief and acceptance of Jesus as Lord and Savior. There is no alternative!

This personal relationship with God is a "faith" thing! You cannot have it unless you have faith that the Bible is true, that God is real, that your personal relationship with God is as real as your relationship with your earthly father or mother. Faith has many benefits for the believer. George Muller offers a unique insight into the benefits of faith for the believer: "The beginning of anxiety is the end of faith; the beginning of true faith is the end of anxiety."[19] Being anxiety-free is a source of confidence for the spiritual warrior.

Eden is no longer a place, but a relationship. A relationship with God through Jesus is today's Eden. It is what God wants, and He tolerates no other relationship. Humans who do not have a personal relationship with God continue to live east of Eden. This is what the Bible teaches.

Non-Christians can be good, moral, honest, kind people; after all, they are made in God's image. They just do not have the relationship with God, which God requires. They do not have God's presence in their lives.

Only people who accept Jesus as the Son of God and the salvation He offers will receive the Holy Spirit to **live in** them. Only these people have God living in them. The effort to yield to the Holy Spirit's growth and control is the essence of the Type 2 Personal (Internal) Spiritual Warfare.

As stated earlier, the devil is not present in Type 2 battles. This is not a struggle between the Christian and the devil. This is the internal struggle between the two natures of man. Paul states, "Parts of me covertly rebel." It is a matter of the will of man. Does man choose to be holy? Does man make the conscious choice to seek to do like Jesus, "not my will but Thine"?

When the new nature begins in the new Christian, a war begins. It is a lifelong struggle. Man will always be more human than spiritual. There is only one person who was 100% human and 100% spiritual, and that was Jesus.

The conversion to our second nature is our march to holiness. The theologians call this process sanctification. The sanctification of the Christian will never be 100% complete this side of heaven. That part of us that is not sanctified has to be our focus of concern. It is the source of our sin in this Type 2 Spiritual Warfare.

God expects this effort toward holiness of the true believer. It is critical that we win this battle every day as preparation for the spiritual war that we face with Satan, which is the Type 3 Counter-Terrorism Spiritual Warfare. *"Pursue righteousness...fight the good fight of faith"* (1 Timothy 6:11-12 NIV).

Hypostatic Union

We have a theological term for the embodiment of God and man in Jesus. It is "hypostatic union."[20] It occurs only in Jesus. We need to understand that we can never be 100% like Jesus, because we are not capable of a hypostatic union. That is, we can never be Jesus. Since only Jesus was capable of a hypostatic union, we Christians cannot be like Jesus' God side, but we can be like His human side. That is our goal. When we pray to God the Father that He will help us be like Jesus, we should be conscious that we are praying to be like Jesus' human side. Keep the two separate. We are incapable of being like Jesus' God side. In fact, to pray to be like Jesus' God side is blasphemy. We should never pray to be God. *(Judge Laws Cross)*

We can be like Jesus' human side. Jesus' human side did the following: Jesus prayed to God, "Our Father, which art in heaven." Jesus resisted the temptations presented by the devil. Jesus befriended the poor, the despised, and the sinner. Jesus argued with the Church when it was wrong. Jesus overturned the moneychangers' tables when they disrespected the Church and God. Jesus witnessed to all he met about God and having a relationship with God. Jesus spent a lot of time with the apostles who would later be called Christians.

We can strive to be like Him (His human side) in behavior, attitude, and relationship with God and man. That must be our goal. When engaging in Type 2 Personal Spiritual Warfare, just remember you will always be more human than spiritual. However, in Type 2 Spiritual Warfare, you are trying to conquer your human side. The spiritual warrior will always be involved in Type 2 Spiritual Warfare. The Type 2 spiritual war is analogous to a soldier working his body and mind into shape to prepare for entry into battle with external forces.

In Type 2 Spiritual Warfare, sin may occur and be in the Christians life. The presence of the devil is not a requirement for the Christian to sin. **All sin is not caused by the devil.** In Type 2 Spiritual Warfare, sin comes from our human nature, but sin still has the consequences of separating us from God.

God saw the Ten Commandments
Jesus saw - Matt (5 - 17)

Behold, the LORD'S hand is not shortened, that it cannot save; neither his ear heavy, that it cannot hear. But your iniquities have separated between you and your God, and your sins have hid his face from you, that he will not hear (Isaiah 59:1-2 NIV).

The "old nature" is not from the devil; it is from God. The free-will nature often does not choose to obey God, because it can choose. It is hard! Type 2 spiritual wars are hard.

"The missing element in much teaching about the normal Christian life is the full biblical dimension of spiritual warfare. Part of that dimension includes our dealing realistically with the very real difficulties of everyday life."[21]

"We live all the time in the deep end of the pool with no time outs allowed."[22] In Peter Gilquist's article, "Spiritual Warfare: Bearing the Bruises of the Battle," the successful Christian life must have built into it a certain expectation of failure.[23] As my pastor has said, "The only way to be faithful in the Christian life is to play hurt."[24] This is not unlike the athlete who is called to participate even though he is not 100%. He must still play through his pain to perform at his best in order for the team to win. **Christianity is a contact sport.** Christians who fight this fight will tell you the hard knocks received are worth achieving a real relationship with God.

This book helps define Type 2 Personal (Internal) Spiritual Warfare. However, this book will not help you with Type 2 Personal (Internal) Spiritual Warfare.

Type 3: Counter-Terrorism Spiritual Warfare

What is terrorism? The Terrorism Research Center defines terrorism:

> "Terrorism is a criminal act that influences an audience beyond the immediate victim. The strategy of terrorists is to commit acts of violence that draw the attention of the local populace, the government, and the world to their cause. The terrorists plan their attack to obtain the greatest publicity, choosing targets that symbolize what they oppose. The effectiveness of the terrorist act lies not in the act itself, but in the public or government's reaction to the act. For example, in 1972 at the Munich Olympics, the Black September Organization killed 11 Israelis. The Israelis were the immediate victims. But the true target was the estimated 1 billion people watching the televised event."

"Terrorism has often been an effective tactic for the weaker side in a conflict."[25] These characteristics of physical and earthly terrorism also characterize spiritual terrorism.

Then there is the war the Christian fights:

> *not against flesh and blood, but against the rulers, against the authorities, against the powers of this dark world and against the spiritual forces of evil in the heavenly realms*" (Ephesians 6:12 NIV).

This, we will call Type 3 Counter-Terrorism Spiritual Warfare.

Chip Ingram (Bestseller #6) states, "...there is guerrilla fighting all around us, and the strategy of the guerrillas is to deceive, discourage, divide, and destroy God's people and God's program. They employ terrorist tactics, and our alert signals should always be on 'code red.'"[26]

God will ultimately win the Type 1 spiritual war, but there is no guarantee that He will win any one of the Type 2 or Type 3 spiritual battles because both are dependent on the believer's behavior. This book starts with the assumption that the serious spiritual warrior will win the Type 2 personal battles daily, becoming more holy (sanctified). **Remember holiness is necessary but not sufficient to win spiritual wars.** Victories in Type 3 battles are dependent on disciplined, focused, smart actions of the believer. If the warrior does his job with Type 2 battles, this book will help him win the Type 3 battles with our spiritual terrorist, the roaring lion.

Paul was a man of action. Paul did not talk about spiritual warfare until his ninth book in 62 AD when he wrote Ephesians chapter 6. Before Paul addressed the issue of spiritual warfare, he had written 80 percent of the 87 chapters of the thirteen books he wrote.

In the first ten years of Paul's ministry, he was preoccupied with setting standards for the early church, making the case that Gentiles did not have to become Jews in order to become Christians, and establishing the legitimacy of his ministry to the Gentiles. You can get an idea of where Paul's head and heart were by reading the topics he addressed in the first ten years and the first eight books he wrote. Most Christian Bibles give the topic as a heading to each chapter and section.

Paul's emphasis was understandable when you realize how early he wrote in the life of the Christian church. Remember, Paul was a contemporary of Jesus, born during the first decade of the first century and dying in 67 A.D.

Before his conversion, Paul was an enemy of Jesus and Christians, keeping the coats of the men who stoned Stephen to death:

> *And when the blood of your martyr Stephen was shed, I stood there giving my approval and guarding the clothes of those who were killing him* (Acts 22:20 NIV).

Ephesians 6 is the first and only time, in the thirteen books that Paul wrote from 52 AD until he was beheaded in 68 AD, that he offered specific behavior to counter the *roaring lion*. Read again what Paul said about spiritual warfare. Look for his emphasis on being alert and taking action.

> *Finally, be strong in the Lord and in his mighty power. **Put on** the full armor of God, so that you can take your stand against the devil's schemes. For our struggle is not against flesh and blood, but against the rulers, against the authorities, against the powers of this dark world and against the spiritual forces of evil in the heavenly realms. Therefore, **put on** the full armor of God, so that when the day of evil comes, you may be able to **stand your ground**, and after you have done everything, to stand. **Stand firm** then, with the belt of truth buckled around your waist, with the breastplate of righteousness in place, and with your feet fitted with the readiness that comes from the gospel of peace. In addition to all this, **take up the shield** of faith, with which you can extinguish all the flaming arrows of the evil one. **Take the helmet** of salvation **and the sword** of the Spirit, which is the word of God. And pray in the Spirit on all occasions with all kinds of prayers and requests. With this in mind, **be alert** and always keep on praying for all the Lord's people* (Ephesians 6:10-18 NIV).

Look at the action words Paul uses in his advice to deal with the "strategies and tricks of the Devil": Put on, stand your ground, stand firm, take up the shield, take the helmet and the sword, and be alert.

The actions Paul advocates help counter the surprise attacks from the dark forces of Ephesians 6. These are battles between the Christian and the devil. These forces of darkness are full of trickery:

> *Put on the full armor of God, so that you can take your stand against the devil's schemes* (Ephesians 6:11 NIV).

Chapter Summary

The Christian layman is involved in all three types of spiritual warfare. With his ministry, he is involved with evangelism of the never-believer. This is Type 1 Universal Spiritual Warfare. This book does not help you with Type 1 Spiritual Warfare.

The spiritual warrior is compelled to be involved with Type 2 Personal (Internal) Spiritual Warfare. This is necessary if he is gong to be successful with Type 3 Counter-Terrorism Spiritual Warfare. This book does not help you with Type 2 Spiritual Warfare.

The remainder of the book will help the spiritual warrior fight the Type 3 battles.

By defining the three types of spiritual warfare, the warrior can better identify the battle in which he is engaged and avoid the fog of war.

Not all believers are spiritual warriors. Those who are not become victims of this warfare.

The Next Chapter

So, what is a spiritual warrior? This is the subject of our next chapter.

Extra Life Insights

(If you can't know great men and women you can know their words!)
"You don't think your way into a new way of living; you live your way into a new way of thinking."
-Henri Nouwen
"The only true wisdom is knowing that you know nothing."
- Socrates

Notes

1. Ed Murphy, *The Handbook for Spiritual Warfare Revised and Updated* (Nashville, TN: Thomas Nelson Publishers, Inc., 2003), 344.
2. David Powlison, "The Classical Model", in *Understanding Spiritual Warfare: Four Views,* James K. Beilby, Paul Rhodes Eddy, Ed., (Grand Rapids, Michigan: Baker Academic, 2012), 92.
3. Walter Wink, "The World System Model", in *Understanding Spiritual Warfare: Four Views,* James K. Beilby, Paul Rhodes Eddy, Ed., (Grand Rapids, Michigan: Baker Academic, 2012), 47 - 71.
4. Powlison, 89 – 111.
5. Gregory Boyd, "The Ground-Level Deliverance Model", in *Understanding Spiritual Warfare: Four Views,* James K. Beilby, Paul Rhodes Eddy, Ed., (Grand Rapids, Michigan: Baker Academic, 2012), 129 - 157.
6. C. Peter Wagner, Rebecca Greenwood, "The Strategic-Level Deliverance Model", in *Understanding Spiritual Warfare: Four Views,* James K. Beilby, Paul Rhodes Eddy, Ed., (Grand Rapids, Michigan: Baker Academic, 2012), 173 - 198.
7. Murphy, xii.
8. Borgman, Brian S. and Rob Ventura, *Spiritual Warfare: A Biblical and Balanced Perspective* (Reformation Heritage Books: Grand Rapids, Michigan, 2014), Kindal Location = 1910
9. Murphy, 177.
10. "The World, the Flesh, and the Devil," Grantian Florilegium, http://grantian.blogspot.com/2011/06/world-flesh-and-devil.html (accessed December 11, 2013).
11. Karl Payne, *Spiritual Warfare: Christians, Demonization, and Deliverance*, (Washington, D.C.: WND Books, 2011), 45.
12. Francis Frangipane, *The Three Battlegrounds* (Cedar Rapids, Iowa: Arrow Publications, Inc., 2006), 22.
13. Frangipane, 29.
14. Timothy M. Warner, *Spiritual Warfare: Victory over the Powers of This Dark World* (Wheaton, Illinois: Crossway Books, 1991), 48.

15. The U.S. Census Bureau, Population Division, http://www.census.gov/ipc/www/popclockworld.html (accessed December 11, 2013).
16. Murphy, 65.
17. Murphy, 61.
18. Robert McMillan, *I'm Human Thank Go*d! (New York: Thomas Nelson, 1973), 91.
19. George Mueller Quotes, Christian Quotes, file://localhost/http/ (accessed December 11, 2013).
20. Hypostatic Union, Dictionary, Catholicculture.org, http://www.catholicculture.org/culture/library/dictionary/index.cfm?id=34037 (accessed December 12, 2012).
21. Murphy, 93.
22. Murphy, 92.
23. Murphy, 93.
24. Dr. Bill Shiell, First Baptist Church, Tallahassee Florida, Sermon "A Resilient Faith," http://prezi.com/4boxt369v4nj/a-resilient-aith/?utm_campaign=share&utm_medium=copy (accessed December 12, 2013).
25. "What is Terrorism?" International Terrorism and Security Research, http://www.terrorism-research.com (accessed December 11, 2013).
26. Chip Ingram, *The Invisible War: What Every Believer Needs to Know about Satan, Demons, and Spiritual Warfare* (Grand Rapids, Michigan: Baker Books, 2006), 74.

Chapter 2: What is a Spiritual Warrior?

This chapter presents the spiritual warrior as a layman/laywoman. It restores a long-ago-held definition of a layperson as someone whose work is separate from the work of ministers. This chapter will present the job of a layperson as legitimate as is the job of a minister and the ministry of a layperson as being different from the job of a layperson.

(Note: You cannot be a successful spiritual warrior unless you are confident in your personal relationship with God. If you have any doubts about your Christian conversion experience, go to Appendix E, page 231).

A spiritual warrior is a Christian engaged in battle with the "dark forces" of Ephesians 6. This book is addressed to those spiritual warriors who are laymen/laywomen in the workplace. It is necessary to untangle our thinking from years of misguided preaching and Bible teaching to understand the context of daily living for the Christian in the workplace.

Lt. Col. Dave Grossman writes in *On Combat: The Psychology and Physiology of Deadly Conflict in War and in Peace:*

> "There are only two kinds of people once the bullets start to fly: warriors and victims, those who fight and those who are unprepared, unable or unwilling to defend themselves."[1]

Not only is this true in a physical war, but it is also true in the spiritual war. **When the bullets are not flying you cannot tell the Christian who is a victim, from the Christian who is a spiritual warrior.** When Christians are not out in the world living out their God defined calling in their job, mingling with those who need to know God, ministering to the believer and the never-believer they work with, and taking spiritual risks, they are not a threat to the devil. Therefore, the devil leaves those Christians alone to their own entropy.

As my pastor has preached, living the Christian life means playing out on the edge of risk.[2] That is where the Christian needs to be a spiritual warrior. A true warrior runs toward the sound of the battle.

Initially, all Christians are vulnerable and often victims. They are "babes" in Christ, immature. These new Christians need to be protected and nurtured to maturity. Many long-term Christians continue to be victims. They never become warriors. They may have been Christians for 40 years. However, in terms of experience they never got past year one.

They have 40 first-year experiences. To develop the new Christian, it has been suggested that churches need a new category of church membership: the apprentice church member.

Saying you are a spiritual warrior does not make you a spiritual warrior any more than a soldier saying he is an operator with Delta Force makes him a special operations soldier.[3] The training, education, conditioning, mental preparation and experience are what make a Delta Force operator. It is a persistent, hard-nosed commitment to the mission. This same mindset is required of the spiritual warrior.

I have not had courses in systematic theology. Like most Christians, I have accumulated my theology through the years by listening to many sermons and participating in many Bible studies. As a result, like me, most Christians have developed their own systematic theology of the Christian life and ministry. Some of what has been learned is just wrong. The concepts are not scriptural. Some of the concepts may not be consistent with each other.

It is my opinion churches, preachers, and the Faith-At-Work movement outside the church walls are wrong in claiming that all that Christian laymen do is "ministry." These same well-intentioned Christians preach that a layman's job is nothing more than a platform for evangelism and ministry. **In my opinion, forcing the non-ministry work of laymen into a ministry format has caused laymen to take actions in the workplace that are unethical and often illegal.** A layman's employer is not paying him to "do evangelism or ministry." The non-ministry work that laymen do is important and subject to a "calling from God" as much as is the calling of a person to be a minister.

This book is about spiritual warfare in the workplace, but it focuses on a very narrow slice of the broader definition of spiritual warfare. Spiritual warfare is very much about demons and demonization. Spiritual warfare is the battle of the mature Christian *"against the rulers, against the authorities, the powers of this dark world and against the spiritual forces of evil"* (Ephesians 6:12 NIV).

The Spiritual Ambush is about what a spiritual warrior can do (his behavior) when attacked by the "roaring lion." Among categories of Christian literature, this narrow focus might be more accurately labeled "Christian living" or "Christian ethics" than "spiritual warfare." The serious spiritual warrior needs to understand the spiritual implications of his work in the workplace. What is the relationship of your work to God, and what is the relationship of God to your work?

I want to challenge you to rethink your understanding of a number of concepts that I think are critical to the life of the spiritual warrior in the workplace. These are concepts that I have struggled with in the past that I now believe are mature and scriptural. They include the following: Holiness, Work, Minister, Layman, Ministry, God's Will, God's Calling, and The Christian Approach to a Job.

Definitions

(Note: I will often use "laymen" in the text in order to facilitate the flow of the narrative. The reader needs to understand "laymen" to include "laywomen" and "laypersons.")

For purposes of this discussion, there are two types of Christian workers in our society: laymen and ministers. In their work life, each has a job. **A job is the substantive activities/tasks for which an employer pays.**

"Holiness" Defined

No Christian is more vulnerable on the spiritual battlefield than the Christian who is solely dependent on his holiness (sanctification) for protection from Satan's attack.

Jesus' holiness did not deter the devil's attacks. Jesus' holiness did protect him from succumbing to the devil. If you are as holy as Jesus, your sanctification will protect you. If you are that holy, this book has nothing to offer you. Do not get me wrong; your holiness (sanctification) is necessary but not sufficient for you to be victorious in spiritual warfare.

Therefore, the first step in becoming a spiritual warrior is to work on your holiness daily. It is necessary!

> The LORD said to Moses, "Speak to the entire assembly of Israel and say to them: 'Be holy because I, the LORD your God, am holy (Leviticus 19:1-2 NIV).
>
> "Consecrate yourselves and be holy, because I am the LORD your God Keep my decrees and follow them. I am the LORD, who makes you holy (Leviticus 20:7-8 NIV).
>
> He has saved us and called us to a holy life—not because of anything we have done but because of his own purpose and grace. This grace was given us in Christ Jesus before the beginning of time (2 Timothy 1:9 NIV).

Make every effort to live in peace with everyone and to be holy; without holiness no one will see the Lord (Hebrews 12:14 NIV).

As obedient children, do not conform to the evil desires you had when you lived in ignorance. But just as he who called you is holy, so be holy in all you do; for it is written: "Be holy, because I am holy" (1 Peter 1:14-16 NIV).

One part of your work to become holy is to read your Bible every day. The Scripture is the principal source of our knowledge of God, how He works, and how we should think and behave. Jerry Bridges, author of *The Pursuit of Holiness*, stated he does not believe reading the Bible would make one holy, but he has never known a holy person who did not read his Bible daily.[4]

As Dietrich Bonhoeffer points out, "The deceit, the lie of the devil, consists of this: that he wishes to make man believe that he can live without God's word."[5]

There are many plans for daily Bible reading. I like the one that guides you in reading the Bible through in a year and the Psalms twice, by reading one chapter out of the Old Testament, one chapter out of the New Testament, and one Psalm each day. One of the more respected Bible teachers at First Baptist Church of Tallahassee has read the Bible through each year for 52 years. He starts over with a new Bible each year that is a different translation than the one he just completed.

Jesus said a lot about holiness (sanctification) in the Book of John:

They are not of the world, even as I am not of it. Sanctify them by the truth; your word is truth. As you sent me into the world, I have sent them into the world. For them I sanctify myself, that they too may be truly sanctified (John 17:16-19 NIV).

Sanctification is a state of separation unto God; all believers enter this state when they are born of God:

"It is because of him that you are in Christ Jesus, who has become for us wisdom from God—that is, our righteousness, holiness and redemption (1 Corinthians 1:30 NIV).

However, that initial sanctification must be developed. That sanctification must be "battle hardened" if the spiritual warrior is going to prevail in his battles with the dark forces of Ephesians 6.

"Work" Defined

In the beginning, God did work:

> *By the seventh day God had finished the **work** he had been doing; so on the seventh day he rested from all his **work**. Then God blessed the seventh day and made it holy, because on it he rested from all the **work** of creating that he had done* (Genesis 2:2-3 NIV).

Then He created man and put him in the "garden" of Eden to "work it" and "care for it," in other words, to work:

> *The LORD God took the man and put him in the Garden of Eden to work it and take care of it* (Genesis 2:15 NIV).

Work was good! Work was Godly! There is no mention of "ministry" here!

Enter sin. Work got harder! No more "easy pickings" in the garden. Note that the curse because of sin was not on man or work, but on the ground.

> *To Adam he said, "Because you listened to your wife and ate fruit from the tree about which I commanded you, 'You must not eat from it,' "Cursed is the ground because of you; through painful toil you will eat food from it all the days of your life. It will produce thorns and thistles for you, and you will eat the plants of the field. By the sweat of your brow you will eat your food until you return to the ground, since from it you were taken; for dust you are and to dust you will return"* (Genesis 3:17-19 NIV).

East of Eden, work was going to be harder.

Tony Watson, in his book, *Sociology, Work & Industry*, gives a brief summary of what went before the Christian Bible's view of work. This sets the context in which the New Testament was written:

> "The ancient Greeks regarded the most desirable and the only good life as one of leisure. Work, in the sense of supplying the necessities of life, was a degrading activity which was to be allocated to the lowest group within the social order and especially, to slaves. The Romans tended to follow the Greek view, whilst the Hebrews had a view of work as unpleasant drudgery, which could nevertheless play a role of expiating sin and

recovering a degree of spiritual dignity. A corresponding modification of the extremes of the Greek view is to be seen in early Christianity which recognized that work might make one healthy and divert one from sinful thoughts and habits."[6]

The work of laymen was just not important to the culture of the writers of the New Testament and therefore was not a subject to which they devoted any energy.

"Minister" Defined

Paul is explicit in his definition of the ministry and the "ministry" job of ministers and laymen:

> *So Christ himself gave the apostles, the prophets, the evangelists, the pastors and teachers, to equip his people for works of service, so that the body of Christ may be built up* (Ephesians 4:11-12 NIV).

Ministers' ministries are being apostles, prophets, evangelists, pastors and teachers and equippers of the saints. This is also the minister's job; it is what he is paid to do. **A minster's job is ministry!**

Organizations that hire ministers have goals to develop and expand the Church and to minister to the spiritual and earthly needs of believers and never-believers. The focus of that effort is man's soul - bringing it closer to God. The role of pastor also involves comforting, encouraging and educating the believer, "equipping of the saints for the work of service, to the building up of the body of Christ." Thus the Bible states that the minister's job is to equip the layman to do ministry. Nothing in this verse implies that the minister is to help the layman select or do his non-ministry job. **The non-ministry job of the layman was not on the radar of the New Testament writers.**

Ministers also share with all Christians the mission of the "Great Commission":

> *"Therefore go and make disciples of all nations, baptizing them in the name of the Father and of the Son and of the Holy Spirit, and teaching them to obey everything I have commanded you. And surely I am with you always, to the very end of the age"* (Mathew 28:19-20 NIV).

"Layman" Defined
Ephesians 4:11-12 also defines the layman regarding his ministry. The laymen are "the saints for the work of ministry." Paul defines the ministry for the layman but not the non-ministry job, for which his employer pays him. **The job of a layman and the ministry of a layman are two different things.** The work of the layman was just not important in the culture when the Christian Bible was written. It is not part of the story the New Testament tells.

The goals of organizations that hire laymen today are not about saving people's souls or "building" the Church. In America, the focus of those organizations is all of the services and products necessary for civil society to exist, other than the service and products provided by the Church. The "non-religious" organization that hires the layman is not paying him to do ministry.

There is a Christian approach to a layman's job however, but that is not ministry. A layman takes a Christian approach to his job, not in order to have a ministry to people in his workplace, but because it is the Christian thing to do. Not to take a Christian approach would undermine any opportunity the Christian might ever have for ministry to those from the workplace. The layman's Christian approach to his job and to his ministry is addressed below.

"Ministry" Defined
Ministry is bringing never-believers to a saving knowledge of Jesus Christ and caring for, encouraging, supporting, and developing believers to be "Christ-like" in all of their endeavors. Ministry also includes behavior that helps and heals never-believers.

For emphasis, let me state again that the minister's ministry is also his job; it is what the minister is paid to do. The layman's ministry is not his job. If it is not in the layman's job description, he should not do it on the job or, as it is sometimes termed, "on the clock." The layman's employer is not paying the layman to do ministry. The layman should not be involved in any ministry when he is on his job.

My late brother-in-law, Russell Barron, best captured the correct attitude of a Christian layman toward his lay job when he stated, "I believe anything brought to the workplace should be work related" (See his complete statement in Appendix H, page 261).

I accept the observations of Sherman and Hendrix in their seminal 1984 work, *Your Work Matters to God.* In that book Sherman states, "I believe the workplace is the most strategic arena for Christian thinking and influence today. And, our greatest need in the workplace right now is for Christians whose lifestyle and work style are so unique and so distinctive that coworkers will want to know why."[7]

> "The only Christian work is good work well done. Let the Church see to it that the workers are Christian people and do their work well, as to God: then all the work will be Christian work, whether it is church embroidery, or sewage farming. As Jacques Maritain says: 'If you want to produce Christian work, be a Christian, and try to make a work of beauty into which you have put your heart; do not adopt a Christian pose.' He is right."[8]

This will be fulfilled by Christians who take a Christian approach to their job; however, doing so is not ministry. The unique lifestyles and work styles of the Christian will lead to opportunities for the layman to do ministry, including evangelism, off the job, to individuals from his workplace.

Just to reemphasize this important principle, the layman should not do direct evangelism or ministry during the hours his employer is paying him to do his job. The confusion within the Faith-At-Work movement, and among many ministers, regarding this important principle, often occurs because of a lack of understanding of the New Testament regarding the calling of a layman to his non-ministry lay job.

Often ministers cannot understand the work of laypeople unless it involves evangelism. It is as though the minister is telling the layman that the best way to deal with the dark forces of Ephesians 6 is to first lead everyone in the workplace to Christ. There will be less room for the devil if everyone is a Christian. Most individuals who work at a church are Christians. Seldom are there more than 25% to 30% of the laymen in a non-church workplace are Christians. This approach of first evangelizing the workplace is like telling the warrior that the best way to be successful on the battlefield is to first convince the enemy to change their worldview and behavior. Before that happens to a sufficient degree, the spiritual warrior is going to be "eaten alive."

"The Layman's Ministry" Defined

As established earlier, all laymen are called to ministry, which is different and parallel to their calling to a lay profession or a lay job. One task of the layman is to find a way to minister to individuals in his workplace in such a way that it does not distort his secular non-ministry job, as well as a way to do his secular non-ministry job so that it does not distort his ministerial work. In fact, one task of the layman is to find a way to practice his job that will facilitate his exercise of his obligations for ministry in some appropriate way.

The job God calls the layman to do in the secular world is just as important to God as what the minister is called to do in the religious world. I want the layman to come away from this chapter confident in his calling to a job in the secular world as well as his calling to a ministry to the people he meets in the workplace.

It is critical that the serious spiritual warrior understand the relationship of his job to his God and ministry. Understanding the relationship of his ministry to his God is easy. He has the Bible for guidance of his ministerial activities. However, there is confusion created for the layman about his non-ministerial job, because much of today's Christian literature and today's ministers attempt to force his non-ministerial job into a ministry format in order to legitimate it in the eyes of the Christian community. This is particularly true of the non-church-based "Faith-At-Work" movement discussed in Chapter 6.

Some ministers mask the real need of Christians in the workplace by forcing everything the layman does into a ministry format. This keeps real issues like the following from one of Doug Spada's WorkLife truth modules from driving church programs, sermons, and Bible study:

Are my God-given talents, passions, and temperament aligned to my present job?

Is my work ethic free from compulsions such as meaningless goals, accumulating temporary success, and a desire to please everyone?

Do I honor my earthly employer with competency and integrity in order to accomplish God's purpose?

Do I earn the respect of my coworkers in a way that blends a gracious spirit, keen intellect, courageous heart, and cultural sensitivity?

Do I regularly grow my practical work skills in order to serve my employer and God?

Do I operate with virtues that honor God (fairness, graciousness, and compassion)?

Do I keep promises and tell the truth at work when subtle pressure is used to encourage hype, false appearance, white lies and spin?

Am I willing to go against the grain at work when biblical values are at stake?

Do I effectively deal with a difficult boss, serve an unreasonable client, or cooperate with a cynical coworker?

Do I resolve conflict involving office politics, gossip, slander, favoritism, and unfounded criticism?

Do I effectively deal with lust at work, including everything from travel temptations to office affairs, from risqué jokes to sexual harassment?

Do I protect and help the weakest members of my workplace and society in a "survival of the fittest" world?[9]

The Christian Community is so desperate to keep what the layman is doing in his job in the realm of "Christian work" that it defines any component of the job that is service to people as a ministry. Let us lay that notion to rest by saying that non-Christians cannot do Christian ministry. Yet, many non-Christians are involved in providing services to people. If that same service is provided by a Christian, that does not make it ministry.

My goal for this chapter is for the layman to understand that you not only have a responsibility for ministry to those you come in contact with in your workplace, just as a minister does, but you also have a lay job that is not ministry, the one you get paid to do. The layman must find God's will for his job and for his ministry to those in the workplace. You need to understand that the "non-ministry" job is important, and it must be done in a manner that does not hinder ministry or let ministry hinder it.

Sherman and Hendrix caution that we should not take a "two-story view of work." This view of work "is a system that sets up a dichotomy or hierarchy among things. Things are separated into two categories, one of which is inherently superior." When it comes to work, they say this theory of work is "sub-biblical." Ministry is not a superior profession to that of a layman's "non-ministry" job.[10]

"God's Will for Your Life" Defined

In all things, Christians should search for God's will.

*Do not conform any longer to the pattern of this world,
but be transformed by the renewing of your mind. Then
you will be able to test and approve what God's will is
–his good, pleasing and perfect will* (Romans 12:2
NIV).
*I desire to do your will, O my God; your law is within
my heart* (Psalm 40:8 NIV).

So how do you, a Christian layperson, determine if a lay-job is
God's will for your life and therefore your calling? One approach is that
recommended by George Muller, a 19th century evangelist and
philanthropist, who wrote the following concerning finding God's will:

"Knowing God's will is the key to prayer, spiritual
growth and fruitfulness in our individual lives. I seek at
the beginning to get my heart into such a state that it has
no will of its own about a given matter. Nine-tenths of
the trouble with people generally is just here. Nine-
tenths of the difficulties are overcome when our hearts
are ready to do the Lord's will, whatever it may be.
When one is truly in this state, it is usually but a little
way to the knowledge of what His will is. Having done
this, I do not leave the result to feeling or simple
impression. If so, I make myself liable to great
delusions.

I seek the Will of the Spirit of God through, or in
connection with, the Word of God. The Spirit and the
Word must be combined. If I look to the Spirit alone
without the Word, I lay myself open to great delusions
also. If the Holy Ghost guides us at all, He will do it
according to the Scriptures and never contrary to them.

Next, I take into account providential circumstances.
These often plainly indicate God's Will in connection
with His Word and Spirit. I ask God in prayer to reveal
His Will to me aright.

Thus, through prayer to God, the study of the Word,
and reflection, I come to a deliberate judgment
according to the best of my ability and knowledge, and
if my mind is thus at peace, and continues so after two
or three more petitions, I proceed accordingly. In trivial

matters, and in transactions involving most important issues, I have found this method always effective."[11]

For the first seventy-two years of my life, this was the process I used to determine what God was "calling me to do." Not always successfully, I might add! This approach was dependent on feelings, a feeling of peace about the decision. In fact, for me, that "peace" was the litmus test. It was the bar that all decisions had to get over.

Sherman and Hendrix capture the difficulty of divining God's will based on our feelings:

> "But I certainly would advise against basing a career decision on the notion that God has somehow committed Himself to giving a mystical, inner prompting one way or another. While inner impressions and feelings are valid and normal, it is impossible to define with certainty either their source or their meaning. Consequently, we must not invest these subjective impressions with divine authority."[12]

This approach is what my friend Josh Hall, the Minister to Young Adults at First Baptist Church of Tallahassee (2015), calls "the personal guidance model." Through a series of Bible studies in 2012, Josh Hall introduced me and our congregation to the work of Garry Friesen in a book titled *Decision Making and the Will of God.*[13] Dr. Friesen presents a scriptural approach to making godly decisions, what he calls "the Way of Wisdom." Friesen shows that the dysfunctional "personal guidance model" is like finding a dot within God's moral will, which is defined by the Bible. That "dot" is buried in the Bible like a needle in a haystack. That is the traditional view of God's individual will. That is what Mueller describes above. I used that process until I discovered Friesen. Friesen shows within God's moral will, there is an area of freedom and responsibility for the individual decision maker. Nothing more simply explains Friesen's model of finding "the Way of Wisdom" (God's will) than Friesen's parable of "The First Supper":[14]

> Adam was hungry. He had had a long, challenging day naming animals. His afternoon nap had been refreshing, and his post-siesta introduction to Eve was exhilarating, to say the least. But as the sun began to set on their first day, Adam discovered that he had worked up an appetite.

"I think we should eat," he said to Eve. "Let's call the evening meal 'supper.'"

"Oh, you're so decisive, Adam," Eve said. "I like that in a man. I guess all the excitement of being created has made me hungry, too."

As they discussed how they should proceed, they decided that Adam would gather fruit from the garden, and Eve would prepare it for their meal. Adam set about his task and soon returned with a basket full of ripe fruit. He gave it to Eve and went to soak his feet in the soothing current of the Pishon River until supper was ready. He had been reviewing the animal's names for about five minutes when he heard his wife's troubled voice.

"Adam, could you help me for a moment?" "What seems to be the problem, dear?"

"I'm not sure which of these lovely fruits I should prepare for supper. I've prayed for guidance from the Lord, but I'm not really sure what He wants me to do. I certainly don't want to miss His will on my very first decision. Would you go to the Lord and ask Him what I should do about supper?"

Adam's hunger was intensifying, but he understood Eve's dilemma. So he left her to go speak with the Lord. Shortly, he returned. He appeared perplexed.

"Well?" Eve said.

"He didn't really answer your question."

"What do you mean? Didn't He say anything?"

"Not much. He just repeated what He said earlier today during the garden tour: 'From any tree of the garden you may eat freely; but from the tree of the knowledge of good and evil you shall not eat.' I assure you, Eve, I steered clear of the forbidden tree."

"I appreciate that, but that doesn't solve my problem," Eve said. "What fruit should I prepare for tonight?"

From the rumbling in his stomach, Adam discovered that lions and tigers were not the only things that growl. So he said, "I've never seen such crisp, juicy apples. I feel a sense of peace about them. Why don't you prepare them for supper?"

"All right, Adam. I guess you've had more experience at making decisions than I have. I appreciate your leadership. I'll call you when supper's ready."

Adam was only halfway back to the river when he heard Eve's call. He jogged back to the clearing where she was working, but his anticipation evaporated when he saw her face. "More problems?" he asked.

"Adam, I just can't decide how I should fix these apples. I could slice them, dice them, mash them or bake them in a pie, a cobbler, fritters, or dumplings. I really want to be your helper, but I also want to be certain of the Lord's will on this decision. Would you be a dear and go just one more time to the Lord with my problem?"

Adam was not keen on bothering the Lord again, but after Eve said some very nice things about him, he agreed to go. When he returned, he said, "I got the same answer as before: 'From any tree of the garden you may eat freely; but from the tree of the knowledge of good and evil you shall not eat.'"

Adam and Eve were both silent for a moment. Then with light in his eye, Adam said, "You know, Eve, the Lord made that statement as though it fully answered my question. I'm sure He could have told us what to eat and how to eat it, but I think He's given us freedom to make those decisions. It was the same way with the animals today. He told me to name the animals, but He didn't whisper any names in my ear. Assigning those names was my responsibility."

Eve was incredulous. "Do you mean that we could have any of these fruits for supper?" Eve said. "Are you telling me that I can't miss God's will in this decision?"

"The only way you could do that is to pick some fruit from the forbidden tree. But none of these fruits are from that tree. Why, I suppose we are free to eat a little from each one of them." Adam snapped his fingers and exclaimed, "Say, that's a great idea! Let's have fruit salad for supper!"

And so they did.

Although some biblical scholars state that the story of Adam and Eve is historical symbolism, this parable helps us understand Friesen's model of the Way of Wisdom.[17] If we know the Scripture and stay within the boundaries of God's moral law, we are free to decide what God wants us to do. There are no magic feelings. As George Muller stated, God's will is never contrary to his Word. It is just that simple.

(Author's Note: in the beginning there was only one rule. If Adam and Eve could have kept that one rule, humanity would still be fellowshipping with God in the Garden of Eden. They didn't and we are not. God's first plan for human companionship failed! So he killed all but eight humans with the flood. Then God chose the Hebrews and gave them 613 rules in the Torah. God also failed in this arrangement. The Jews just could not keep the rules to God's sanctification. So God sent Jesus to have a personal relationship with each human.

> *"Do not think that I have come to abolish the Law or the Prophets; I have not come to abolish them but to fulfill them* (Matt 5:17 NIV).

So, when Jesus fulfilled the law we are now back being ruled by one law. We are ruled by the singular personal relationship that each human can have with God. Now how is that for a "heavenly design?")

"Calling" and "Called" Defined

A "calling" from God or to be "called" by God is very important in today's Christian culture, particularly in the Faith-At-Work movement discussed in Chapter 6. This usually means a calling from God to do something. So, what is a "calling" from God? Let's look at the Scripture instead of "leaning on our own understanding."

Twenty-one verses in the New Testament (NIV) include the word "calling." (See Appendix F, page 235 which lists each verse.) Not one of these verses is a "calling" to do a task or a job. They are all about being called to holiness or to God.

There are 202 verses in the New Testament (NIV) that contain the word "called." (See Appendix G, page 238 for complete listing of those verses.) Only four involve being called to do a task. The following summary table categorizes the use of the word "called" in each verse:

NUMBER OF VERSES IN THE BIBLE IN WHICH THE WORD "CALLED" APPEARS	
MEANING OF "CALLED"	**NUMBER OF VERSES**
SUMMONED	80
LABELED	38
NAMED	57
SHOUTING	17
SPOKE	6
CALLED TO A JOB OR TASK*	4
TOTAL	202

*The only verses in which God calls to a specific job or task, which is what many Christians consider the word "calling" to mean.

An example of how so much of the use of the word "calling" is misconstrued is the verse Ephesians 4:1 (NIV): *"As a prisoner for the Lord, then, I urge you to live a life worthy of the calling you have received."*

Many a sermon using this verse has been preached telling laymen that they need to be in jobs into which God called them. Sherman and Hendrix point out that the "calling" Paul is talking about in this verse is the calling of God that all Christians are called to, not a call to a lay job.[15] It is a calling to come to God. It is a calling to holiness and ministry.

A reading of the translation of this verse in The *Message* makes that more apparent,

> *I want you to get out there and walk--better yet, run! -- on the road God called you to travel...and mark that you do this with humility and discipline...pouring yourselves out for each other in acts of love, alert at noticing differences and quick at mending fences* (Ephesians 4:1 The Message).

Sherman and Hendrix state that there are only four verses in the New Testament where God called an individual to a specific task:

1. God's call of Paul to be an apostle:
Paul, a servant of Christ Jesus, called to be an apostle and set apart for the gospel of God— (Romans 1:1 NIV).

2. A second verse regarding Paul's calling:
Paul, called to be an apostle of Christ Jesus by the will of God, and our brother Sosthenes (I Corinthians 1:1 NIV).

3. God's call of Barnabus and Saul to be the Church's first missionaries:
While they were worshiping the Lord and fasting, the Holy Spirit said, "Set apart for me Barnabas and Saul for the work to which I have called them" (Acts 13:2 NIV).

4. God's call to Paul and his companions to take the gospel to Macedonia:
During the night Paul had a vision of a man of Macedonia standing and begging him, "Come over to Macedonia and help us." After Paul had seen the vision, we got ready at once to leave for Macedonia, concluding that God had called us to preach the gospel to them (Acts 16:9-10 NIV).

Sherman and Hendrix also point out that these four verses are the exception rather than the rule.

Please note even these three incidences of a calling to do a specific task were to some task of ministry, not to a non-ministry job.

An example of a minister's failure to recognize the importance and significance of the layman's non-ministry job in modern times is my experience with the Navigator Ministry in 1965-66.

In the fall of 1965, I arrived at my new assignment to the 1st Brigade, 2nd Battalion, 38th Infantry, 2nd Infantry Division in the Republic of South Korea. At that time, everything was going to Vietnam. Our infantry platoons were so depleted of U.S. soldiers that South Korean soldiers were assigned to our units as Korean Augmentations To the U. S. Army (KATUSA). We also did not get chaplains assigned to our battalion. To take up the slack, missionaries were asked to fill those responsibilities. A missionary from the Navigator Ministry was assigned to our Battalion.[9] I eagerly got involved in their weekly Bible studies and scripture memory program led by the Navigator Missionary.

When I returned to Ft. Benning in 1967, I lived in the "Navigator Home" and was heavily involved in the Navigator Ministry at Ft. Benning. When my active duty separation date came up in the summer of 1967, the director of the Navigator ministry told me that he would like me to remain in Columbus and be involved in the ministry at Ft Benning. He said, "Get a 40-hour-a-week job to pay your bills, but one that will not interfere with ministry at night and weekends. Also don't get involved in "churchy" activities that will interfere with our ministry." Well, I felt 40 hours a week was a very important block of time, and I had specific ideas of how I wanted to spend those 40 hours earning a living. I did not stay!

I point this out because it was the Navigator Press that published the Sherman and Hendrix book quoted above, just 20 years later (1987). That book is 180 degrees opposite the position of the Navigator staff I left at Ft. Benning. That book states emphatically that "What you Do Matters to God."

The only passage in the New Testament that speaks directly to a non-ministry task of a layman is Ephesians 6:7-8:

> Serve wholeheartedly, as if you were serving the Lord,
> not people, because you know that the Lord will reward
> each one for whatever good they do, whether they are
> slave or free (NIV).

Note that Paul has nothing to say in this verse about the merits of the tasks the slaves were doing. Paul focuses on how the person does the task. This is an issue of quality of work. To approach every task as though we were doing it for the Lord tells us to do the task with excellence. But what that task is, is important to God whether it is ministry or non-ministry. For the Christian lay-person, neither the New Testament nor his Church does very little to help him in this critical decision. In spite of the absence of Christian guidance, the individual needs to find his calling in each.

Levoy, in a non-religious book about a calling, offers several criteria for selecting a calling:

> "What do you love? As you listen for callings, keep such a question poised in your mind to help tune out some of the static. In fact, "What do you love?" is the question that callings pose. Focus on whether a particular call has integrity or not, whether it makes us feel more or less authentic, more or less connected to ourselves and others, more or less right, not morally but intuitively. Better to ask whether a call will give us a feeling of aliveness."[16]

"Authentic aliveness" should also drive the search for a Christian layman's calling to his non-ministry job.

Steve Jobs in his June 14, 2005 Stanford Commence Speech stated, "Do what you love!"[17]

Even that great philosopher George Burns weighed in on loving what your do: "I honestly think it is better to be a failure at something you love than to be a success at something you hate."[18]

Both Levoy and Jobs are right! The calling of non-Christians and Christians is the same. The calling of a layperson and a preacher are also the same. To have a calling, the Christian and non-Christian as well as the layperson and the minister must love what they do and be driven by authentic aliveness. Also, in my opinion, what the layperson chooses to do as his paid lay job is just as holy as is what the minister does in the ministry job he is paid to do. This equal "holiness" comes from both being Christians and finding God's will for their lives. As seen above in the word analysis of "calling" the New Testament just has nothing to say about the layperson's non-ministry job.

If the most important things about your job is your pay, prestige, position or power, that is not a calling. The work needs to be bigger than yourself. I am reminded of Steve Jobs' challenge to John Scully, when Jobs was recruiting Scully from CEO of Pepsi Cola to Apple, "Do you want to sell sugar water for the rest of your life or do you want to come with me and change the world?"[19]

For his job to be a calling the individual needs to believe that what he is doing is making a contribution to something bigger than himself.

Dr. Barry Schwartz, in his book *Why We Work (TED Books)*, describes the research of Amy Wrzesniewski, professor at Yale's School of Management, that demonstrates that an individual can find a calling even in the menial job he finds himself in.[20]

Dr. Wrizesniewski's research includes interviews with hospital custodians. See the description of the work of Luke:

> "Luke works as a custodian in a major teaching hospital. In an interview with researcher Wrzesniewski and her collaborators, Luke reported an incident in which he cleaned a comatose young patient's room – twice. He had already done it once, but the patient's father, who had been keeping a vigil or months, hadn't seen Luke clean the room and had snapped at him. So Luke cleaned it again. Graciously, why? Luke: I kind of knew the situation about his son. His son had been here or a long time and…from what I hear, his son had got into a fight and hew was paralyzed. That's why he got there, and he was in a coma and he wasn't coming out of the coma…Well…I went and cleaned the room. His father would stay here every day, all day, but he smoked cigarettes. So, he had went out to smoke a cigarette and after I cleaned the room he cam back up to the room. I ran into him in the hall, and he just freaked out…telling me I didn't do it. I didn't clean the room an all this stuff. And at first, I got on the defensive, and I was going to argue with him. But I don't know Something caught me and I said, "I'm sorry. I'll go clean the room."
> Interviewer: And you cleaned it again?
> Luke: Yeah, I cleaned it so that he could see me clean it…I can understand how he could be. It was like six months that his son was here. He'd be a little frustrated, and so I cleaned it again. But I wasn't angry with him. I guess I understand."[21]

Dr. Wrzesniewski found that Luke and other hospital custodians were going far beyond their job descriptions.

> "The custodians "real job" was to make the patient and their families feel comfortable, to cheer them up when

they were down, to encourage them and divert them from their pain and their fear, and to give them a willing ear if they felt like talking. Luke wanted to do something more than mere custodial work."[22]

Dr. Schwartz states that what Luke sought was shaped by the purpose of the hospital.[23] Aristotle would call it the telos of the hospital. Telos is defined as "the end term of a goal-directed process; especially, the Aristotelian final cause."[24]

The custodians found and lived out these aims in spite of their job descriptions. " These custodians shaped their jobs with the central purpose of the hospital in mind."

These custodians found a calling in even a menial task. The calling they found was not the result of Christian motivation or belief.

What a calling is, is the same for Christian and non-Christian. How you get there is the difference. The difference for Christians is that a calling must not only be authentic, create aliveness and an activity you love, but it also must be God's will for your life.

How does the Christian discover and select his "calling" from God to a "non-ministry" job? The same way a non-Christian searches and finds his calling. There is no difference in how a Christian and non-Christian finds Levoy's "authentic" job that you love and makes you feel alive, Swartz's identifying and embracing the telos of your organization, or Wrzesniewski's crafting your job with the central purpose of our organization in mind. All of these will help you find your calling. The calling of a Christian is not higher than that of a non-Christian. What makes the calling of the Christian different is that the Christian's search and embracing what he loves must be done within the "moral law of God." This difference is huge.

The degree of difference between the Christian and non-Christian calling can be seen in one example, the search for a spouse. The Christian's search must be within the boundaries set by the Bible, e.g., no sex before marriage, no dishonesty in the relationship, Godly purity honoring the marriage vows, etc. The non-Christian has no boundaries. If it "feels good" do it. Do all and anything in the relationship that your animal instincts lead you to do. I am reminded of the lyrics from the 1977 song by Debbie Boone, *You light Up My Life*, "It can't **be wrong** when it **feels so** right." The idea is that feelings trump all Godly wisdom. Feelings are unleashed and they alone rule the relationship. In my opinion, this is a formula for disaster.

In my opinion, a church "calls" a minister to be its preacher, not God. However, if the minister has chosen that church job consistent with God's will for his life, he can say that God has "called" him to that church. If a person has chosen the ministry as his profession, consistent with his understanding of God's will for his life, he can say that God has called him to be a minister. If a Christian layman chooses a "lay" job that is God's will for him, then he can say God has called him to that job, whether it is as an engineer, accountant, governmental employee, farmer, lawn care person, ditch digger or something else. A calling in this way is true for laymen and ministers. *In all your ways submit to him, and he will make your paths straight* (Proverbs 3:6 NIV).

I strongly recommend that the layperson and minister first find their calling and then find God's will within that calling.

"The Christian's Approach to Work" Defined

The Christian approach to work has to go beyond the Protestant Work Ethic. The Christian approach to a job has to go way beyond just an honest day of work for an honest day of pay if, as Sherman declares, the Christian's "work style (is) so unique and so distinctive that coworkers will want to know why."

Before we discuss the Christian's approach to his job, let us first look at some of the attributes of the Protestant Work Ethic that lay the foundation of the Christian's approach to his job. "Max Weber, the German economic sociologist, coined a term for the new beliefs about work, calling it the 'Protestant ethic.' The key elements of the Protestant ethic were diligence, punctuality, deferment of gratification, and primacy of the work domain" [25]

The *Complete Book of Everyday Christianity* offers the following:
"Generally the term Protestant work ethic refers to some of the following attitudes and behavior: (1) believing that work gives meaning to life; (2) having a strong sense of duty to one's work; (3) believing in the necessity of hard work and of giving work (even before the family) the best of one's time; (4) believing that work contributes to the moral worth of the individual and to the health of the social order; (5) viewing wealth as a major goal in life; (6) viewing leisure as earned by work and as preparation for work; (7) viewing success in work as resulting primarily from the amount of

personal effort; (8) viewing wealth that accrues from work as a sign of God's favor."[26]

The Protestant work ethic is the context for what we will call "the Christian layman's approach to his job." Note that not all of the elements of the Protestant Work Ethic are necessarily Christian. For example, number 8 in the above list. After the Spiritual Warrior has found his calling within God's will for his life following Friesen's The Way, the serious Spiritual Warrior must consciously do his work in a Christian manner.

The following are approaches to one's work that will make the Christian's "work style so unique and so distinctive that coworkers will want to know why." They are not all of the attributes of a Christian's approach to his lay job, but they are certainly a minimum. Each goal is biblically based.

Goal 1: Excellence

> *Slaves, obey your earthly masters in everything; and do it, not only when their eye is on you and to curry their favor, but with sincerity of heart and reverence for the Lord. Whatever you do, work at it with all your heart, as working for the Lord, not for human masters, since you know that you will receive an inheritance from the Lord as a reward. It is the Lord Christ you are serving. Anyone who does wrong will be repaid for their wrongs, and there is no favoritism* Note: The Message ends this passage with, *Being Christian doesn't cover up bad work* (Colossians 3:22-25 NIV).

This was Paul's admonition to slaves. Paul did not address the merits of the tasks the slaves performed. However, they were to approach the job they had as though they were doing it for God.

There is nothing in this Scripture that in the least implies that Paul thought that the tasks being performed were ministry. Those tasks were not ministry. Paul did not pass judgment on the merits of the tasks the slave performed, or whether the jobs the slaves were assigned had any intrinsic value. His admonition to them sets a standard for all believers that whatever you are doing to "earn" a living should be done as though you were doing it for God. The **gold standard** for the Christian is to perform his job with excellence. So, what is excellence?

Jim Collin's book *Good to Great* shows that effort alone may not be enough in doing an excellent job.[27] He looked at companies that were good but became extraordinary when compared to like companies. Taking the right approach is important. Knowing what you are doing is important. He found that the CEOs of the excellent companies were not absorbed with themselves but with what was best for the company. They focused on "getting the right people on the bus." These were people who had a great work ethic and integrity. Believers need to focus not on what is best for them but on what is best for the work organization.

The following are some elements of Excellence:

Attention to Detail: Avoid sloppiness in work products. Make sure you have addressed everything that should be addressed. Make sure the final product is complete. If the final product is a written document, make sure the spelling, sentence structure, and grammar are correct.

Rehearse presentations before others. After six years of graduate school and three graduate degrees, I can say the best instruction I ever received was at the U.S. Army Infantry School at Fort Benning, GA, where instructors were required to rehearse six hours before a committee for each hour's presentation before a class. To my knowledge no college professor has ever practiced his classroom presentation in front of other faculty six hours for each hour to be presented to students.

Timeliness: Be punctual in assignments and attendance. The Christian will not be late for work or leave early, ever. The Christian will deliver assignments on time. This requires discipline.

Knowledge and Skill: Continue to develop your knowledge and skill about your job and your company via self-study and company-sponsored education.

Think Ahead: The motto of the Florida Department of Health Emergency Operations is, "Never let the unexpected be a surprise!" Plan ahead! Be prepared!

"Excellence can be obtained if you:
Care more than others think is wise,
Risk more than others think is safe,
Dream more than others think is practical,

Expect more than others think is possible."[28]

The Redeemer Presbyterian Center for Faith and Work states "Any answer to **what makes a work 'Christian'?** is, in the end, reductive. But, we unabashedly adopt Dorothy I. Sayer's working definition: **Good work, done well.**"[29]

A Christian approach to a job requires a commitment to excellence in performance!

Goal 2: Be an Encourager
The following Scripture is Paul's guidance on how Christians should act toward other Christians. In my opinion, it is also how Christians should act toward their work colleagues, be they Christian or non-believer.

> *Hold them in the highest regard in love because of their work. Live in peace with each other. And we urge you, brothers and sisters, warn those who are idle and disruptive, encourage the disheartened, help the weak, be patient with everyone. Make sure that nobody pays back wrong for wrong, but always strive to do what is good for each other and for everyone else* (1 Thessalonians 5:13-15 NIV).

Encourage others! Be patient with others! Help others do their best!

Tom Peters, author of *In Search of Excellence* (2004) has also published, *The Little Big Things: 163 Ways to Pursue Excellence*, in which he states:

> "In this book I argue that 'the stuff that matters' is the likes of intensive and engaged listening and showing appreciation of the work and wisdom of others, any and all others. And I argue and fervently believe that you can study these full-blown disciplines and practice these full-blown disciplines and become, say, a full-fledged professional listener."[30]

Becoming a "full-fledged professional listener" is how the Christian learns what his work colleagues need for encouragement.

One of Zig Ziggler's principles was the way to get to the top of an organization was to help others get to the top, because reciprocity works.[31] When the Christian takes on this principle, he does this because it is the Christian approach, not because he is going to get something out of it.

A Christian approach to a job requires attentiveness to the needs of colleagues, as well as finding ways to do things and say things that will encourage them!

<u>Goal 3: Love Your Coworkers</u>

> "You have *heard that it was said, 'Love your neighbor and hate your enemy.' But I tell you, love your enemies and pray for those who persecute you, that you may be children of your Father in heaven. He causes his sun to rise on the evil and the good, and sends rain on the righteous and the unrighteous. If you love those who love you, what reward will you get? Are not even the tax collectors doing that? And if you greet only your own people, what are you doing more than others? Do not even pagans do that? Be perfect, therefore, as your heavenly Father is perfect* (Matthew 5:43-48 NIV).

This is one goal non-Christians will have a hard time achieving. Achieving this goal as a Christian will set your work style apart from the crowd and make your work colleagues ask why are you acting that way.

Many coworkers will not be loveable. Those are the ones who need your love most. You can love them by being alert to their personal and professional needs. Forward Internet sites or materials to a colleague that might be helpful for something your colleague is working on or has an interest in. Acknowledge personal tragedy. Celebrate joyous occasions appropriately.

The American author Leo F. Buscaglia said "To love is to risk not being loved in return. To hope is to risk pain. To try is to risk failure, but risk must be taken because the greatest hazard in life is to risk nothing".[32]

A Christian approach to a job will be genuinely to love others with whom you interact and to find ways to express that love, particularly to those who are the least loveable. The world preaches that people need to be tolerant of people that are different from them. "Love trumps tolerance!"[33]

<u>Goal 4: Service</u>

> *The greatest among you will be your servant* (Matthew 23:11 NIV).

Andy Stanley, communicator, author, pastor and founder of Atlanta based North Point Ministries, has preached about the "servant leader" approach to the job. This can be lived by asking coworkers and your boss, "What can I do to help you?"[34]

Pete Blaber, one of the absolutely great field commanders of the U.S. Army Delta Force, related what one of his first commanders called the keys of success for a commander, "the 3 Ms."

> "The 3 Ms are the keys to being successful in life. They stand for the mission, the men, and me." He then drew a line from the top M, through the middle M, down to the bottom M. "They're all connected," he continued. "So if you neglect one, you'll screw up the others. The first M stands for the mission; it is the purpose for which you are doing what you are doing. Whether in your personal or professional life, make sure you understand it, and that it makes legal, moral, and ethical sense, then use it to guide all your decisions. The second M stands for the men. Joshua Chamberlain, a Medal of Honor-receiving schoolteacher in the Civil War, once said that 'there are two things an officer must do to lead men; he must care for his men's welfare, and he must show courage.' Welfare of the troops and courage are inextricably linked. When it comes to your men, you can't be good at one without being good at the other. Take care of your men's welfare by listening and leading them with sound tactics and techniques that accomplish your mission, and by always having the courage of your convictions to do the right thing by them. The final M stands for me. Me comes last for a reason. You have to take care of yourself, but you should only do so after you have taken care of the mission, and the men. Never put your own personal well-being, or advancement, ahead of the accomplishment of your mission and taking care of your men."[35]

The Christian approach to a job is that of a servant!

Goal 5: Honesty
The Christian must be absolutely honest in all things.

"Whoever can be trusted with very little can also be trusted with much, and whoever is dishonest with very little will also be dishonest with much. So if you have not been trustworthy in handling worldly wealth, who will trust you with true riches? And if you have not been trustworthy with someone else's property, who will give you property of your own (Luke 16:10-12 NIV).

The Merriam-Webster Dictionary defines honesty as "fairness and straightforwardness of conduct."[36]

I believe the first challenge in honesty is the effort to be honest to oneself. I believe most people know when they are being honest. The challenge then is to represent to others what you know to be true and honest.

The Christian approach to a job will always be honest and truthful.

Goal 6: Sexual Purity

Don't *allow love to turn into lust, setting off a downhill slide into sexual promiscuity, filthy practices, or bullying greed* (Ephesians 5:3 The Message).

You know the guidelines we laid out for you from the Master Jesus. God wants you to live a pure life. Keep yourselves from sexual promiscuity. Learn to appreciate and give dignity to your body, not abusing it, as is common among those who know nothing of God. (1 Thessalonians 4:3-5 The Message).

But what comes out of the mouth gets its start in the heart. It's from the heart that we vomit up evil arguments, murders, adulteries, fornications, thefts, lies, and cussing. That's what pollute (Matthew 15:19-20 The Message).

Your heart can be corrupted by lust even quicker than your body. Those leering looks you think nobody notices-they also corrupt (Matthew 5:28 The Message).

Sexual behavior on the job should be controllable, even for men. See how to avoid and deal with this spiritual danger area in Chapter 5, "Something More." One anonymous blogger on the Internet blog "Revolution" stated:

"You will inevitably adopt the morality of the programs, movies, books, magazines, music, internet sites and conversations you participate in. GIGO—Garbage in, garbage out; Godliness in, Godliness out. You become what you choose to feed your mind on."[37]

Frangipane reminds us: "We cannot be successful in the heavenly war if we are not victorious in the battlefield of our minds. There is only one realm of final victory against the enemy: Christ-likeness."

> *I will strike her children dead. Then all the churches will know that I am he who searches* **hearts and minds***, and I will repay each of you according to your deeds* (Rev 2:23 NIV).

Our victory in every matter begins here, in our "minds and hearts."[38]

The Christian approach to a job will not permit even a hint of sexual impurity.

Goal 7: Humility

> Whosoever *therefore shall humble himself as this little child, the same is greatest in the kingdom of heaven (Matthew 18:4 NIV).*
> *And whosoever shall exalt himself shall be abased; and he that shall humble himself shall be exalted* (Matthew 23:12 NIV).

Be courteously respectful, not arrogant, not proud or self-serving. Benjamin Franklin put it this way:" To be humble to superiors is duty, to equals courtesy, to inferiors nobleness."[39]

My brother-in-law gave me a great example of Christian humility on the job (see Appendix H, page 261). He recalls when another employee inappropriately confronted him:

> "My first reaction on the inside of me was to find his manager, put this person in his place, and continue my job as planned. My second reaction involved thoughts and words of response not necessary to explain. My third reaction came from my spirit inside, and thank God, I responded to this reaction only. From inside there was a very soft and gentle urge to say, 'We have just finished, that will be fine.' David escorted us past the guards and held the door open for us to leave. During the walk back to my office, my colleague said David was extremely ugly and rude. I said, "I have seen

ugly and rude and David was not. He was just doing
what he felt he should do."

The Christian will approach his job and all the people with whom
he interacts with humility.

Goal 8: Consistency

> *There should be a consistency that runs through us all.*
> *For Jesus doesn't change-yesterday, today, tomorrow,*
> *he's always totally himself* (Hebrews 13:8 The
> Message).

Paul was encouraging the church members to be consistent in their
Christian living. The Christian layman must be consistent in all of his
behavior on the job.

The Christian approach to a job will be the same day in and day
out. This requires discipline.

Goal 9: Clean Language

> *Watch the way you talk. Let nothing foul or dirty come*
> *out of your mouth. Say only what helps, each word a*
> *gift* (Ephesians 4:29 The Message).
> *Though some tongues just love the taste of gossip,*
> *Christians have better uses for language than that. Do*
> *not talk dirty or silly. That kind of talk doesn't fit our*
> *style* (Ephesians 5:4 The Message).
> *Post a guard at my mouth, God, set a watch at the door*
> *of my lips. Don't let me so much as dream of evil or*
> *thoughtlessly fall into bad company* (Psalms 141:3-4
> The Message).

The Christian will not use even a "damn or a hell" nor will he pass
along an inappropriate email or joke.

The Christian approach to a job will not allow inappropriate words
and expressions in his communication.

Goal 10: Christian Ethics

> *One of the religion scholars came up. Hearing the*
> *lively exchanges of question and answer and seeing*
> *how sharp Jesus was in his answers, he put in his*
> *question: Which is most important of all the*
> *commandments?" Jesus said. "The first in importance*

is, Listen, Israel: The Lord your God is one, so love the Lord God with all your passion and prayer and intelligence and energy. And here is the second: Love others as well as you love yourself. There is no other commandment that ranks with these (Mark 12:28-31 The Message).

The Interpreter's Bible states "Christianity has no monopoly on ethical teachings or moral ideals. Christian ethics differs radically, however, in the motives which it calls into play."[40]

The Merriam-Webster Dictionary defines ethic as "the discipline dealing with what is good and bad and with moral duty and obligation."[41]

The All-About-Ethics website relates one's ethics to his behavior:

"What are ethics? My ethics are the rules or standards governing the conduct by which I live my life and make all my decisions. One of the best ways of thinking about ethics is to take a quick look at what you believe and then think about how you would react when those beliefs are challenged. Your ethics govern your thought process so that when a problem arises or you need to try to work your way through a situation your solution is based on your ethics. So exactly where do these come from?"[42]

The answer to that question is found in the greatest commandment quoted above. The values that underlie the behavior of Christians emanate from love of God and others.

The Christian approach to a job must be ethical.

Summary of Christian Work Ethics

The Christian layman will always strive for excellence in all work efforts, be an encourager to other employees, love and serve others humbly, and consistently exhibit clean language, sexual purity, honesty and the highest ethical standards possible. In so doing, the Christian layman will have a work life and work style that will be so different that colleagues will ask, "Why?"

This is how the Christian layman practices his faith in the workplace. How could any employer complain about an employee practicing their faith on the job when his single focus is to be a competent and enthusiastic contributor to the work organization's goals?

Jobs that Christian Laymen Should Not Take

We Christian laymen are not free to choose just any job. Sherman and Hendrix state, "In our work we should strive to make the greatest contribution we can to people in light of the resources and responsibilities God has given us."[43]There are jobs and industries that Christians should avoid. Jobs that harm God's creation are not something a Christian should be involved in. Jobs in the tobacco industry are one example.

The Tobacco Industry

One example of prohibited jobs is found in the tobacco industry. That industry produces a product that kills and maims a lot of people.

> "Around 5.4 million deaths a year are caused by tobacco. Smoking is set to kill 6.5 million people in 2015 and 8.3 million humans in 2030, with the biggest rise in low-and middle-income countries. Every 6.5 seconds a current or former smoker dies, according to the World Health organization (WHO). An estimated 1.3 billion people are smokers worldwide (WHO). Over 443,000 Americans (over 18 percent of all deaths) die because of smoking each year. Secondhand smoke kills about 50,000 of them. 1.2 million people in China die because of smoking each year. That is 2,000 people a day. Tobacco use will kill 1 billion people in the 21st century if current smoking trends continue. 33 percent to 50 percent of all smokers are killed by their habit. Smokers die on average 15 years sooner than nonsmokers."[44]

In testimony before Congress, the CEOs of seven American tobacco companies perjured themselves when under oath on April 14, 1994; they stated that nicotine was not addictive.[45]

The work of a Christian in that industry would be promoting all of the bad things that the tobacco industry represents.

Jobs in illegal and immoral businesses are not options for Christians, (e.g., prostitution).

Some have argued that a Christian can make a positive contribution for the Kingdom in any job. That may be true, but equally true is that if a Christian is getting paid to do ungodly things, his acts undermine any Christian influence he may have.

Chapter Summary

The spiritual warrior this book is written for is a Christian layman in his workplace, approaching the tasks of the job he is paid to do with a Christian approach. This spiritual warrior is also alert to the human and spiritual needs of his colleagues and finds appropriate ways to meet those needs at times when he is "off the clock."

You now understand how you choose your lay job. You are now confident that your choice can be a calling that you love and is authentic and makes you feel alive, and that calling is from God because you have made decisions consistent with God's moral will as stated in the Bible.

The Next Chapter

Now we turn to help you be more informed about your Bible. Knowledge about how you got this miraculous book will help you to follow its direction. The Bible is the Spiritual Warrior's Global Positioning System.

Extra Life Insights

(If you can't know great men and women you can know their words!)

"Be who you are and say what you feel, because those who mind don't matter, and those who matter don't mind."
-Dr. Seuss

"But nothing worth having comes without some kind of fight--Got to kick at the darkness 'till it bleeds daylight."
-Bruce Cockburn

"Courage is Contagious. When a brave man takes a stand the spines of others are stiffened." -Billy Graham

"You have all the reason in the world to achieve your grandest dreams. Imagination plus innovation equals realization." -Denis Waitley

"Nothing resists a human will that stakes its very existence upon the achievement of its purpose."
-Benjamin Disraeli

"Weakness of attitude becomes weakness of character."
–Albert Einstein

Notes

1. Lt. Col. Dave Grossman with Loren W. Christen, *On Combat: The Psychology and Physiology of Deadly Conflict in War and in Peace* (PPCT Research Publications, 2007), xix.
2. Dr. Bill Shiell, Pastor First Baptist Church of Tallahassee, FL, Sermon: "The March of Faith," October 28, 2013.
3. Eric L Haney, *Inside Delta Force* (New York: Delacorte Press, 2006), Charlie A. Beckwith, Donald Knox, *Delta Force: A Memoir by the Founder of the U.S. Military's Most Secretive Special-Operations Unit*, William Morrow: New York, 1983).
4. From an email from Jerry Bridges, author of *The Pursuit of Holiness* (Colorado Springs: NavPress, 1985), on September 14, 2010: "As to the quote you attribute to me, I do not remember making it. It was probably an extemporaneous thought in the course of a message that was given. Feel free to use it either with or without crediting it to me. Cordially in Christ, Jerry Bridges"
5. Azquotes, http://www.azquotes.com/quote/849656 (accessed December23, 2015).
6. Tony Watson, *Sociology, Work & Industry*, (London: Routledge & Kegan Paul, 1980), 83.
7. Sherman and Hendricks, 51.
8. Dorothy L. Sayers, *Letters to a Diminished Church: Passionate Arguments for the Relevance of Christian Doctrine* (W. Publishing Group, a division of Thomas Nelson, Inc., 2004), Kindle location = 1611.
9. Truth Modules, WorkLife, http://www.workliferhythm.org/CC_Content_Page/tm_ser ies.html (accessed December 23, 2013).
10. Sherman and Hendricks, 47.
11. "Knowing God's Will – Insight from George Muller," All About Following Jesus, http://www.allaboutfollowingjesus.org/knowing-gods-will.htm (accessed December 23, 2013).
12. Sherman, 142.
13. Garry Friesen, *Decision Making and the Will of God* (Colorado Springs, CO: Multmonah Books, 2004).
14. Friesen, 139.
15. Doug Sherman and William Hendricks, *Your Work Matters To*

God, (Colorado Springs: NavPress, 1987), 136.

16. Gregg Levoy, *Callings, Finding and Following an Authentic Life* (New York: Three Rivers Press, 1997), 31.

17. "Steve Jobs: Find What you Love, WST, October 6, 2011 http://www.wsj.com/articles/SB1000142405297020338880457661 3572842080228 (Accessed November 10, 2015)

18. http://www.brainyquote.com/quotes/quotes/g/georgeburn121344.html

19. John Scully, Bio, http://www.biography.com/people/john-sculley-21187457

20. (page 15 of Swartz)

21. Barry Schwartz, *Why We Work (TED Books)*, Simon & Schuster/ TED (September 1, 2015), 12.

22. Schwartz, 14

23. Ibid., 15

24. Dictionary, (http://dictionary.reference.com/browse/telos?s=t) (accessed December 23, 2015).

25. History of Work Ethic. accessed May 10, 2014. http://workethic.coe.uga.edu/htpp.html

26. *"Protestant Work Ethic," Complete Book of Everyday Christianity,* Intervarsity Urbana, www.urbana.org/complete-book-of-everyday-christianity/work-ethic-protestan (accessed May 10, 2013).

27. Jim Collins, *Good to Great* (New York: Harper Collins, 2001).

28. Collins, xxvi

29. What/Why, http://www.faithandwork.com/about/1-what-why (accessed December 23, 2015).

30. Tom Peters, *The Little Big Thing*, (New York: Harper Collins, 2010), 10

31. Zig Zigler, *Meet You at the Top* (Gretna, LA: Pelican Publications, 2000).

32. Quotes, http://thinkexist.com/quotation/to_love_is_to_risk_not_being_loved_in_return-to/9949.html accessed December 23, 2013.

33. Shiell, Bill, At Presentation of the Village Square in Tallahassee in 2015.

34. Andy Stanley, "Leading Great", Follow Sermon Series, Northpoint Community Church,

http://northpoint.org/messages/follow/leading-great/ (accessed December 23, 2013).

35. Blaber, Pete, *The Mission, The Men and Me: Lessons from a Delta Force Commander*, (The Berkley Publishing Group: New York, 2008), 111-112.

36. Honesty, Merriam-Webster, (accessed December 23, 2013). http://www.merriam-webster.com/dictionary/honesty.

37. Sexual purity begins in the mind, not the body, Revolution, http://hanieumoh.blogspot.com/2013/05/sexual-purity-begins-in-mind-not-body.html (accessed December 23, 2013).

38. Francis Frangipane, *The Three Battlegrounds* (Cedar Rapids, IA: Arrow Publications, Inc., 2006), 146.

39. Benjamin Franklin Quotes, Thinkexist, http://thinkexist.com/quotation/to_be_humble_to_superiors_is_duty-to_equals/146119.html (accessed December 23, 2013).

40. *The Interpreter's Bible: Volume 10*, (Abingdon Press: New York, 1953), 682.

41. Ethics, Merriam-Webster, http://www.merriam-webster.com/dictionary/ethics (accessed December 23, 2013).

42. "What Are Work Ethics?" All About Philosophy, http://www.allaboutphilosophy.org/what-are-work-ethics-faq.htm (accessed December 34, 2013).

43. Sherman and Hendrix, 167

44. Arthur A. Hawkins II, "Smoke-free: The Complete Guide to Stop Smoking," http://www.inforesearchlab.com/smokingdeaths.chtml (accessed October 7, 2010).

45. "Tobacco CEO's Statement of Congress 1994 News Clip Nicotine is not addictive," http://senate.ucsf.edu/tobacco/executives1994congress.html

Chapter 3: What is the Spiritual Warrior's Global Positioning System?

This chapter will give the Spiritual Warrior a deep understanding of how the Bible came to exist as he now depends on it as his principal tool for guidance. The chapter will help educate the Spiritual Warrior as to how he got the Bible he now uses daily. It will identify and discuss major issues about the Bible so that the Spiritual Warrior may have an informed understanding when the world attacks this critical and basic guidance for his life.

Introduction

The Bible is the Spiritual Warrior's Global Positioning System! The Bible is the principal source for experiencing and understanding God and getting direction for life. The spiritual warrior needs to have confidence in his Bible. I believe that confidence in God's Word comes from being informed about the evolution of the Bible we now have. **"Blind faith" regarding the Bible is dangerous!** It is lazy and unnecessary. "Blind faith" makes the spiritual warrior vulnerable. What the spiritual warrior needs is "informed faith." Knowledge can help the warrior be unshakeable in his faith in the scriptures in the face of criticism of this incredible Book.

Rabbi Joshua Heschel (1907 – 1972) describes the paradox of our belief in God and the Bible.

> "We are moving in a circle. We would accept the Bible only if we could be sure of the presence of God in its words. Now, to identify His presence we must know what He is, but such knowledge we can only derive from the Bible. No human mind, conditioned as it is by its own perspectives, relations and aspirations, is able on its own to proclaim for all men and all times "This is God and nothing else." Thus we must accept the Bible in order to know the Bible; we must accept its unique authority in order to sense its unique quality. This, indeed, is the paradox of faith, the paradox of existence."[1]

Rabbi Heschel is talking about the Hebrew Bible. As a Christian I believe this is also true of the New Testament. I think what Heschel is saying is that in order to know God we must accept the Bible as the inspired

Word of God, but the Bible is our principal source for knowing God. Now that is a paradox!

How the world got the Bible we have today is a rich and complicated story. It is not as simple as an old deacon's statement, "If the King James Version (KJV) was good enough for the disciples, it is good enough for me!" Of course that is not the case, but the King James Version of the Bible has been a cherished translation through the years from its first printing in 1611. Countless numbers of souls have become Christians as a result of reading and being taught from the KJV. Nothing can take away from the significant impact of the KJV on Christianity. (Author's Note: the 1611 King James Version included 14 books of the Apocrypha.) [2]

I would never disparage anyone from his or her love and respect for the KJV. However, I hope here to challenge the spiritual warrior to consider some of the current information we have about the Bible, all of which aims to know the original manuscript and its message more completely. I learned as a freshman at Howard College (Samford University in Birmingham, Alabama) there is no question too big to ask of God, even to how we got the Bible.

A metaphor may help to explain why the following is presented. To accept the KJV as the only or preeminent English translation is like a man standing in a field in the year 1400 and experiencing the earth only by what he sees, hears and feels. That may be all he needs to get through the day, but there is so much more happening that will enrich and inform his life. Our man in the field is not aware that the earth he is standing on is spinning on its axes at 1,040 miles per hour (at the equator). Not only does the sun not rotate around the earth as thought in 1400, but also it is orbiting the sun at 67,108 miles per hour. Those specks of light in the night sky are stars and planets; many are like our sun but billions of light years away. Many are moving away from us at great speeds. A recent estimate is that the universe is expanding at a rate of 46.2 miles per second per megaparsec. A megaparsec is roughly three million light-years. That is very fast! [3]

What we now know about the original manuscripts of the Bible is just as dramatic and extensive as the difference between what our 1400 man in the field knew about his universe to what a man in a field could know today.

Another metaphor may help impress the reader with the value of understanding how we got this extraordinary Book. For purpose of our metaphor, imagine four people sitting down to eat one of the most exquisite gourmet entrees prepared by a world-renowned chef. All four people agree that it is the tastiest dish they have ever eaten. Three of our people have no knowledge of gourmet cooking and have never cooked a meal for someone else and they have no interest in what went into creation of such a dish. The fourth person is himself a gourmet cook with extensive knowledge of the skill that went into preparing the meal. Because of his knowledge of and experience with cooking, He is aware of the subtleties of what he is tasting and appreciates all that went into preparation of the meal. Although all four are having similar taste experiences, it is our fourth person, the chef, that is having a "higher" experience. So too is the reader of scripture who knows how that scripture came to him and what it contains.

One more metaphor to help us understand how we Christians have come to this sad state of ignorance of the creation of the most important book in our lives. This has happened because Christian parents who have seen their children become Christians approach their children's education on what is in the Bible and how we got it, the same way we have provided our children with sex education. Leave them on their own and let them learn the details from their peers and common knowledge on the street. This approach is not good for either subject.

This chapter will present information on the Old Testament and the New Testament.

The Old Testament: The Back Story of the New Testament

The Old Testament (OT) (the Hebrew Bible) is critical to the Christian's understanding of the New Testament (NT). There are 31,103 verses in the Christians Bible: 23,145 in the OT and 7,958 in the NT. By count of verses, the OT is 74.4% of the Christian Bible.

There were precursors to establishment of chapter and verse numbers in the Bible. Chapter numbers were developed by Stephen Langton (1150 – 1228), an Archbishop of Canterbury from 1207 to his death in 1228. Verse numbers were added to the Old Testament by a Jewish rabbi named Nathan in 1448. Robert Estienne (Stephanus) assigned verse numbers to the New Testament in 1555. Estienne used the work by Rabbi Nathan and assigned verses to the Old Testament at the same time. These chapter and verse numbers have remained unchanged since the publication of the Geneva Bible in 1555.[4]

The Geneva Bible was the first Bible brought to America. It arrived on the Mayflower in 1620. The Geneva Bible had extensive marginal notes by the likes of John Calvin and John Knox. It predated the King James

Version by 56 years. In fact, the Geneva Bible with its marginal notes that undercut the authority of kings, was in part the motivation of King James to authorize his Bible, without marginal notes.

Orthodox Jews and fundamentalist Christians believe that God gave Moses the entire Torah (first five books of the Bible, in Greek, Pentateuch) on Mount Sinai when (Moses) (1391 – 1271 BCE) received the Ten Commandments. Many Bible scholars do not believe this.

The development of the Hebrew Bible cannot be separated from the history of the Hebrew people.

The Israelites coming out of Egypt were an amalgam of thirteen tribes. We normally think of them as twelve tribes because twelve tribes received land, see Appendix M, page 281. The thirteenth tribe was the Levites.

> "If one tribe were to withdraw from the union or to be absorbed into another, the number twelve would be preserved, either by splitting one of the remaining tribes into two or by accepting a new tribe into the union. For example, when the tribe of Levi is considered among the twelve tribes, the Joseph tribes are counted as one. However, when Levi is not mentioned, the Joseph tribes are counted separately as Manasseh and Ephraim."[6]

The Levites were the priests. They received the temple tax of ten percent of all the animal sacrifices they performed at the Temple. Within each **tribe** there were **clans**. Within each clan there were **families**.

> *Eleazar son of Aaron married one of the daughters*
> *of Putiel, and she bore him Phinehas. These were*
> *the heads of the Levite **families**, **clan** by **clan***
> (Exodus 6:25 NIV).

King David (1040 BCE - 970 BCE) was not allowed to build the First Temple to house the Ark of the Covenant that contained the Ten Commandments because he had "shed so much blood."

> *But God said to me, 'You may not build a house for my*
> *name, for you are a warrior and have shed blood'* (I
> Chronicles 28:3 NIV).

So David's second son, Solomon (1000 BCE – 931 BCE) built the First Temple in 957 BCE.

The Israelites divided into two kingdoms: The northern 10 tribes were called Israel; the southern two tribes of Judah and Ruben were called Judah.

The Northern Kingdom of Israel was conquered by Assyria in 722 BCE and disappeared from history.

The Southern Kingdom of Judah was conquered by Nebuchadnezzar in 597 BCE and about 10,000 of the most prominent citizens of Judah were deported to Babylon.[7] Solomon's Temple in Jerusalem was destroyed in 587 BCE.

The Hebrews prospered in Babylon. Many Biblical scholars state it was during this exile that the Torah was put down in writing. When the Torah (Genesis, Exodus, Leviticus, Numbers and Deuteronomy) was written down it was written in ancient Hebrew. There were no vowels and no spaces between words in the text and was written from right to left.

The exile lasted 59 years and ended when Cyrus of Persia conquered Mesopotamia and let the Israelites return to Jerusalem in 538.

The Second Temple was begun in Jerusalem in 519 BCE in the second year of the reign of Darius Hystaspes (550 – 486 B.C.E.).[8] The second Temple was not nearly as ornamented as Solomon's, so much so that when men who had lived to see Solomon's temple saw this temple, they wept.

> But many of the older priests and Levites and family
> heads, who had seen the former temple, wept aloud
> when they saw the foundation of this temple being laid
> (Ezra 3:12 NIV).

Herod the Great (73 BCE – 4 BCE) became King of Judea in 37 BCE. He rebuilt the Second Temple on a grander scale from 20 BCE to 19 BCE. It took another eight years to complete. This rebuilt Second Temple was the central place of Judaism for 79 years until Rome destroyed it in 70 CE.

It was in the Second Temple period when Rabbis began to use translations of the Hebrew Bible into Aramaic in order for the people to understand the Torah, because Aramaic was the common everyday language of the people. These translations are called Targum.[9]

> They read from the Book of the Law of God, making it
> clear and giving the meaning so that the people
> understood what was being read (Nehemiah 8:8 NIV).[10]

The existence of Targum demonstrates the interest of the clergy to make God's word understandable to common people. This is much of the reason behind all of the translations since.

There are 613 commandments in the Torah. These included the Ten Commandments, which Jews today prefer to call the "ten sayings." Tracey

R. Rich has compiled a list, with references, of all 613 laws at http://www.jewfaq.org/613.htm

One group that played a major role in the written Hebrew Bible we have today, was the Masoretes. They lived in Palestine in the 6th to the 10th centuries CE. They were committed to develop a "correct" written Hebrew Bible. They would judge from all of the copies available at the time, which were the most accurate text. The Masorites also helped preserve the oral tradition by developing and adding vowels to the Hebrew text and adding "vocalization and cantillation marks."[11] The earliest existing manuscript of the complete Hebrew Bible is the **Codex Leningradensis** housed in the National Library of Stalingrad since the 1800s.[12] This codex is a Masoretic Text and is a complete copy of the Hebrew Old Testament completed in 1010 CE.[13]

Many of the modern Hebrew Bibles and Christian Old Testaments use the Leningradensis Codex as their source.

The JPS Tanakh is one modern Hebrew Bible used in many synagogues today. It was first published by the Jewish Publication Society in 1917 to give American Jews an up-to-date English translation. It drew heavily on the Protestant Revised Version with an effort to "remove all un-Jewish and anti-Jewish phrases, expressions, renderings, and usages…) and introduce traditional Jewish interpretation to reflect Jewish feeling, law, faith and tradition."[14] Updated translations were developed over twenty years in the 60's and 70's and published in 1985. A further updated edition was published in 2001 and is available on Amazon @ http://www.amazon.com/Hebrew-English-Tanakh-Jewish-Publication-Society/dp/0827606974/ref=sr_1_2?ie=UTF8&qid=1436644019&sr=8-2&keywords=jps+Tanakh

The Hebrew Cannon

The Hebrew Bible has the same books as does the Christian Old Testament but arranged in a different order (see Appendix L, page 279). There are 35 books in the Hebrew Bible and 39 in the Christian Old Testament. The difference of four is because the Hebrew Bible combines 1 & 2 Chronicles into one book, 1 & 2 Samuel as one book, 1 & 2 Kings as one book and Ezra-Nehemiah as one book.

The Hebrew Bible groups the books into three sections: The Torah, The Prophets and the Writings. The Hebrew Bible is often referred to as the Tanakh, which is the first two letters of the Hebrew name for each section.

"Canon," a Greek word meaning "reed," came to refer to any straight stick that could be used for measuring.[15] Canon was applied to a selection of Greek writings that were set apart as having a high standard of content and value. The sense of canon being applied to books of the Bible is found in a rabbinic comment on Ecclesiastes 12:12

> *Of anything beyond these, my child, beware. Of making many books there is no end* (Ecclesiastes 12:12 NRSV).

The rabbinic comment states:

> Those who bring more than twenty-four books (the standard number in the Hebrew Bible) into their house introduce confusion into their house (Qoh Rab 12.12).

The number twenty-four comes from some books in the Hebrew Bible which are grouped as one book, "e.g., Samuel, Kings, and the Twelve Prophets."[16]

There is no one event at which books of the Hebrew Bible were to be determined as the canon.

> "Torah (first five books) was canonized in the Persian period (538 BCE – 333 BCE), followed by the canonization of the Nevi'im (Prophets) in the late Persian or early Greek period (333 BCE – 63 BCE), while the Ketuvim (The Writings) were canonized last, around the time of the destruction of the Second Temple (70 CE)."[17]

"The (complete) Hebrew Bible canon was not finalized until the second century CE..."[18]

Few Biblical scholars today believe that Moses wrote the Torah. He could not have written the last chapter of the Torah, Deuteronomy 34, which tells of his death. So, if Moses did not write the Torah, who did? How did the Torah get written down?

Some biblical scholars hypothesize that it was Ezra. Ezra (480 – 440 BCE) was born in Babylon during the exile. Ezra "probably wrote Chronicles I and Ezra and was the final editor of the Torah." King Artaxerxes of Persia sent Ezra back to Jerusalem with a large group of exiles in 458 BCE. Nehemiah says that Ezra read the law at the Water Gate of the Temple at the Feast of Tabernacles (444 BCE).[19]

> All the people came together as one in the square before the Water Gate. They told Ezra the teacher of the Law to bring out the Book of the Law of Moses, which the LORD had commanded for Israel. So on the first day of

the seventh month Ezra the priest brought the Law before the assembly, which was made up of men and women and all who were able to understand. He read it aloud from daybreak till noon as he faced the square before the Water Gate in the presence of the men, women and others who could understand. And all the people listened attentively to the Book of the Law (Nehemiah 8:1-3 NIV).

Bible scholars theorize that there were source documents for the Hebrew Bible. None of these source documents exist today, but the clue that they did exist comes in the duplication, conflicting and disjointed stories told in the Torah.

The Documentary Hypothesis

One theory of the sources for the Torah is called the Documentary Hypothesis. It had precursors but came together in the work of Julius Wellhausen (1844 – 1918).[20] Wellhausen was a German biblical scholar and university professor (University of Greifswald). He saw in the scripture four different documents, which he called J, E, P, and D.

J — the Yahwist. J gets its name because it uses and allows humans to use the name Yahweh for "God" (Jahwe in German) before Israel exists (see Genesis 4:26; cf. E and P, below). J appears to have been composed in Judah (the southern Hebrew kingdom), perhaps during Solomon's day, around 950 BCE.

E — the Elohist. The name is derived from E's use of Elohim (Hebrew for "God") rather than Yahweh in the early period. E reserves the name Yahweh for the time from Moses on (see Exodus 3:13-15). E appears to have been written by priest living in the northern Hebrew kingdom, around 850 BCE.

P — the Priestly source. P is especially concerned with stories and laws relevant for priests. Like E, it reserves the name YHWH (Yahweh) for the period from Moses on (see Exodus 6:3). Many scholars date P either during the exile (6th century BCE.) or shortly after (5th century BCE.). Others date it as early as the beginning of the 7th century BCE.

D — is essentially the book of Deuteronomy. It is not

mingled with J, E and P.[21]

Commentary in The New Oxford Annotated Bible (NRSV) validates the Documentary Hypothesis as a tool for biblical analysis:

> "(Wellhausen's) formulation of the Documentary Hypothesis became a classic statement, the theory that subsequent scholars up to the present have built upon, accepted, modified, or rejected. Despite initial and continuing conservative opposition, and, in the case of Roman Catholics especially, institutional interdict, it is widely adopted by liberal Protestant scholars and eventually by Roman Catholic and Jewish scholars, resulting in a large consensus that is still dominant."[22]

Richard Elliot Friedman (1946 - --) wrote two books that further refines the Documentary Hypothesis: *Who Wrote the Bible* (1987) and *The Bible with Sources Revealed* (2003). In the second book Dr. Friedman presents the five books of the Torah by source using colors and fonts to distinguish one source from another. He also defines and explains the "seven main arguments for the hypothesis."

1. Linguistic: The text reflects usage consistent with several different ages of Hebrew history. This analysis includes archeological evidences spread out over time and dated to different historical periods. This evidence in the Bible is supported by non-biblical anthropological sources found in scrolls and engravings on pottery. The different periods can be distinguished by language usage much as the King James Version (1611 CE) can be distinguished from the New International Version (1984 CE) translations of Psalms 23:1-3:

   > *The LORD is my shepherd; I shall not want. He maketh me to lie down in green pastures: he leadeth me beside the still waters. He restoreth my soul: he leadeth me in the paths of righteousness for his name's sake* (KJV 1611).
   > *The LORD is my shepherd, I lack nothing. He makes me lie down in green pastures, he leads me beside quiet waters, he refreshes my soul. He guides me along the right paths for his name's sake* (NIV 1984).

2. Terminology: Dr. Friedman states that "Certain words and phrases occur disproportionately or even entirely in one source but not in

others." He identifies twenty-five incidents where this happens. Two of his examples are presented here:

A. The mountain that is called Sinai in J and P (twenty times) is called Horeb or "the Mountain of God" in E and D (fourteen times). In thirty-four occurrences of these names, there is no exception to this distinction.

B. The word "congregation" occurs more than one hundred times in the Torah, all in P, without a single exception.

3. Consistent Content:

A. The Revelation of God's name.

Different words are used for the name of God by different sources: YHWH (Yahweh) is used by the J source and Elohim is used by the E source. Yahweh is the Hebrew word for the God of the covenant. Hebrews considered the name to be so holy that it could not be spoken aloud. When spoken aloud Jews today use the word Adonai. This use of two different names is important but Dr. Friedman states the most significant evidence of different sources is when the name Yahweh begins to be used.

"According to J, the name was known since the earliest generations of humans. Referring to a generation before the floods J says explicitly, "Then it was begun to invoke the name YHWH" (Gen 4:26). The use of the name by humans may go back even earlier in J, because Eve uses it when she names Cain (Gen 4:1). But in E and P it is stated just as explicitly that YHWH does not reveal this name until the generation of Moses. In Genesis YHWH instead tells Abraham that his name is El Shadday. YHWH appeared to Abram and said to him, "I am El Shadday." (Gen 17:1) and then when YHWH speaks to Moses in Exodus, the text says: "And God spoke to Moses and said to him,

"*I am YHWH. And I appeared to Abraham, to Isaac, and to Jacob as El Shadday, and I was not known to them by my name, YHWH* (Exodus 6:2-3)."[23]

B. The Sacred Objects:

"The Tabernacle is mentioned 200 times in P, but never mentioned in J or D. "In E, miracles are performed with Moses' Staff, but in P, it is Aaron's staff that is used for performing miracles."[24]

C. Numbers:

"Ages, Dates, measurement, numbers, orders, and precise instructions are an obvious, major concern in P. There is nothing even nearly comparable in degree in J, E, or D."[25]

4. Continuity of Texts (Narrative Flow)

When J and E are separated, each presents a complete narrative without the help of the other.

5. Connections with Other Parts of the Bible

Each source has a unique "affinity" to other books in the Old Testament. They share a common view and vocabulary. Dr. Friedman writes:

"D has well-known parallels of wording with the book of Jeremiah; P has such parallels with the book of Ezekiel. J and E are particularly connected with the book of Hosea."[26]

6. Relationships Among the Sources To Each Other and to History

Dr. Friedman points out that from 922 to 722 BCE Israel was divided into two kingdoms, the northern ten tribes were called Israel and the southern tribes of Judah and Ruben were called Judah. Dr. Friedman's analysis shows that the J source has a lot of connections with Judah, whereas the E source has connections to Israel.

A. J Source and Judah

Among the many connections Dr. Friedman establishes, only in J is Judah a significant figure, i.e., it is Judah that is the brother who saves Joseph from his bother's plan to kill him and "it is Judah who speaks for his brother and defends Benjamin to Joseph in Egypt." Also, the Ark is important in J but never mentioned in E. J states that the Ark was located in Judah.[27]

B. E Source and Israel

E has specific connections to the Levites and the priesthood of Shiloh, a city in Ephraim, which was one of the 10 Northern tribes of Israel. E develops a "special standing" for Joshua. Joshua was from the tribe of Ephraim. J never mentions Joshua.[28]

P is the priestly source. In P only Levite ancestors of Aaron serve as priest. All other Levites "serve as lesser clergy." In P all sacrifices occur only at the Temple. In J and E "people sacrifice at various locations."

7. Convergence

Dr. Friedman states, "the strongest evidence establishing the

Documentary Hypothesis is that several different lines of evidence converge." The "convergence" occurs when the different names for God line up with the different ages in which sources wrote and the complete stories told when the doublets are separated. Doublets are two or more accounts of the same event that have conflicting facts. There are thirty-one doublets. They are listed in Appendix N, page 282.[29]

Criticism of the Documentary Hypothesis

The Documentary Hypothesis is not without criticism. "The time has long passed for scholars of every theological persuasion to recognize that the Graf-Wellhausen theory, as a starting point for continued research, is dead" so states Duane Garrett of the Associates of Biblical Research.[30] In his article he addresses each of the issues presented by the advocates of the Documentary Hypothesis:

1. The name of God. Referencing Umberto Cassuto, "To put it simply, Elohim is what God is and Yahweh is who He is." Therefore, the use of the two names is reasonable and does not support "two sources."

2. Repetition, Parallel Accounts (Doublets), and Redundancy. This duplication is a strong argument of the Documentary Hypothesis until it is recognized as a very common literary attribute of ancient writing. Examples are given in non-biblical writings.

3. Contradictions in the Text. "Genesis 6:2 says to bring one pair of every kind of animal, but 7:2 says to bring seven pairs of clean animals." Genesis 6:2 is nothing more than a general number given so the builders can know how large to build the ark compared to a specific number (seven clean pairs in Gen 7:2) as instruction for the provisions they would need given right before the flood.

4. The Criterion of Style. "We know nothing of the common speech of the people of ancient Israel, and we cannot be sure that the words cited as synonymous pairs are in fact synonymous." Quoting from authors of a recent computer-aided analysis of the text, "with all due respect to the illustrious Documentarians past and present, there is *massive evidence* that the pre-Biblical triplicity [i.e., of J, E, and P] of Genesis, which their line of thought postulates to have been worked over by a late and gifted editor into a trinity, is actually a unity (1985:190 italics added)."

5. The Theological Unity of Each Document. "Under continued scholarly scrutiny, the Elohist has disappeared from view entirely

and the Yahwist is fast fading from existence, even as P grows beyond all reasonable bounds. The hypothesis has no value as a guide for continued research."

6. The Hypothesis Proven in Some Specific Texts. The author does state that there does appear to be sources for passages in Genesis: "I want to make a single point here. It is possible that Genesis 1:1 and Genesis 2:4ff. do in fact spring from separate sources, but that these sources have nothing to do with the four documents of the Documentary Hypothesis."

7. The Hypothesis Verified by the History of the Priesthood. The author of this article states that the reason many biblical scholars hold to "the hypothesis seems to offer the best explanation of why the term *Levite* is used inconsistently in the Old Testament." He states, "A far better solution can be obtained by reading the Pentateuch as a work that was substantially produced, as the text affirms, during the period of the Exodus.

The author concludes that the Documentary Hypothesis must be abandoned because it is "methodologically unsound."

Rof Rendtorff states the Critical-Historical (Documentary Hypothesis) method is a powerful tool but takes the focus off the real intent of the scripture. Regardless of how the text occurred, it needs to be read in the final form that has come to us:

"We have to interpret it, not change it. The Bible, in its final, canonical form, is always our teacher."[31]

The above criticism not withstanding, the Documentary Hypothesis continues to have great legitimacy among modern Biblical Scholars.

The Dead Sea Scrolls

Until the discovery of the Dead Sea Scrolls beginning in 1946, the earliest manuscript of the Hebrew Bible was the Masoretic Text published in CE 1010. The earliest complete copy of the Masoretic Text is the **Codex Leningradensis.**[32]

The Dead Sea Scrolls were produced by the Essenes, a Jewish sect, which was a third party alternative to the Pharisees and Sadducees. The Essenes chose a monastic life in Qumran on the Northwestern shore of the Dead Sea.

From 1946 to 1956, 941 scrolls were recovered from eleven caves near Qumran. 240 were biblical scrolls and 701 non-biblical. The biblical scrolls included copies of every book of the Hebrew Bible except Ester. "They are dated [based on] paleographic and radiocarbon grounds to between 250 BCE and 68 CE, when the site was destroyed by the Romans." Among the scrolls are "19 copies of the Book of Isaiah, 25 copies of Deuteronomy and 30 copies of the Psalms."[33]

The scrolls have validated the existing manuscripts and augmented some. The Dead Sea Scrolls are 1,000 years earlier than the Masoretic text. When the two are compared the Scrolls "reflect the Masoretic Text of the Torah only 48% of the time, while the remaining books outside the Torah reflect the Masoretic Text only 44 percent of the time."[34] For example, the scrolls provided the missing verse of the "acrostic Psalm 145 and "is now included as verse 13b in the HCSB, RSV, NRSV, and NIV." The portion added is:

The Lord is faithful in all His words and gracious in all His actions. (Psalm 145:13b NIV).

Check your Bible. If it does not have this phrase included in Psalm 145 then the translators of the version you are reading did not update the Hebrew they were using with the Dead Sea Scrolls.

It is interesting that the Christian Bible, The New Revised Standard Version (NRSV) has a more complete translation of Psalm 145:13 than the Jewish Publication Society's Tanaka because the former updates the Masoretic text with the Dead Sea Scrolls while the latter does not. "At least 100 such examples using the Dead Sea Scrolls have gotten modern Bible translators closer to the original text."[35]

The Talmud and Midrashim
There is some ancillary Jewish literature that is very important to the Jewish community and important in understanding the Hebrew Bible. Few Christians have ever read any of these, an omission that serious Christian Bible students should correct.

The Talmud
The Talmud contains the Mishnah, which is the Jewish Oral law written down. Rabbi Judah (The Prince) (150 CE - 220 CE) organized and edited the Mishnah in its final form in 200 CE.

The Mishnah has six "orders." Each order has a number of "tractates." Each Tractate has a number of chapters. The names of the "orders" are:

1. Zera'im (Seeds) (11 Tractates). These are the agricultural rules that include how they   are to be presented as an offering.
2. Mo'ed (Festivals) (12 Tractates). These deal with laws of the Shabbat (Sabbath) and the Holy Days.
3. Nashim (Women) (7 Tractates). These deal with marriage and divorce.
4. Nezikin (Damages) (10 Tractates). These deal with civil and criminal law.
5. Kodshim (Holly Things) (11 Tractates). These deal with laws about the sacrifices, the Holy Temple and the dietary laws.
6. Taharot (Purities) (12 Traactates). These deal with laws of ritual purity and impurity, including impurity of the dead, laws of ritual purity for the priests (Kohanim), and laws of "Family Purity" and others.[36] One of the 63 tractates has no Jewish laws. It is *Pirkei Avot*, "The Ethics of the Fathers." It is a collection of sayings and proverbs from the Rabbis through the ages.

One of my favorite passages from the Pirkei Avot is inscribed in the foyer of Temple Israel in Tallahassee. It is Pirke Avot 2:5:

"The more Torah the more life
The more study the more wisdom
The more counsel the more understanding
The more righteousness the more peace."

My take on Pirke Avot 2:5 is that we get righteousness (holiness) by reading and studying the Bible and talking to others about what we read and study. This righteousness leads to peace.[37]

As soon as the Mishnah was published, Rabbis began to discuss and debate it. There grew up a compilation of these debates over the centuries. For each law there was an explanation by one Rabbi and then a debate by another Rabbi. These Rabbis didn't always live at the same time, so the debates were across generations. The compilation of the debates/discussions of the different elements of the Mishnah is called the Gemara.[38]

The Mishnah and the Gemara together is the Talmud. There are two versions of the Talmud. "The first, known as the Jerusalem Talmud, was compiled around 350-400 CE. The Babylonian Talmud, completed around 500 CE, is considered the more authoritative version."[39] The Babylon Talmud is available on-line @ http://halakhah.com.

Midrashim

Midrashim is plural for Midrash. There are a lot of Midrash!

> "Midrash is a form of rabbinic literature. There are two
> types of midrash: midrash aggada and midrash halakha.
> Midrash aggada can best be described as a form of
> storytelling that explores ethics and values in biblical
> texts. It can take any biblical word or verse and interpret
> it to answer a question or explain something in the text.
> For instance, a midrash Aggada may attempt to explain
> why Adam didn't stop Eve from eating the forbidden
> fruit in the Garden of Eden. One of the best-known
> midrashim deals with Abraham's childhood in early
> Mesopotamia, where he is said to have smashed the
> idols in his father's shop because even at that age he
> knew there was only One God. Midrash aggadah can be
> found in both Talmuds, in midrashic collections and in
> Midrash Rabbah, which means "Great Midrash."
> Whereas midrash aggada focuses on biblical characters
> as they pertain to values and ideas, midrash halakha
> focuses on Jewish law and practice. Midrash halakha
> attempts to take biblical texts that are either general or
> unclear and to clarify what they mean. A midrash of this
> nature may explain why, for instance, tefillin are used
> during prayer and how they should be worn."[40]

For four years I have been involved in a weekly study of a book of
aggada Midrash at Temple Israel of Tallahassee. The study is called "Lunch
and Learn with Rabbi Romberg." Rabbi Romberg is a Hebrew scholar. The
Midrash we have used for several years is *Pirke De Rabbi Eliezer*.[41] The
author is unknown. A "Spanish scribe of the twelfth or thirteenth century"
probably wrote it.[42] It is attributed to Rabbi Eliezer, who lived in the last
half of the first century.[43]

As Rabbi Romberg explained these are teachings where the Rabbi
will take a verse(s) of the Torah and squeeze it until he gets all of the
possible meaning from it. From time to time Rabbi Romberg would say,
"Here the Rabbi is stretching the meaning of the verse." It reminded me of
sermons I have heard Baptist preachers preach where they stretched the
meaning of a verse so far that you wonder how did we get to that point from
the verse we started with. But the lessons in the Midrash are powerful.

One of my favorite examples is the story about Jacob, Rachel and Leah. Poor ole Jacob worked seven years for Rachel's father before he was allowed to marry Rachel. Then the father allowed Jacob to marry Rachel but extracted a promise from Jacob for another seven years after the wedding. Then to Jacob's surprise, the father substituted Leah, the older daughter, for Rachel the night of the wedding. In the Midrash, the Rabbi speculates what Jacob said when he woke up the next morning and discovered it was Leah. The Rabbi has Jacob asking Leah, "How could you deceive me like that?" Leah's response, "who are you to talk about deception?" That is powerful!

Rabbi Romberg and members of his congregation that attend consider Lunch and Learn to be a Jewish Bible Study. I consider it a Christian Bible Study of the Old Testament led by a Hebrew scholar. Something I have never experienced in a Baptist Church.

Apocrypha and the Pseudepigripha

Growing up in a Baptist Church, I never heard any reference to any passage from the Apocrypha from any Bible teacher or preacher. I learned that the books of the Apocrypha were written between the writing of the Hebrew Bible and the New Testament. I was told that the "Catholic Bible" contained the Apocrypha. Beyond that I knew nothing about the Apocrypha.

I now have learned a number of the sixteen books of the Apocrypha are included in the Bibles of four Christian Churches: Roman Catholic, Greek Orthodox, Slavonic (Russian Orthodox) and Protestant Anglican Church (See Appendix I, page 263). None of the books of the Apocrypha are included in the Hebrew Bible. All of the books of the Apocrypha were written between 200 BCE and 200 CE.[44]

> The Roman Catholic Church consider several Apocryphal books to be 'Deuterocanonical,' meaning 'second canon,' but their secondary status refers to the late date at which they were approved at the Council of Trent in 1546, not to a lesser spiritual value.[45]

The books of the Apocrypha that are in the Catholic Bible are Tobit, Judith, Additions to Esther, 1 Maccabees, 2 Maccabees, Wisdom, Sirach, and Baruch/Letter of Jeremiah.

We Christians today have a hard time understanding just how "fluid" the scriptures were in the First Century, e.g., the cannon of the Hebrew Bible was not finalized until 200 CE and the New Testament was being written and circulated in the First Century and the New Testament cannon established in the Fourth Century:

> "In the eastern church the 39th Paschal Letter of Athanasius, the Bishop of Alexandria, dates to A.D. 367. This document was the bishop's letter to the faithful, written on the occasion of Passover. In this letter Athanasius mentions 27 books the church accepted as being the New Testament. In the western church the Council of Carthage met in A.D. 397. Part of the council's work was to publish the names of the 27 books that the church held to be genuine Scripture. Putting these two dates together makes evident that by the middle-to-late fourth century the church had no question about the 27 books that would comprise the New Testament. No really serious question has risen since."[46]

The Septuagint

In the First Century the Septuagint, the Greek translation of the Hebrew Bible, was very often the Old Testament used by the writers of the New Testament. That makes a lot of sense since Greek was the common language in the Greek-Roman world and the New Testament was written in Greek.

> "The Old Testament in modern Bibles is a translation from the Hebrew Bible, but in quoting the Old Testament, the writers of the New Testament used almost exclusively the Greek Septuagint."[47]

The Septuagint included six of the books of the Apocrypha. So it is easy to understand that, given the "fluid" nature of the scripture at the time, the writers of the New Testament not only drew on the Hebrew Bible but also from the Apocrypha.

> "The most important books outside of the canonical Hebrew Bible for the new Testament writers were Sirach, the Wisdom of Solomon, Tobit, and 2 Maccabees. It has long been pointed out that the famous Prologue of the Gospel of John (John 1:1-18), in the discourse about the divine Logos, shares many similarities with if not outright dependence on the Wisdom of Solomon."[48]

This is plausible in that Biblical scholars date the writing of "The Wisdom of Solomon" in 20 B.C.E[49] before the writing of the Book of John in 90 C.E.[50]

Another example of a New Testament writer drawing from books of the Apocrypha is Jude 14-15. The NRSV attributes that scripture to 1 Enoch 1.9. Enoch is a book classified as one of several in the Pseudepigripha. The Pseudepigripha is defined as:

> "Spurious or pseudonymous writings, especially Jewish writings ascribed to various biblical patriarchs and prophets but composed within approximately 200 years of the birth of Jesus Christ."[51]

The apparent fact that New Testament writers quoted from Apocryphal and Pseudepigripha books should not shake the Spiritual Warrior's confidence in the Bible. As one strong Christian stated, "none of this shakes my faith in the scripture." To use her words, "if it happened this way it was God's intent that caused it to happen this way."

While it is believed that at least the Synoptic Gospels (Matthew, Mark and Luke) were written in the first century, we do not have any surviving manuscripts from that century and only a handful of canonical gospel manuscripts from the second century, with the earliest being P52. Most of the early Christian manuscripts come from the third century or later.[57]

The New Testament

Mark is a major source for Matthew and Luke. The author of Mark is unknown. Mark is the shortest and earliest written Gospel. From the content of Mark, it appears to have been written in 66 CE just before the Jewish revolt that included the destruction of the Temple in 70 CE.[52] The Gospel of Matthew includes 82% of the 678 verses of Mark. Luke includes 70% of the verses of Mark.[53]

The development of the New Testament we use today is very much intertwined with the development of the printing press. From the creation of the original 28 manuscripts by eight writers till the invention of the printing press, the New Testament was passed down by way of hand copies by scribes. There were errors in that process, some unintentional and some intentional. The invention of the printing press by German printer Johannes Gutenberg (1398 – 1468) in 1450 eliminated the errors from hand copying in future printed copies.

The first printed book on Gutenberg's moveable type press was the Gutenberg Bible in 1452.[54] It was a translation of the Hebrew and Greek into Latin. It was called the Latin Vulgate.

The first English translation of the Bible was by John Wycliffe (1324 – 1384). He began his translation of the New Testament in 1381. It was a translation from the Latin Vulgate to English.[55]

A lot went on from when the books of the New Testament were first written and the King James Version was printed. We don't have a copy of the original text of any of the New Testament books. "Textual Criticism" is a method of study used by biblical scholars to determine the original text.[56] There are more than five thousand hand copied "manuscripts" that exist today. Some are only fragments. The Biblical Archaeology Review had a photocopy of the earliest known manuscript in its March/April 2015 issue. It was the first time I had ever seen it. It has been labeled as P52 for Papyrus 52. It is a copy of a copy of a copy of a copy of the original. That is to say it is four times removed from the original. So, if you want to see what the original looked like, the next page is an image of P52. The image and narrative are from the Biblical Archeology Review article referenced above. The image is used by permission from the University of Manchester. The text is used by permission of the Biblical Archeology Review.

Earliest Existing New Testament Fragment

Containing part of the Gospel of John, P52 dates
to the early second century. Most experts regard
the fragments of P52 as the oldest extant canonical
Christian text. On the front appears John 18:31-33
(shown above). John 18:37-38 is on the back.
This is the scripture in which Pilate questions
Jesus before the crucifixion. Written in Greek,
this fragment came from a codex, not a scroll.

Discovered in Egypt, Papyrus 52 (P52) was
published in 1935 and is housed in the John
Rylands Library in Manchester, England. (Its full

name is "John Rylands Papyrus P52", with the
acquisition number "John Rylands Greek 457".)
The fragment measures 3.4 by 2.5 inches.

Authorities Kurt and Barbara Aland date the
fragment to "about 125" A.D., allowing for a
margin of error of 25 years on either side. should
not shake the Spiritual Warrior's

Bible Issues

The Bible has its critics. The strong Spiritual Warrior needs to know and
understand these criticisms so that when they confront him, his faith is not
shaken.

Christians and Jews should always be honest in all things. Honesty
is imperative in their knowledge and interpretation of the Bible. The two
issues presented below are examples where Christians and Jews have not
always been honest.

The Messiah

The Jewish Messiah

My pastor, Dr. Bill Shiell at First Baptist Church of Tallahassee (2015), has
said that Christianity was a Jewish religion until the 15th Chapter of Acts.
As a Christian, I have come to believe I cannot understand Christianity
without understanding my Jewish heritage. To pursue knowledge of that
heritage, I have taken the sixteen-week "Introduction to Judaism" course at
Temple Israel, a Reformed Jewish Congregation, twice (2 hours each
Sunday night). As mentioned earlier, I have also attended "Lunch and
Learn" with Rabbi Romberg each Wednesday at noon for four years. The
class averages twenty people, which includes eight Christians. There is no
effort on anyone's part in that class to convert one to the other's religion.
There is a mutual respect in an effort to understand the truth of the Bible
and the worldview of each other.

Studying my Bible "Old Testament" under the leadership of a
Hebrew scholar has been critical to my spiritual growth as a Christian. The
Jews and Rabbi Romberg consider this study to be a "Jewish Bible Study."
I consider this to be a study of the Christian Old Testament under the
leadership of a Hebrew scholar.

I am often asked by my Christian friends, "Why don't Jews see the
prophesy of Jesus in the Old Testament?" This section will help the spiritual
warrior understand the answer to that question.

The Messiah is important to some Jews. One of the greatest Rabbis, Rabbi Maimonides (1134 CE – 1204 CE) developed a list of thirteen principles of the Jewish faith. Number 12 is about the Messiah. They are:

1. God exists.
2. God is one and unique.
3. God is incorporeal (having no material existence).
4. God is eternal.
5. Prayer is to be directed to God alone and to no other.
6. The words of the prophets are true.
7. Moses' prophecies are true, and Moses was the greatest of the prophets.
8. The written Torah. (the first 5 books of the Bible) and the Oral Torah (teachings now contained in the Talmud and other writings) were given to Moses.
9. There will be no other Torah.
10. God knows the thoughts and deeds of men.
11. God will reward the good and punish the wicked.
12. The Messiah will come.
13. The dead will be resurrected.[58]

Temple Israel sponsored a lecture by Rabbi Michael J. Cook, PhD. In his book *Modern Jews Engage the New Testament*, Rabbi Cook identifies four scriptural passages that prophecy the Jewish Messiah.[59]

> *In the last days the mountain of the LORD's temple will be established as the highest of the mountains; it will be exalted above the hills, and all nations will stream to it. Many peoples will come and say, "Come, let us go up to the mountain of the LORD, to the temple of the God of Jacob. He will teach us his ways, so that we may walk in his paths." The law will go out from Zion, the word of the LORD from Jerusalem. He will judge between the nations and will settle disputes for many peoples. They will beat their swords into plowshares and their spears into pruning hooks. Nation will not take up sword against nation, nor will they train for war anymore* (Isaiah 2:2-4 NIV).
> *At that time they will call Jerusalem The Throne of the LORD and all nations will gather in Jerusalem to honor the name of the LORD. No longer will they follow*

Throne of the God — The Holy Land.

the stubbornness of their evil hearts (Jeremiah 3:17 NIV).

In that day the mountains will drip new wine, and the hills will flow with milk; all the ravines of Judah will run with water. A fountain will flow out of the LORD's house and will water the valley of acacias (Joel 3:18 NIV).

This is what the LORD Almighty says: "In those days ten people from all languages and nations will take firm hold of one Jew by the hem of his robe, and say, 'Let us go with you, because we have heard that God is with you.' (Zechariah 8:23 NIV).

All of these verses have to do with "end times," not the reign of an individual. Rabbi Cook explains the Jewish view of the Messiah:

"In terms of its own redemption need, ancient Judaism envisioned the Messiah as a restored human king in Jerusalem, likely descended from King David preoccupied with the entire people (not individuals), and a strong leader who will vindicate God in demonstrating the political, military, and economic freedom and strength of God's People by overthrowing Israel's foreign oppressors, fulfilling biblical prophesies as Jews interpret them, and ushering in God's Kingdom."[60]

Another verse in Isaiah also prophesies that the Jewish Messiah will bring world peace:

The wolf will live with the lamb, the leopard will lie down with the goat, the calf and the lion and the yearling together; and a little child will lead them (Isaiah 11:6 NIV).

Regarding the last verse, the Jewish Virtual Library quotes a modern day Jewish "commentator" Woody Allen who cautions: "And the lamb and the wolf shall lie down together, but the lamb won't get any sleep.[61]

The Virtual Jewish Library also summarizes the characteristics of the Jewish Messiah:

1. He will be a descendant of King David,
2. He will gain sovereignty over the land of Israel,
3. He will gather the Jews there from the four corners of the earth,

4. He will restore them to full observance of Torah Law, and

5. He will bring peace to the whole world.[62]

Jews will point out that Jesus only fulfilled one of these five Jewish prophecies, a descendant of King David. Never in any Jewish prophesy of a Messiah is there the idea that the Messiah would be God.

Christians need to understand that the concept of the "Jewish Messiah" is totally different from the concept of the "Christian Messiah."

In summary: the idea of the Jewish Messiah has to do with the "end times." The Messiah will be a man that is not God. All Jews will gather in Israel. There will be worldwide peace. These things did not occur when Jesus came. Therefore, from a Jewish perspective Jesus could not be the Messiah of the Old Testament and the Jews.

The Christian Messiah

For Christians, there are some rock solid prophesies of the coming of Jesus as the Messiah. The Holman Illustrated Bible Dictionary identifies 122 Old Testament prophesies of the coming of the Christian Messiah that are fulfilled by Jesus in the New Testament.[63] They are all listed in Appendix K, page 274. Here are ten of them that also includes the prophecy fulfilled in the New Testament:

The Messiah will be born of a woman.

> Prophesy: *And I will put enmity between you and the woman, and between your offspring and hers; he will crush your head, and you will strike his heel* (Genesis 3:15 NIV).
>
> Fulfillment: *But when the set time had fully come, God sent his Son, born of a woman, born under the law, to redeem those under the law, that we might receive adoption to sonship* (Galatians 4:4-5 NIV).
> *Since the children have flesh and blood, he too shared in their humanity so that by his death he might break the power of him who holds the power of death—that is, the devil—* (Hebrews 2:14 NIV).

The Messiah will be born in Bethlehem.

> Prophesy: *But you, Bethlehem Ephrata, though you are small among the clans of Judah, out of you will come for me one who will be ruler over Israel, whose origins are from of old, from ancient times* (Micah 5:2 NIV).

Fulfillment: *After Jesus was born in Bethlehem in Judea, during the time of King Herod, Magi from the east came to Jerusalem* (Matthew 2:1 NIV).

The Messiah would come from the line of Abraham.

Prophesy: *I will bless those who bless you, and whoever curses you I will curse; and all peoples on earth will be blessed through you* (Genesis 12:3 NIV).

Fulfillment: *This is the genealogy of Jesus the Messiah the son of David, the son of Abraham* (Matthew 1:1 NIV).

The Messiah would be a descendant of Isaac.

Prophesy: *Then God said, "Yes, but your wife Sarah will bear you a son, and you will call him Isaac. I will establish my covenant with him as an everlasting covenant for his descendants after him* (Genesis 17:19 NIV).

Fulfillment: *Nor because they are his descendants are they all Abraham's children. On the contrary, "It is through Isaac that your offspring will be reckoned* (Romans 9:7 NIV).

The Messiah would be a descendent of Jacob.

Prophesy: *"I see him, but not now; I behold him, but not near. A star will come out of Jacob; a scepter will rise out of Israel. He will crush the foreheads of Moab, the skulls of all the people of Sheth* (Numbers 24:17 NIV).

Fulfillment: *and he will reign over Jacob's descendants forever; his kingdom will never end* (Luke 1:33 NIV).

The Messiah would be heir to King David's throne.

Prophesy: *When your days are over and you rest with your ancestors, I will raise up your offspring to succeed you, your own flesh and blood, and I will establish his kingdom* (2 Samuel 7:12-13 NIV).

Fulfillment: *He will be great and will be called the Son of the Most High. The Lord God will give him the throne of his father David, and he will reign over Jacob's descendants forever; his kingdom will never end* (Luke 1:32-33).

A messenger would prepare the way for Messiah.

Prophesy: *A voice of one calling: "In the wilderness prepare the way for the LORD; make straight in the desert a highway for our God* (Isaiah 40:3 NIV).

Fulfillment: *The beginning of the good news about Jesus the Messiah, the Son of God, as it is written in Isaiah the prophet: "I will send my messenger ahead of you, who will prepare your way." "A voice of one calling in the wilderness, 'Prepare the way for the Lord, make straight paths for him.'" And so John the Baptist appeared in the wilderness, preaching a baptism of repentance for the forgiveness of sins* (Mark 1:1-4 NIV).

The Messiah would be crucified with criminals.

Prophesy: *Therefore, I will give him a portion among the great, and he will divide the spoils with the strong, because he poured out his life unto death, and was numbered with the transgressors. For he bore the sin of many, and made intercession for the transgressors* (Isaiah 53:12 NIV).

Fulfillment: *And with him they crucify two thieves; the one on his right hand, and the other on his left. And the scripture was fulfilled, which saith, and he was numbered with the transgressors* (Mark 15:27-28 NIV).

The Messiah would resurrect from the dead.

Prophesy: *But God will redeem me from the realm of the dead; he will surely take me to himself* (Psalm 49:15 NIV).

Fulfillment: *"Don't be alarmed," he said. "You are looking for Jesus the Nazarene, who was crucified. He has risen! He is not here. See the place where they laid him* (Mark 16:6 NIV).

The Coming of Elijah.

Prophesy: *"See, I will send the prophet Elijah to you before that great and dreadful day of the LORD comes* (Malachi 4:5 NIV).

Fulfillment: *The disciples asked him, "Why then do the teachers of the law say that Elijah must come first?" Jesus replied, "To be sure, (Elijah) comes and will restore all things. But I tell you, Elijah has already come, and they did not recognize him, but have done to him everything they wished. In the same way the Son of Man is going to suffer at their hands." Then the disciples understood that he was talking to them about John the Baptist* (Matthew 17:10-13 NIV).

Christians have never had a problem in finding Old Testament prophesies of Jesus coming as the Messiah. One of the major issues for Christians about the Messiah is that one of the key verses we Christians have always used is not about Jesus' coming.

Christians often quote Isaiah 7:14 regarding the birth to a "virgin" of a boy named Immanuel as a prophesy of Jesus. Matthew 1:23 is a direct quote of Isaiah 7:14.

> *Therefore, the Lord himself will give you a sign: The **virgin** will conceive and give birth to a son, and will call him Immanuel* (Isaiah 7:14, NIV).
> *All this took place to fulfill what the Lord had said through the prophet: "The **virgin** will conceive and give birth to a son, and they will call him Immanuel"* (which means "God with us") (Matthew 1:22-23, NIV).

Spoiler Alert! Isaiah 7:14 is not a prophesy of Jesus. Let me explain. The actual Hebrew for the Isaiah verse does not use the word "virgin." The Hebrew is "young woman."

> *Therefore, the Lord himself will give you a sign. Look, **the young woman** is with child and shall bear a son, and shall name him Immanuel* (Isaiah 7:14, NRSV).

The JPS Tanakh is a Jewish Bible published by the Jewish Publication Society and used today in many synagogues. Its English translation of this verse is

> *Assuredly, my Lord will give you a sign of His own accord! Look, the **young woman** is with child and about to give birth to a son. Let her name him Immanuel* (Isaiah 7:14, JPS Tanakh).

The first Hebrew Bible translation to use "virgin" in Isaiah 7:14 was the Septuagint, the first Greek translation of the Hebrew Bible, begun by Jews in 300 BCE. The Septuagint was probably translated by Jews in Alexandria, Egypt.[64] However, its history was described in *The Letter of Aristeas*, which most biblical scholars think to be a work of fiction. This work of fiction was probably written in 200 BCE by an Alexandrian Jew to put Jews in Alexandria in a positive light. It is a letter written by Aristeas to his brother Phalocrates telling of the event. According to Aristeas, the king of Egypt, Ptolemy II Philadelphus (285 – 246 BCE) requested that a translation in Greek of the Jewish Law (the Torah) be added to the Library in Alexandria. The King appointed Aristeas to go to the Jewish High Priest in Jerusalem to secure 72 Jewish scholars (six from each of the twelve tribes) to come to Alexandria to produce the book. The scholars came, divided into six work groups and in seventy days produced the translation of the first five books of the Hebrew Bible, the Torah. For payment the King released 30,000 Jewish slaves captured by his father, paying their owners 20 drachmas per head. The King also sent a gift to High Priest Eleazar of 100 talents of silver for temple sacrifices, a sacred table, gold and silver bowls and golden vials.[65]

Septuagint is the Latin word for seventy and sometimes the Septuagint is labeled "LXX", the Roman numeral for 70.

"Virgin" got into the Christian Old Testament Bible because early English translations, including the King James Version, used the Septuagint or the Latin Vulgate, which also used the Greek translation instead of the Hebrew Masoretic text. The use of the word "virgin" in Matthew 1:23 also comes from the fact that the writer of Matthew was using the Septuagint as his source.[66] The Septuagint got the translation of Isaiah 7:14 wrong:

> *Therefore, the Lord himself shall give you a sign; behold, a **virgin** shall conceive in the womb, and shall bring forth a son, and thou shalt call his name Emmanuel* (Isaiah 7:14 Septuagint).[67]

There are 306 verses in the New Testament that are direct quotes from the Old Testament (See Appendix J, page 265). Some of these quotes are from the Septuagint instead of the Hebrew Masoretic Text.[68] This kind of error in the New Testament is what drives Jews crazy about Christianity because Jews know the Hebrew Bible does not say the young woman was a virgin, nor is the verb future tense, it is present tense, that is "she is with child". Also, nowhere in the New Testament is Jesus ever called Immanuel.

In Jewish eyes, this misinterpretation of the Hebrew by the writer of Matthew as well as the use of "virgin" in Isaiah 7:14 in many Christian Bibles (KJV, NIV, HCSB, and NASB) discredits Christianity. Christians can get their theology of the virgin birth of Jesus from the gospel of Matthew without the prophesy of Isaiah 7:14 or Matthew 1:23:

> *This is how the birth of Jesus the Messiah came about: His mother Mary was pledged to be married to Joseph, but before they came together, she was found to be*

pregnant through the Holy Spirit. Because Joseph her husband was faithful to the law, and yet did not want to expose her to public disgrace, he had in mind to divorce her quietly. But after he had considered this an angel of the Lord appeared to him in a dream and said, "Joseph son of David, do not be afraid to take Mary home as your wife, because what is conceived in her is from the Holy Spirit (Matthew 1:18-20 NIV).

Beyond the miss-translation of "young woman", the story in Isaiah 7 is not a prophesy of the coming of Jesus but about the evil King of Judah, Ahaz. He was king from 735-715 BCE. He was a contemporary of Isaiah and Micah and father to King Hezekiah.[69] King Ahaz was afraid of the King of Syria who had joined with Pekah and they were coming to destroy Jerusalem. Isaiah was trying to assure Ahaz that God was with Israel and he should not be afraid. Isaiah told Ahaz to ask God for a sign. Ahaz would not ask God for a sign. So Isaiah said God would give him a sign. That sign would occur before a young woman who was now with a child (present tense) would bear a son she would name Immanuel. Before Immanuel was old enough to *"reject wrong and choose the right"* (about 3 years old) *"the land of the two kings you dread will be laid* waste" (Isaiah 7:16, NIV).

The Interpreters *Bible* makes a strong case that the historical context about what Isaiah 7 addresses trumps all of the arguments for interrupting Isaiah 7:14 as a prophesy of the coming of Jesus by stating:

> "This method of reasoning is not convincing, if for no other reason, than that a prediction of the miraculous birth of a Messiah more than seven centuries later could hardly have served as a sign to Ahaz."[70]

It is also interesting to me that Jews object to Christians using "virgin" in Isaiah 7:14, when it was the Jewish translators of the Septuagint who made this translation error.

Inerrancy

"Inerrancy" is the theological position that there is no error in the Bible. This position holds that every word in the Bible is the "inspired" word of God and therefore not capable of having error. Inerrancy has become an icon in the political correctness of the Christian community. Yet it is not well defined. Several Christian denominations and organizations have developed statements regarding inerrancy. Although these are official statements, the writer understands not all members of a denomination/group adhere to the official statements of doctrine.

1. The *International Council on Biblical Inerrancy* (ICBI) (**Accepts Inerrancy**.)

   The ICBI was formed in 1978 and produced the Chicago Statement of Biblical Inerrancy signed by 300 "noted" biblical Scholars. That statement includes the following:

   > "Holy Scripture, as the inspired Word of God witnessing authoritatively to Jesus Christ, may properly be called *infallible* **and** *inerrant*. These negative terms have a special value, for they explicitly safeguard crucial positive truths. *Infallible* signifies the quality of neither misleading nor being misled and so safeguards in categorical terms the truth that Holy Scripture is a sure, safe, and reliable rule and guide in all matters. Similarly, *inerrant* signifies the quality of being free from all falsehood or mistake and so safeguards the truth that Holy Scripture is entirely true and trustworthy in all its assertions."[71]

2. The Southern Baptist Faith and Message (2000) (**Accepts Inerrancy**.)

   > "The Scriptures: The Holy Bible was written by men divinely inspired and is God's revelation of Himself to man. It is a perfect treasure of divine instruction. It has God for its author, salvation for its end, and truth, **without any mixture of error**, for its matter. Therefore, all Scripture is totally true and trustworthy."[72]

3. The United Methodist Church (**Accepts Inerrancy**)

   The Articles of Religion were adopted by the Methodist Church in 1784 and revised in 1808. They have basically remained unchanged:

   > "Article V: The Holy Scripture containeth all things necessary to salvation; so that whatsoever is not read therein, nor may be proved thereby, is not to be required of any man that it should be believed as an article of faith, or be thought requisite or necessary to salvation. In the name of the Holy Scripture we do understand those canonical books of the Old and New Testament of whose authority was never any doubt in the church."[73]

4. Catholic Church (**Accepts Inerrancy**)

The traditional understanding of the doctrine of biblical inerrancy is perhaps most powerfully and clearly expressed for Catholics by St. Augustine in one of his letters to St. Jerome:

> "For I confess to your Charity that I have learned to yield this respect and honour only to the canonical books of Scripture: of these alone do I most firmly believe that the **authors were completely free from error**. And if in these writings I am perplexed by anything which appears to me opposed to truth, I do not hesitate to suppose that either the MS. (manuscript) is faulty or the translator has not caught the meaning of what was said, or I myself have failed to understand it . . . I believe, my brother, that this is your own opinion as well as mine."[74]

In 1965 the Second Vatican Council did not change this doctrine. However, as a part of the debate that led up to the Second Vatican Council, Cardinal Franz Konig of Vienna in December 1964 gave a speech on behalf of the German-speaking Bishops' Conference arguing against the doctrine of inerrancy. In his speech he states: "that the Bible does, in fact, contain errors of science, history and incorrectly-attributed quotations. He then proceeded to provide several examples of apparent contradictions and misinformation."

> "According to Mark 2:26 David had entered the house of God under the high priest Abiathar and eaten the bread of the Presence. In fact, however, according to 1 Sam 21:1 ff., it was not under Abiathar, but under his father Abimelech. In Matthew 27:9 we read that in the fate of Judas a prophecy of Jeremiah was fulfilled. In fact, it is Zechariah 11:12 f. that is quoted. In Daniel 1:1 we read that King Nebuchadnezzar besieged Jerusalem in the third year of King Jehoiakim, i.e. 607 B.C., but from the authentic chronicle of King Nebuchadnezzar that has been discovered we know that the siege can only have taken place three years later."[75]

Therefore, Cardinal Konig urged the Council to change its position on inerrancy. They did not!

Inerrancy Summary

The New Testament writers often used the Septuagint as their Old Testament. As seen in the section above on the Messiah, there are translation errors in the Septuagint that were incorporated into the New Testament. Those are "errors." Law states:

> "The New Testament authors almost always used the Septuagint to access the Jewish scriptures they so often quote. Examples from the Gospels from the apostle Paul, and from the writer of Hebrews demonstrate that the Greek Septuagint had a profound impact on the development of the New Testament thought. Whether or not they were aware of the divergence between the Septuagint and the Hebrew Bible is irrelevant, as is whether or not they thought that the Septuagint's authority was based on the Hebrew. Whether consciously or not, they were transmitting a message based on the theological reading of the Jewish scriptures that was often different from the Hebrew Bible's message. We can also see that the New Testament authors sometimes use Septuagint readings we know to be mistranslations of the Hebrew, **an unsettling reality but a reality nonetheless.**"[76]

It is my opinion that "educated" ministers who promote the political correctness of "inerrancy" are doing a grave disservice to their parishioners. It is though they do not trust them with the truth. They prefer to keep them ignorant sheep that are easier to lead. This mentality leads to statements like that of Randy Frazee in his book, *Think, Act, Be Like Jesus*:

> "...in the New Testament, only 400 words carry any question as to their original penning, none of which relate to actual doctrine. This is a 99.9 percent accuracy rate."[77]

This statement by Frazee is irresponsible and discredits the rest of the message of his book.

Many Bible scholars state that Mark 16:9-20 was not a part of the original text. Here is the note from the NRSV:

> "Some of the most ancient authorities (manuscripts) bring the book to a close at the end of verse 8. One authority concludes the book with the shorter ending; others include the shorter ending and then continue with

verses 9 – 20. In most authorities verses 9 – 20 follow immediately after verse 8, though in some of these authorities the passage is marked as being doubtful."

Even the Southern Baptist Bible, The Holman Christian Standard Bible, notes "These verses do not appear in the oldest and best manuscripts of Mark's Gospel."[78]

Bart Ehrman, a biblical scholar who trained under Bruce Metzger at Yale states:

"Actually, the view that the Bible is inerrant is a completely modern idea. It is not the traditional "Christian" view since time immemorial."[79]

(Arthur's note: Dr. Ehrman now considers himself a "happy agnostic."[80] This does not diminish my opinion of his biblical scholarship.)

Dr. Ehrman identifies ten verses that were not in the original manuscripts of the New Testament. He states:

"They were added by later scribes. These scribal additions are often found in late medieval manuscripts of the New Testament, but not in the manuscripts of the earlier centuries. But because some of the best known English editions of the New Testament, such as the King James Bible (the Authorized Version), were based not on early manuscripts, but later ones, these verses became part of the Bible tradition in English-speaking lands." [81]

The verses are:

And the Spirit is the witness, because the Spirit is the truth. There are three witnesses, the Spirit, the water, and the blood; and these three agree (1 John 5:7-8 NIV).

And as they continued to ask him, he stood up and said to them, "Let him who is without sin among you be the first to throw a stone at he"
(John 8:7 NIV).

"No one, sir," she said. "Then neither do I condemn you," Jesus declared. "Go now and leave your life of sin." (John 8:11 NIV).

And being in anguish, he prayed more earnestly, and his sweat was like drops of blood falling to the ground (Luke 22:44 NIV).

*In the same way, after the supper he took the cup,
saying, "This cup is the new covenant in my blood,
which is poured out for you* (Luke 22:20 NIV).
*And these signs will accompany those who believe: In
my name they will drive out demons; they will speak in
new tongues;* (Mark 16:17 NIV).
*they will pick up snakes with their hands; and when
they drink deadly poison, it will not hurt them at all;
they will place their hands on sick people, and they
will get well"* (Mark 16:18 NIV).
*From time to time an angel of the Lord would come
down and stir up the waters. The first one into the pool
after each such disturbance would be cured of
whatever disease they had* (John 5:4 NIV).
*Peter, however, got up and ran to the tomb. Bending
over, he saw the strips of linen lying by themselves,
and he went away, wondering to himself what had
happened* (Luke 24:12 NIV).
*While he was blessing them, he left them and was taken
up into heaven* (Luke 24:51 NIV).

So are there errors in the Bible? Yes, without a doubt. So how does the Spiritual Warrior incorporate his knowledge of textual errors into his perception of his Bible so as not to undermine his use of it for his guidance, his Global Positioning System? (Note to Reader: be brave! Don't fear to consider ideas and concepts that are contrary to those you grew up with. The goal of every believer needs to be the search for Biblical truth no matter where it leads. Christian warrior, contrary to what you may have been led to believe, rejecting inerrancy and infallibility of the Bible does not put your "salvation" in jeopardy.)

My answer to the question of inerrancy comes from Rabbi Abraham Joshua Heschel. The Bible is not a book; it is an experience.

"The Bible is an eternal expression of a continuous concern; God's cry for man: not a letter from one who sent out a message and remained indifferent to the attitude of the recipient. It is not a book to be read but a drama in which to participate, not a book about events but itself an event; the continuation of the event, while our being involved in it is the continuation of the response. The event will endure so long as the response will continue. When we open it as if it were a book, it is silent; as a spiritual power it is a voice."[82]

The written text of the Bible has error because it was men that wrote it down and transmitted it through the ages, often via hand copies. The book is not inerrant nor is it infallible. However, the message about God in the Bible is consistent and without error! That consistent message is that God loves man and man is to love God and other men:

Hear, O Israel: The LORD our God, the LORD is one. Love the LORD your God with all your heart and with all your soul and with all your strength. These commandments that I give you today are to be on your hearts. Impress them on your children. Talk about them when you sit at home and when you walk along the road, when you lie down and when you get up. Tie them as symbols on your hands and bind them on your foreheads. Write them on the doorframes of your houses and on your gates (Deuteronomy 6:4-9 NIV).

(Note: Jews call these four verses the "Shema." They are expected to say it twice a day.)

Do not seek revenge or bear a grudge against anyone among your people, but love your neighbor as yourself. I am the LORD (Leviticus 19:18 NIV).

"Teacher, which is the great commandment in the law?" "The most important one," answered Jesus, "is this: 'Hear, O Israel: The Lord our God, the Lord is one. Love the Lord your God with all your heart and with all your soul and with all your mind and with all your strength. The second is this: 'Love your neighbor as yourself.' There is no commandment greater than these. On these two commandments depend all the law and the prophets (Matthew 22:36-40 NIV).

The LORD your God is with you, the Mighty Warrior who saves. He will take great delight in you; in his love he will no longer rebuke you, but will rejoice over you with singing. (Zephaniah 3:17 NIV)

For God so loved the world that he gave his one and only Son, that whoever believes in him shall not perish but have eternal life (John 3:16 NIV).

The spiritual warrior can be confident in the mission and the message he finds in the Bible and not be thrown off balance by the errors he may find in the book written by men.

Spiritual Warrior you need to select a Bible to read and study that you are confident is as accurate a translation as is possible. I recommend you consider *The New Oxford Annotated Bible*. It contains the New Revised Standard Version. The translators compared the Masoretic Text of the Hebrew Bible to the Dead Sea Scrolls and included the differences from the scrolls in their translation. It is the Bible that is used at George W. Truett Theological Seminary at Baylor University. The sixty-eight-page essay following Revelations is a graduate course in the history of the Bible. It includes the Apocrypha, 14 maps and a number of helpful appendixes.

Chapter Summary

To know God, you must read and understand the Bible as the inspired Word of God. However, you can only understand the Bible as the inspired Word of God if you know God. Rabbi Heschel explains that this knowing and experiencing God is circular. It is a paradox! God will continue to engage the reader in experiencing God as the believer reads and understands God's word. Heschel warns us not to look upon the Bible as a book but as an experience.

Because it was men that wrote down the word of God and transmitted it through the ages via hand copies, the Bible we have today has errors. The spiritual warrior needs to be aware of these errors so that his **informed** faith will not be shaken when the Bible is challenged by the world. The spiritual warrior can be confident that the **message of God** is consistent and is without error from the first verse of Genesis to the last verse of Revelations. That message is that God loves His creations and His creation must love their God and his fellow man "because He is the Lord."

Spiritual Warrior, listen and follow Psalms 119:105

> *By your words I can see where I am going. They throw*
> *a beam of light on my dark path* (The Message).

The Next Chapter

The next chapter will present information about your work organization. You need to know your jungle!

In the Army's Ranger School, instructors not only teach you how to be a better soldier but also teach you about the jungle they are going to put you into.

Col. Pete Blaber, a senior field commander in Delta Force, led the special operations assault into the Shahikot Valley in Afghanistan in 2002. Operation Anaconda was the largest ground battle in Afghanistan following 9/11.[83] In preparation, Col. Blaber took his troop of Delta Force operators to the Bob Marshall Wilderness area in Montana during the winter to traverse the continental divide. The troop was broken down into groups of four or five men. They were to hike 100 miles over four mountain ranges, including the Continental Divide, with forty-pound backpacks in five to seven days.

Before they started, a local confronted them.

"I been awatchin you boys since you first pulled in here. You ain't no normal backpackers. Most backpackers snack on fruit and nuts and move around real slow. They're nice enough folks, but they don't really care about getting' anywhere in particular. You move with a purpose, and you're asking people their opinions cause you care about what you're gonna be doin, and you know this is the best information you can get. I reckon you boys are military and you got reasons for going up in them crazy mountains."

Blaber's response: "Well, sir, you guessed right, we are in the military, but it usually takes one to recognize one, and we've been watching you too. Someone as fit and observant as you are, I'm guessing you're a Vietnam vet." He stated, "Special Forces, 66-68" He turned serious again and asked why we were so hell-bent on crossing the Continental Divide before the snow melted. I leaned in close to him and whispered, "Same reason you went to the jungles of Panama before you went to Vietnam."[84]

The next chapter is a visit to your jungle: the workplace.

Extra Life Insights

(If you can't know great men and women you can know their words!)

"The beginning of anxiety is the end of faith; the beginning of true faith is the end of anxiety." -George Muller

"Faith is to believe what we do not see, and the reward of the faith is to see what we believe." -St. Augustine

Notes

1. Heschel Rabbi Abraham Joshua, *God in Search of Man: A Philosophy of Judaism*, (Farrar, Straus and Giroux, New York), p 253.
2. Original Bibles. http://www.originalbibles.com/the-original-king-james-bible-1611-pdf/ (accessed December 22, 2015).
3. Clara Moskowitz, "Speed of UIniverse's Expansion Measured Better Than Evere," http://www.space.com/17884-universe-expansion-speed-hubble-constant.html XXX (accessed August 23, 2015).
4. "The Bible : Its Divisions, Chapters, Verses, Titles, and Subscriptions, http://www.stempublishing.com/authors/Walter_Scott/WS_Story_English_Bible8.htmla (accessed August 8, 2015).
5. Moses Biography, Society for Recognition of Famous People, http://www.thefamouspeople.com/profiles/moses-103.phpa (accessed on June 7, 2015).
6. Ancient Jewish History: The Twelve Tribes of Israel https://www.jewishvirtuallibrary.org/jsource/Judaism/tribes.html (accessed December 22, 2015).
7. The Jewish Temples: The Babylonian Exile (597 - 538 BCE), http://www.jewishvirtuallibrary.org/jsource/History/Exile.html (accessed August 10, 2015).
8. "The Second Temple," JewishEncyclopedia.com, http://jewishencyclopedia.com/articles/14309-temple-the-second (accessed June 8, 2015).
9. "Targum," The Jewish Encyclopedia, http://jewishencyclopedia.com/articles/14248-targum (accessed on June 8, 2015).
10. "The Jewish Talmud cites this passage as the source of the Targums, The Aramaic paraphrases of the Hebrew texts that become increasingly important as fewer Jewish people could read Hebrew. Targums were prepared for most of the OT books but not for Ezra-Nehemiah or Daniel." Study Notes, Holman Christian Standard Bible, (Holman Bible Publishers, 2010), 788.
11. The Aleppo Codex, "The Masoretes," http://www.aleppocodex.org/links/8.html (accessed August 18, 2015).

12. "The Leningrad Codex," Educational Site: Biblical Manuscripts, West Semitic Research Project, accessed August 18, 2015. http://www.usc.edu/dept/LAS/wsrp/educational_site/biblical_manu scripts/LeningradCodex.shtml (accessed August 18, 2015).
13. "What Early Manuscripts of the Bible Exist Today? The Old Testament: the Masoretic Text and Others," http://www.provethebible.net/T2-Integ/B-0801.htm. (accessed August 18, 2015).
14. "The Holy Scriptures, Tanakh 1917 edition, According to the Masoretic Text (JPS 1917 Edition)," The Jewish Publication Society, http://jps.org/product/9780827611269/the-holy-scriptures-tanakh-1917-edition (accessed August 18, 2015).
15. *The New Oxford Annotated Bible New Revised Standard Version*, (Oxford: Oxford University Press, 2010), 2185.
16. Law, Timothy Michael, *When God Spoke Greek: The Septuagint and the Making of the Christian Bible* (Oxford: Oxford University Press, 2013), 59
17. I14bid., 2186.
18. Law, 57.
19. "Ezra," Holman Illustrated Bible Dictionary, (Holman Bible Publishers: Nashville, Tennessee: 2003), 542.
20. "Julius Wellhausen: German Scholar," Encyclopedia Britannica, http://www.britannica.com/biography/Julius-Wellhausen (accessed on August 18, 2005).
21. "A Summary of the Documentary Hypothesis: introduction to Biblical Literature," Department of Hebrew & Semitic Studies, University of Wisconsin – Madison, http://hebrew.wisc.edu/~rltroxel/Intro/hypoth.html (accessed on August 18, 2015).
22. The New Oxford Annotated Bible New Revised Standard Version. p. 2222.
23. Richard Elliott Friedman, The Bible with Sources Revealed: A New View Into the Five Books of Moses, (New York: Harper Collins Publishers, 2003), 10.
24. Ibid., 11.
25. Ibid., 12.
26. Ibid., 14.
27. Ibid., 18.
28. Ibid., 19.

29. Ibid., 27.

30. Duane Garrett, "The Documentary Hypothesis, "Associates for Biblical Research, http://www.biblearchaeology.org/post/2010/09/24/the-documentary-hypothesis.aspx. (accessed August 19, 2015).

31. Rendtorff, Rolf. "What We Miss," *Bible Review* 14.1 (Feb 1998): 42-44, http://members.bib-arch.org/publication.asp?PubID=BSBR&Volume=14&Issue=1&ArticleID=19 (accessed July 10, 2015).

32. "The Leningrad Codex," Educational Site: Biblical Manuscripts, West Semitic Research Project, http://www.usc.edu/dept/LAS/wsrp/educational_site/biblical_manuscripts/LeningradCodex.shtml (accessed August 18, 2015).

33. Stetzer, Ed, "A Closer Look: The Significance of the Dead Sea Scrolls," Christianity Today, http://www.christianitytoday.com/edstetzer/2012/february/closer-look-significance-of-dead-sea-scrolls.html (accessed August 9, 2015).

34. Law, 25.

35. Ibid.

36. Rabbi Simcha Bart, "What are the Books of Mishnah?" Ask Moses: Human Questions/Heavenly Answers, http://www.askmoses.com/en/article/190,2180645/What-are-the-books-of-Mishnah.html (accessed Aug 21, 2015).

37. "Tractate Avot: Chapter2," The Jewish Virtual Library, https://www.jewishvirtuallibrary.org/jsource/Talmud/avot2.html (accessed August 21, 2015).

38. "What is the Difference Between the Mishnah and the Gemara?" The Wise Geek, http://www.wisegeek.com/what-is-the-difference-between-the-mishnah-and-the-gemara.htm (accessed August 21, 2015).

39. "Talmud, Jerusalem, " The Jewish Virtual Library, https://www.jewishvirtuallibrary.org/jsource/judaica/ejud_0002_0019_0_19546.html (accessed August 21, 2015).

40. Ariela Pelaia, "What is Midrash?" About Religion, http://judaism.about.com/od/glossary/g/midrash.htm (accessed August 22, 2015).

41. Friedlander, Gerald, Translator and Introduction, *Pirke De Rabbi Eliezer*, (New York: Hermon Press, 1916).

42. Ibid., xiv.

43. Ibid., xiii.

44. Law, 59.

45. Law, 60.

46. Terry L. Wilder, "Establishing the New Testament Cannon." http://www.lifeway.com/Article/bible-study-establishing-new-testament-canon (accessed December 23, 2015).

47. Law, 85.

48. Law, 87.

49. *The New Oxford Annotated Bible New Revised Standard Version*, p. 1427.

50. Ibid., 1879.

51. Oxford Dictionaries · © Oxford University Press), http://www.oxforddictionaries.com/us/ (accessed December 23, 2014).

52. The Gospel According to Mark, *The New Oxford Annotated Bible*, 1791.

53. Throckmorton Jr., Burton H., *Gospel Parallels: A Comparison of the Synoptic Gospels*, (Thomas Nelson Publishers: Nashville, 1992).

54. John E. Steinmeuller, "The History of the Latin Vulgate," Catholic Culture, http://www.catholicculture.org/culture/library/view.cfm?recnum=7470 (accessed June 11, 2015).

55. John Wycliffe, English Bible History, http://www.greatsite.com/timeline-english-bible-history/john-wycliffe.html (accessed August 23, 2015).

56. "Textual Criticism." Merriam-Webster.com, http://www.merriam-webster.com/dictionary/textual criticism (accessed August 26 2015).

57. VanderKam, James C., "The Dead Sea Scrolls and the New Testament," Biblical Archeaology Review, March/April 2015, Vol 41 No 2, p. 49. (Note: The image of P52 is used with permission from the Reylands Library at the University of Manchester.)

58. "Jewish Concepts: Articles of Faith," Jewish Virtual Library, http://www.jewishvirtuallibrary.org/jsource/Judaism/articles_of_faith.html (accessed August 24 2015).

59. Cook, Michael, *Modern Jews Engage the New Testament:*

Enhancing Jewish Well-Being in a Christian Environment, (Woodstock, Vermont: Jewish Lights Publishing, 2012), 312.

60. Ibid., xxi.
61. "Jewish Concepts: The Messiah"
62. Ibid.,
63. *Holman Illustrated Bible Dictionary*, (Nashville, TN: Holman Bible Publishers, 2003), 1112 – 1114.
64. Law, 39.
65. Anonymous (Author), *The Letter of Aristeas* (English Translation by R.H. Charles), (Publisher: Kindle)
66. Amy-Jill Levine and Marc Zvi Brettler, editors, The Virgin Birth, The Jewish Annotated New Testament: NRSV (Oxford University Press, Oxford: Oxford University Press, 2010), 4.
67. *The Septuagint LXX: Greek and English* by Sir Lancelot C.L. Brenton
    published by Samuel Bagster & Sons, Ltd., London, 1851, http://www.ccel.org/bible/brenton/ (accessed August 10, 2015).
68. Law, 115.
69. "Ahaz", Holman Illustrated Bible Dictionary, (Nashville, Tennessee: Holman Bible Publishers, 2003), 37.
70. *The Interpreter's Bible*, Vol 5, (New Your: Abingdon Press, 1956), 219.
71. International Council on Biblical Inerrancy, Chicago Statement on Biblical Inerrancy with Exposition (1978), http://www.bible-researcher.com/chicago1.html (accessed August 27, 2015).
72. "The 2000 Baptist Faith & Message", Southern Baptist Convention, http://www.sbc.net/bfm2000/bfm2000.asp (accessed August 27, 2015).
73. "The Articles of Religion of the Methodist Church Article V — Of the Sufficiency of the Holy Scriptures for Salvation," The United Methodist Church, http://www.umc.org/what-we-believe/the-articles-of-religion-of-the-methodist-church (accessed August 27, 2015).
74. St. Augustine's Letter 82. http://catholicism.org/biblical-inerrancy.html (accessed December 22, 2015).
75. Mark Joseph Zia, "The Inerrancy of Scripture and the Second Vatican Council," Catholic Culture, http://www.catholicculture.org/culture/library/view.cfm?recnum=8441 (accessed August 28, 2015).

76. Law, 6-7)
77. Frazee, 1-52
78. HCSB, 1720)
79. Ehrman, Bart D., *Misquoting Jesus: The Story Behind Who Changed the Bible and Why* (Harper Collins Publishers: New York, 205) , 249.
80. Ehrman, 258.
81. Ehrman, 265.
82. Heschel, 254.
83. Sean Naylor, *Not a Good Day to Die* (New York: Berkley Caliber Books, 2005).
84. Blaber, Pete, *The Mission, The Men and Me: Lessons from a Delta Force Commander*, (The Berkley Publishing Group: New York, 2008), 11.

Chapter 4: What Is the Spiritual Warrior's Jungle?

This chapter introduces the spiritual warrior to the idea that many of the challenges he faces in the workplace are not spiritual and do not have spiritual solutions. The spiritual warrior will better understand their workplace jungle by understanding the structure and workings of the organization in which they are immersed.

The whole world of daily living is the Christian's spiritual battlefield, his "jungle." In order to address directly what the Christian faces on the battlefield and how to deal with it, this book focuses on the workplace. In the workplace, the spiritual warrior needs to know that his jungle is the work organization.

I first wrote this chapter as an academic review of the literature on theories of organizations. However, that discussion did not focus on the attributes of work organizations that would help the spiritual warrior determine if the un-comfortableness or challenges he felt were coming from elements of the organization or from spiritual challenges "*against the powers of this dark world and against the spiritual forces of evil in the heavenly realms*" (Ephesians 6:12 NIV).

Each battle is unique and requires different knowledge, skill, and actions for success. The spiritual warrior should not blame the devil for challenges that are organizational in nature. Most of us do not see our workplace as a jungle and would not recognize a spiritual danger in it unless it gobbled us up. However, the workplace can be viewed as a jungle full of challenges. Not all of the challenges for the believer in the workplace are spiritual or have spiritual solutions. Therefore, the spiritual warrior needs to understand the maze in which he is immersed.

The view of a spiritual warrior of his workplace is not unlike the view of a soldier of his battlefield in a firefight. The impression is one of total chaos. It is hard to understand what is going on unless he has a "trained eye." With the "trained eye" he can see flows and patterns that give him clues as to what he might do or should not do. This chapter will help train the spiritual warrior's view of his work organization to enable him to better chose what he should do or not do.

You need to know your work organization just as you would need to know a physical jungle into which you were sent to perform some military operation. It would be obvious to you that you needed to know the physical jungle because it would slap you in the face when you walked into it. The jungle may be a hindrance or a help to your mission (job) and that depends on how much you know about all that is in the jungle. There are hindrances in the workplace that could be described metaphorically as those "wait-a-minute" vines and thorn thickets that Rangers get entangled in during night land navigation exercises at Fort Benning, Georgia. However, it is incredible that many of us are ignorant of the workplace "jungle," what it is, its interworking, or its relationship with its environment.

The purpose of this chapter is to help the spiritual warrior tease out of his work experience the challenges that are truly spiritual challenges from challenges that simply come from working in a human organization. To repeat, the challenges from the latter are not spiritual and cannot be addressed with spiritual solutions. The devil is not in these work challenges.

Factoid: In the United States in 2007, there were 7,705,018 private non-farm establishments that employed 120,604,265people. There were another 21,708,021 non-farm non-employer establishments.[1] That is a lot of workplaces and employees!

Why Do Work Organizations Develop?

What is a work organization? One powerful definition is found in the simple equation $1+1=2$. What gives rise to a work organization is a task that requires more than one person. What is in the two that is more than the two 1s is the $+$. The $+$ is the organization and all that goes on to help the two 1s work together. By the way, this equation is also a good definition of synergy. Synergy is more than the sum of the parts of an organization. It comes from the *plus*, the organization of its parts. The Type 3 Counter Terrorism Spiritual Challenges that you read about in Chapter 1 that the spiritual warrior will face at work are often contained in the *plus*. You need to know and understand the plus.

Theories of Work Organizations

For an academic review of the theories of organization literature, see *Sociology, Work & Industry* by Tony Watson.[2]

No other literature on work organizations better conveys my point that the work organization may apply challenges to the spiritual warrior that are not from the "evil forces," than the research of Chris Argyris in the 1950s. He developed what he called "Personality and Organizational

Theory."[3] Argyris showed that attributes of workers and work tasks could be described on a "maturity" continuum.

One of Argyris's studies showed that incompatibility of the maturity of an individual with the maturity required by a job would produce job dissatisfaction. He rated individuals and jobs on a continuum scale that had maturity attributes at one end and infancy attributes on the other end. Attributes of maturity included long attention spans, many skills, some skills in depth, and the ability to work with relative independence. Infancy attributes included short attention span, few skills and no skills in depth. Job satisfaction was missing when an individual who was on the infancy end of the continuum was placed in a job that required maturity attributes or vice versa. Job dissatisfaction came from that incompatibility.

A job challenge that comes from job dissatisfaction caused by this kind of incompatibility is a problem for the believer, but it is **not** a spiritual problem and cannot be solved with spiritual solutions. The discomfort that a worker experiences by being in a job that is not a good fit is not caused by the devil. Type 3 Counter-Terrorism Spiritual Warfare cannot correct it. The believer needs to find and move to a job that is a better fit or become more "mature" that is, more educated and trained to do the mature tasks he is required to do.

It would appear that early on, work organizations do not make conscious decisions as to their organizational structure. They continue to add individuals as the tasks grow, i.e., 1+1+1+1+1+1+1+1+1. At some point the owner of a business or the director responsible in government sees there is a need for organizing the individuals into a hierarchy.

Three types of organizations are presented below as examples of organizations that have been developed: the bureaucracy, the matrix, and the democratic or circular organization.

The Bureaucracy

German sociologist Max Weber (1864-1920) defined sociology as a study of social action.[4] He was one of the founders of sociology. Much of his writing focused on issues of methodology for studying society and the organization of societal units such as work organizations. In one of his publications, *The Protestant Ethic and the Spirit of Capitalism* (1920) Weber postulates that protestant religion gave rise to capitalism. Weber postulated there was "one best way to organize and do work." Weber developed six major principles for a bureaucracy:

    1.   A formal hierarchical structure,

2. Management by rules,
3. Organization by functional specialty,
4. An "up-focused" or "in-focused" mission,
5. Purposely impersonal,
6. Employment based on technical qualifications.[5]

Although Weber addressed many sociological issues, today he is often thought of as the father of bureaucracy because he was one of the first to write about it. Bureaucracy has a bad connotation today as being rigid and debilitating to its incumbents. However, as an organizational model it is alive and well, particularly in government. Weber's principles were somewhat revolutionary because at the time there was not much written about how to organize work organizations.

Matrix Organizations

NASA was the first work organization to develop and employ a matrix organizational structure.[6] The concept was a major break from the traditional bureaucratic structure. The matrix organization has the individual worker reporting equally to two different supervisors. In the matrix organization, the individual worker reports to a supervisor of his or her technical area (welding, engineering, accounting, etc.) and to the project manager, who has day-to-day supervision of a project formed to produce a product. This was a major break from the traditional bureaucracy, which rigidly held to the authority of one person reporting only to one supervisor.

An example of a pure matrix organization was the institutional dentistry program in the State of Florida during the 1980s. Dr. Richard Urwick was the director of the program in 17 institutions, which included prisons and mental hospitals. Dr. Urwick, a dentist, hired the dentists in all of the Florida state institutions. Then, with the institutional administrator, he jointly evaluated and fired dentists. The institutional administrator was responsible for day-to-day supervision of the dental program in his particular institution. Who better to hire and evaluate a dentist than another dentist? It worked!

Factoid: Peter F. Drucker (1909 - 2005) developed the concept of corporations with his book *Concept of the Corporation* (1946) based on his observations of General Motors.[9]

There are some weaknesses in the matrix organization. Five have been identified:

(1) misaligned goals,
(2) unclear roles and responsibilities,
(3) ambiguous authority (in the matrix, leaders can have responsibility without authority as a result of the dual reporting structure),
(4) lack of a matrix guardian, and
(5) silo-focused employees who view their membership and loyalty as belonging to a certain subunit in the organization.[7]

Even with the weaknesses listed above, the failure to go to a matrix structure is in part the reason the corporate structure of the Florida Department of Health and Rehabilitative Services (HRS) failed in the 1980s.[8] Created in the early 1970s, HRS had twelve districts in its original design. Coordinating those districts, which were spread out over 58,664 square miles and stretched from one end of the state to the other (447 miles), and keeping them all on the "same page" was a major effort. At one point, when Lawton Chiles became Governor of Florida, an edict went out that state headquarters could not direct districts to do anything and should have no contact with the district administrators. This was a part of Governor Chiles's effort to decentralize state government. As a result, twelve independent districts, each "doing its own thing" without any coordination statewide, distorted the legislative mandates to the Department.

A matrix organization would have had the state office personnel officer appointing the district personnel officers, jointly evaluating them with the district administrator, and jointly firing them. The district administrator would be responsible for day-to-day supervision. This would have been the procedure for each administrative and program office. Instead, HRS disintegrated and eventually broke up into the Department of Children and Family Services and the Department of Health.

The Democratic or Circular Organization

Russell Ackoff was the Anheuser-Busch Professor Emeritus of Management Science at the Wharton Business School, University of Pennsylvania. Dr. Ackoff first published his ideas of a "democratic circular organization" in 1981. Its basic goal is to integrate the organization horizontally and vertically: "A principal responsibility of managers is to create an environment and conditions under which their subordinates can do their jobs as effectively as their capabilities allow. It is not to supervise them."[10]

The democratic organization structure has been legitimated by its installation in major companies and governments including Metropolitan Life Insurance, Anhauser-Bush, Alcoa Aluminum-Tennessee Operation, Ford, Super Fresh (formally A&P Groceries), and Ministry of Public Works in Mexico. The basic idea is that every manager, supervisor, line executive, etc., will have a board. The board will include all of the employees, the manager/supervisor, and his supervisor. This is the minimum membership. The board may add others including external people who have a stake in the work of that board.

Ackoff states: "Fully empowered boards have six responsibilities:
1. Planning for the unit whose board it is,
2. Policy making for the unit whose board it is,
3. Coordinating plans and policies of the immediately lower level,
4. Integrating plans and policies, its own and those of its immediately lower level, with those made at higher levels,
5. Improving the quality of work life of the subordinates on the board,
6. Enhancing and evaluating the performance of the manager whose board it is."[11]

Membership is mandatory for the manager but voluntary for the employees he supervises. Ackoff was asked, "Are there certain types of organizational structures on which a circular organization cannot be superimposed, for example, a matrix organization?" His answer was, "To the best of my knowledge, no. Since in a matrix organization almost everyone has two bosses, almost everyone participates on at least two boards."

The Legal Constraints of Ministry in the Workplace

The spiritual warrior needs to understand the legal constraints he faces in the workplace. In America, there is paranoia in the workplace regarding forcing or coercing people into religion. Much of this has been codified into laws and ordinances. Spiritual warriors should support this. There is a way to approach ministry to those in the workplace that does not break the law. Spiritual warriors cannot take that approach unless they know the law. Spiritual warriors need to be law followers, not law breakers.

There is a great resource for this education. It is the American Center for Law and Justice (ACLJ). This private, not-for-profit law firm challenges encroachments by the world into the practice of faith. [12]

The following is the ACLJ position on workplace rights:

> Unless an employer is an exempt religious organization, the employer is required to reasonably accommodate its employee's sincerely held religious beliefs in the workplace, unless such an accommodation would impose an undue burden on the employer's business. The most common methods of reasonable accommodation include allowing shift swaps, making exceptions to dress and grooming requirements that are not essential to the business, allowing observance of religious rituals in a quiet area during breaks, allowing the non-disruptive display of religious symbols, and allowing non-intrusive, non-disruptive proselytization.

Title VII of the 1964 Civil Rights Act is the principal law that protects and inhibits religious practices in the workplace. The following is a portion of that Act:

> Title VII applies to most large private employers as well as to governmental employers. With regard to employers, Title VII states: (a) Employer practices. It shall be an unlawful employment practice for an employer-- (1) to fail or refuse to hire or to discharge any individual, or otherwise to discriminate against any individual with respect to his compensation, terms, conditions, or privileges of employment, because of such individual's race, color, **religion**, sex, or national origin; or (2) to limit, segregate, or classify his employees or applicants for employment in any way which would deprive or tend to deprive any individual of employment opportunities or otherwise adversely affect his status as an employee, because of such individual's race, color, religion, sex or national origin...The Title VII definition of religion was amended in 1972 to require employers to reasonably accommodate an individual's sincerely held religious observances or religious practices. The employer can avoid making an accommodation only if to do so would

constitute an undue hardship on the employer's
business. [13]

Title VII applies only to businesses with 15 or more employees.

In summary, employers have an affirmative duty to
reasonably accommodate the religious beliefs and practices of their
employees that they are aware of, unless such accommodation
would place an undue burden on the employer. [14]

In 1997, the Clinton administration's Office of Personnel
Management issued guidelines that cover all civilian-branch employees of
the federal government. The guidelines were prepared by a wide-ranging
coalition of groups, including such diverse organizations as the People for
the American Way, the Southern Baptist Convention, and the Christian
Coalition. The guidelines clarify that "Federal employees may engage in
personal religious expression to the greatest extent possible, consistent with
workplace efficiency and the requirements of law." It also states" Federal
employers may not discriminate in employment on the basis of religion,
"and government agencies "must reasonably accommodate employees'
religious practices."[15]

There is a lot of case law establishing principles that require
work organizations to follow their own written rules governing
employee behavior. I have found when managers in a work
organization go after an employee for whatever reason, the manager
often violates their own written policies. Just remember that it is
hard to do wrong right. Know and follow the rules. Know the rules
better and follow them more faithfully than individuals willing to
violate those rules in order to do you harm.

Chapter Summary

Work organizations are created for job-related tasks that require more than
one person. These organizations are the context in which most Christian
laymen work. There are challenges for the spiritual warrior in the
workplace that comes from the dynamics of working in organizations.
These are not spiritual challenges. They are not from the devil and are not
a part of Type 3 Counter-Terrorism Spiritual Warfare. However, these
challenges are real. The spiritual warrior must deal with them in order to
free himself from constraints and entanglements of organizational dynamics
in order to confront spiritual challenges that come from the "roaring lion."

With the conclusion of these four chapters, the spiritual warrior
now:

- Can avoid much of the fog of war by understanding spiritual warfare and his piece of that battle (Chapter 1),
- Is confident in his calling to a job within God's will for his life. He also understands what he needs to do to keep ministry as a Christian separate from his Christian approach to his work so that one does not inhibit the other (Chapter 2),
- Knows how he got his Bible, enough so that criticisms of his Bible do not shake his confidence in it as the principal source of guidance for his life and knowledge of God (Chapter 3),
- Knows his jungle, the context of his work life, which is set by a work organization (Chapter 4).

The Next Chapter

The next chapter will help the spiritual warrior understand a strategy that will give him an edge in his battle with the roaring lion in the workplace. It is based on what I was taught in the Army's Ranger School for dealing with danger areas in the enemy infested jungle. It is a major tool for the spiritual warrior engaged in Type 3 Counter-Terrorism Spiritual Warfare.

Extra Life Insights

(If you can't know great men and women you can know their words!)
"The test of a first-rate intelligence is the ability to hold two opposing ideas in mind at the same time and still retain the ability to function."
-F. Scott Fitzgerald

Notes

1. "State & County Quick Facts," United States Census Bureau, http://quickfacts.census.gov/qfd/states/00000.html (accessed December 13, 2013).
2. Tony Watson, "The Sociological Analysis of Work and Industry," *Sociology, Work and Industry*, (London: Routledge & Kegan Paul, 1980).
3. Chris Argyris, *Personality and Organization* (New York: Harper & Row, 1957).
4. Watson, 46
5. Crystal Lee, "Six Characteristics of Bureaucracy," http://www.ehow.com/list_7472257_six-characteristics-reaucracy.html (accessed December 13, 2013).
6. Tonn, Greg, "Matrix Management: A Scoping Reviews (August 8, 2007)," http://www.cio.gov.bc.ca/local/cio/kis/pdfs/matrix_management.pdf (accessed December 13, 2012).
7. Tonn, 10.
8. This is the author's observation as an employee of HRS from 1978 till it was broken apart in 1996 into two departments: The Florida Department of Health and the Florida Department of Children and Family Services.
9. Peter F. Drucker, *The Concept of the Corporation* (New York: The John Day Company, 1946).
10. Russell L. Ackoff, *The Democratic Corporation* (New York: Oxford University Press, 1994), 134.
11. Ackoff, 124.
12. American Center for Law and Justice, http://www.aclj.org/ (accessed December 13, 2013).
13. "Religious Discrimination in the Workplace (Title VII)," http://aclj.org/workplace-rights/religious-discrimination-in-the-workplace-title-vii- (accessed December 14, 2013).
14. "Unlawful Employment Practices, Sec. 2000e-2 [Section 703] (a). Employer practices," http://www.eeoc.gov/laws/statutes/titlevii.cfm (accessed December 14, 2013).

15. "Religious Freedom in the Workplace," http://www.religioustolerance.org/wrfa.htm (accessed December 14, 2013).

Chapter 5: How Can the Spiritual Warrior Counter the Spiritual Ambush?

This chapter is the unique contribution this book makes to the Spiritual Warfare literature. It focuses on behavior to carry out the admonition to "Be Alert." It includes U.S. Army Ranger School procedures for the physical jungle that will help the spiritual warrior stay alert to spiritual challenges and be prepared for the unexpected spiritual ambush.

The U.S. Army Ranger School

July 8, 1965, was a very hot day at Ft. Benning Georgia. About 200 men had assembled at Camp Darby to sign in to the new Ranger School class (1-66). The sign-in process was interrupted numerous times when the instructor told a soldier that he could not sign in because his orders had been changed. Each received new orders and was told to report to his new unit immediately. When all was finished, there were about 100 of us left for the class. The others were assigned to units scheduled for immediate deployment to Vietnam.

In 1965, the U.S. Army Ranger School was a "leadership school that used long range patrolling as a teaching vehicle."[1] The course was nine weeks long.

The first three weeks were spent at Fort Benning, learning the basics of long range patrolling and a variety of other skills for living and surviving in the jungle, as well as going through physical conditioning. We were told that our class was the first one to go through the course under a revised curriculum geared toward Vietnam.

The next three weeks of mountain training was held in the Appalachian National Forest near Dahlonega, Georgia, where you could find "DO NOT FEED THE RANGERS" signs posted on the paved roads.

The third three weeks were spent in the swamps in and around the Yellow River at Eglin Air Force Base, near Panama City, Florida. It was conducted out of Auxiliary Field Seven, where General Jimmy Doolittle had trained his people for the first bomber raid on Japan.

A grueling conditioning program was a significant part of the Fort Benning phase. It helped prepare us for walking almost every night to reach and attack an objective at BMNT (Before Morning Nautical Twilight), followed by the return to a base camp, only to start again preparing for the next raid. It was estimated that a Ranger walked about 500 miles during those nine weeks.

Members of the Ranger class were divided into long-range patrols. At some point, each student was assigned to be the patrol leader for each of the five components of a long-range patrol. A student had to get a satisfactory performance rating for three out of the five components in order to pass the course. I did graduate, but not without a struggle. Those who graduated received the coveted Ranger Tab.

Lessons that were pounded into our heads included how to recognize danger areas in the jungle, a course of action to follow if you could not avoid a danger area, and immediate action to take if caught in an ambush in a danger area. Knowing these did not guarantee survival of an enemy attack, but it increased the probability that the patrol would survive and successfully complete the mission.

3D RANGER COMPANY 1ST STUDENT BATTALION July 8, 1965 September 9, 1965

Ranger Class 1-66, from July 8, 1965 to October 9, 1965.[2] I am in the third row from the top, sixth man from the left. (Note: about a third of these men were killed in Vietnam, and two received the Medal of Honor posthumously.)

Captain Jim Croushorn, Group Adjutant, 20th Special Forces preparing for a parachute jump in 1968. Flew out of Birmingham in C119 (Boxcars) and jumped into Ft. Rucker, Alabama.

After Basic Training, Advanced Infantry Training, Infantry Officer Candidate School, Ranger School, and Airborne School, I spent thirteen months in Korea with the Second Infantry Division. I returned to Ft. Benning, Georgia in December 1966 and was separated from active duty on June 22, 1967. I then joined the 20th Special Forces, Alabama National Guard. In the picture above I prepare for a parachute jump with the 20th Special Forces in 1968.[3] I had 35 parachute jumps by the time I resigned my commission as a Captain in 1973. (Note: I like to tell folks: They were all "night jumps. It is always dark when you kept your eyes closed.")

The teachings about danger areas are a miniscule part of the Ranger School curriculum, but I believe they contain many helpful metaphors for the Christian in the world of work. So, let me tell you some of the things I learned in Ranger School about jungle danger areas. (Note: You can find the specific procedures in the *Ranger Handbook*.) [4]

The *Ranger Handbook* defines danger areas as follows:

> "A danger area (DA) is any place on a unit's route where the leader's estimate process tells him his unit may be exposed to enemy observation or fire. Some examples of *d*anger areas are open areas, roads and trails, native villages, enemy positions, and obstacles such as minefields, streams, and barbed wire. Avoid danger areas whenever possible. If they must be passed or crossed, use great caution."[4]

Trails, roads, streams, clear areas, and ridge-tops are danger areas. Why are they danger areas? These are places the enemy sets up ambushes, because they know solders like to take the easy path through the jungle.

Hey, spiritual warrior, can you already see the analogy to the Christian in the workplace? It is human nature to want to take the easy path through any circumstance, whether it is through a thick jungle, administrative procedures, human relationships, or moral dilemmas in the workplace.

Sometimes a long-range patrol could not avoid a danger area. For those times, the Ranger School taught procedures or protocols for negotiating the danger area in such a way as to minimize the danger to the patrol and its mission. The Ranger developed a plan of action for every type of danger area or obstacle that the patrol might encounter. For example, if a patrol was moving along a compass azimuth (yes, this was before GPS when land navigation was done with a compass and a topographical map) that would lead to its objective, and word came back to the patrol leader that the point man had come across a road running perpendicular to the patrol's direction of movement, the patrol leader knew that he had encountered a danger area. There was no discussion about what to do, because there was already a plan that had been rehearsed many times. The patrol leader would put out security on the road to the left and to the right of the path of the patrol. This would be two machine gun teams. Then the patrol leader would send a team across the road to box out the area the patrol was about to enter to make sure no enemy occupied the area. When the team gave the "all clear," the patrol leader would send the main body across the road and then withdraw the security.   The patrol would continue on its way. (See Diagram #1.)

Diagram #1

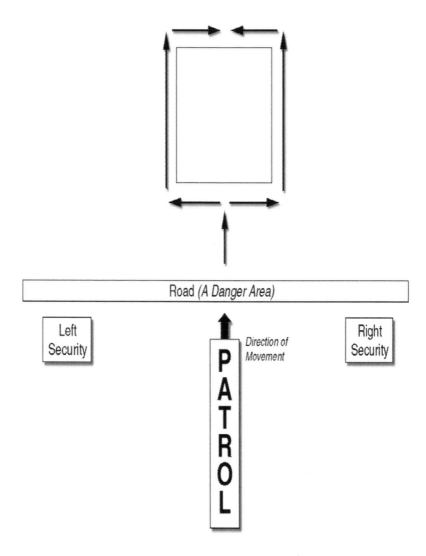

Spiritual Danger Areas

I believe that once you enter into a personal relationship with God, you are "born again," "saved," "converted," whatever you want to call it, and that it is a permanent relationship. It is not unlike your relationship with your parents. Once you are born into their family, you will always be their son or daughter. No matter what you do, that cannot change. You can do things that separate you from your parents, hurt them, move far away from them physically, ethically, emotionally, etc. but you will always be their child.

A spiritual danger area is a situation, a place, a person, or a thought that makes us vulnerable to doing things that separate us from God. The spiritual warrior needs to be alert for those events and have a plan to deal with them before he finds himself in a spiritual danger area.

In preparation for writing this book, I interviewed mature Christians. My research was not scientific in that I did not randomly select people from all the Christians who live in Tallahassee. I selected people I knew were strong and mature Christians and had a reputation as being very good on their job. I interviewed 20 people. I stopped when the danger areas identified began to be repeats of earlier interviews.

I asked those I interviewed to identify spiritual challenges they had encountered on the job. I called these spiritual challenges "spiritual danger areas." I then asked them to describe the situation, how they recognized it and what they did to help them be successful in staying faithful to their personal relationship to God. More specifically, I asked them what actions they took to deal with the danger area. I called these actions "protocols." Through these conversations, I was able to identify eight spiritual danger areas.

Francis Frangipane, in his seminal book on spiritual warfare, states, "The Lord would ask each of us, 'Do you know the areas where you are vulnerable to satanic assault? Jesus would have us not be ignorant of our need'."[5] This chapter will help you answer Frangipane's question.

The protocol for a spiritual danger area must have a behavioral component. Recognition of a spiritual danger area does not just precipitate a cognitive awareness; it demands some behavioral action. I say this in part because my concept of emotion and behavior comes from the behaviorist school, not the psychoanalytic (Freudian) school.

The behaviorist believes that emotion follows behavior, not that behavior follows emotion. The psychoanalytic school believes that you get behavioral change by first changing the person's emotions. My experience as a family therapist, studying the matter in a two-year Master of Social

Work program, and teaching four years at the University of Tennessee Graduate School of Social Work is that the psychoanalytic approach for changing behavior does not work.

The behavioral approach to displaying the correct behavior when confronted with a spiritual challenge is more consistent with a believer's faith approach to life. We act out our predetermined behavior with discipline even though we may be anxious about it. An example of a good protocol can be found in a spiritual challenge I was presented by a building contractor. He said he would go check on the houses under construction by his company after hours. When he made those trips, he had a very difficult time not picking up one or two sheets of plywood and putting them in the back of his pickup truck for personal use.

A good protocol for his danger area that could correct this problem would be for him to ride his motorcycle when he goes to check on jobs after hours. There would then be no way he could carry off sheets of plywood (4 foot X 8 foot).

Henri Nouwen made a great statement about the difference in these two approaches to a change in behavior: "You don't think your way into a new way of living; you live your way into a new way of thinking."[9]

Beth Moore, the prolific Bible teacher, addressed the need for a prior plan to deal with a spiritual challenge in her study of Daniel:

> "How do you specifically guard against self-exaltation? In other words, when you come under this exact temptation, what keeps you from falling for it? I have pressed the question because this temptation will come too often and too insidiously for us not to have a predetermined plan of action. If we are not armed in advance with a mindset, a past experience, or a battery of Scriptures, we're probably going to fall to the temptation to exalt ourselves."[6]

What I would add to Beth Moore's admonition is that there needs to be specific behavior identified as a preplanned protocol.

If a spiritual danger area is a place where something could happen that would separate you from God, and anything that separates you from God is called sin, then your approach to a spiritual danger area is your approach to sin. This chapter presents procedures for dealing with sin. It is my hope you will come away with a highly defined sense of how to approach spiritual challenges in the workplace when they cannot be avoided.

Most of us go through the day without major emergencies. As the Administrative Officer in the Office of Emergency Operations, Florida Department of Health, I spent a lot of time around people who have made it their life to deal with emergencies. You may know some of these types. They quickly recognize emergencies, and they are never at a loss as to what to do, even if they have never been there before! The motto of the Office of Emergency Operations was, "Never let the unexpected be a surprise."

Most of us have a hard time even recognizing that we are in an emergency, much less having a clue as to what we should do. The goal of this book is to sensitize you to spiritual danger areas in the workplace and to provide examples of pre-established protocols for dealing with these in such a way that you will not let what happens in a spiritual danger area penetrate and break down your personal relationship with God.

Knowing what to do and being able to do it are two different things. There is a difference between knowledge and skill. I remember when my son John got his learner's permit to drive. He wanted to drive the moment we walked out the door of the testing station. I told him we would wait until we got to a quiet side street beside our house. I stopped the car as soon as we turned onto the side street and swapped places with John. "OK John, let me tell you how to drive the car."

John looked at me incredulously and said, "I know how to drive!"

John let out the clutch. The car lurched and lurched, stopping and starting with violent jerks for 50 feet before the engine died. This happened four times before we got to the end of the street. He became increasingly open to my suggestion that he release the clutch slowly as he pressed on the gas.

John knew how to drive before he sat in the driver's seat. However, he had few driving skills in the beginning, although the skills quickly came. This is an example of the difference between knowledge and skill. A skill is knowledge applied well!

As Christians, we sometimes fail to understand the difference between the knowledge required to live a Christian life and the skills required to put that knowledge into practice. Just because you know how does not mean you can do it! So, spiritual warrior, how do you get that skill to do what you know? You practice what you preach. Hey spiritual warrior have you ever heard that before? As my friend Dr. George Borders has reminded our Sunday morning Bible study group many times, "It is not walk the talk: it is talk the walk!" I take that to mean let's not talk about it until we have done it. One military veteran stated that if you cannot do it in training, you would never be able to do it for real. The problem in applying this to spiritual warfare is that there is not much of a way to practice these spiritual principles but in the real situation. By its nature, spiritual war is real all of the time. So, look at every minute as an opportunity to put these principles into play. Over time, you will develop the skills.

You might find a spiritual mentor in your workplace. That mentor may be a more mature spiritual warrior who can be a source of counsel and support. An alternative might be a fellow spiritual warrior equivalent to the Ranger Buddy in Ranger School. In Ranger School, you did everything with your Ranger Buddy. Anytime you were separated from your Ranger Buddy, he knew where you were. Each held the other accountable. The Ranger Buddy helped you when you needed help. No one on the Ranger Long Range Patrol cared about or promoted your success more than your Ranger Buddy. In the workplace, one needs a spiritual warrior "buddy" to do spiritually what the Ranger Buddy did for the Ranger. I think of that "buddy" more as a colleague than a mentor. With a colleague there is more of a sense that we are in this together, and we are going to survive the jungle and accomplish our mission. Hey spiritual warrior, do you have a spiritual Ranger buddy at work? If not, get one!

WARNING: The skill of living your faith in the workplace is as distinct and separate from being a Christian as knowing how to drive is from being able to drive. Some of our fellow Christians think that just because they are Christians and the Holy Spirit lives in them, they have taken care of business. In the presence of sin, it is irresponsible to think that the Holy Spirit will compel you to do the "Christian thing" without your making a conscious choice and effort. This side of heaven, you will always be more human than spiritual.

I have tried to describe each of the following spiritual danger areas so that they would be as recognizable to the spiritual warrior in the workplace as is a road encountered by a Ranger in a jungle on a long-range patrol. It should hit you in the face that you have encountered a danger area. The encounter with the road has triggered an alert that should start your implementation of the preplanned protocol you have for that danger area.

Many of the spiritual danger areas in the workplace are not as obvious or recognizable as a road or trail in the jungle. These danger areas are often mental. The workplace jungle is made of office routine, paperwork, and a horde of people with whom you must interact. Your spiritual danger areas are hidden in all of that. Many of my spiritual challenges (danger areas) were people. Therefore, to help you recognize spiritual danger areas, you need explicitly to define triggers or red flags that will prompt you into action. You must first recognize the spiritual danger area. Then you match a predetermined response to that danger area, and do whatever the protocol calls for. A correct response to a spiritual danger area does not require inspiration; it requires discipline!

This book does not contain a comprehensive list of spiritual danger areas. The danger areas included are certainly not all of the danger areas that the spiritual warrior is going to face in the workplace. These eight spiritual danger areas are only representative of what you might encounter in your spiritual jungle. The spiritual danger areas presented may not even be in your jungle. On the other hand, you may not have encountered them yet, since some are more likely to be experienced later in a person's work career than at the beginning.

A soldier does not have to know if a road is paved or just a dirt road in order to know that it is a danger area when he comes across it in the jungle. It is not necessary to know what kind of traffic may pass on the road to know that a road is an ideal place to be ambushed. I am saying this in part to help you understand that you will not find a lot of in-depth explanation or analysis as to why the following spiritual danger areas are dangerous to your personal relationship to God. In order to protect your relationship with God, all you need to do is recognize that an area is spiritually dangerous, and then respond as you have predetermined to respond.

The protocols identified here are not the only responses one might use, but those interviewed have found them to work. The key idea in the development and use of protocols is that you have a predetermined response to recognized spiritual danger areas. It is my hope that you will use the following as a starting point to identify the spiritual danger areas in your workplace and the protocols that work for you.

To enter the same danger area a second time without an alert trigger to help you recognize it and a protocol to deal with it, is not smart. In fact, it is dumb! The dumb soldier, who cannot learn from his mistakes, or the mistakes of others, will not survive the ambushes that wait for him in the jungle. The following danger areas are not presented in any particular order of importance.

Spiritual Danger Area: Something More

Description

Pastor James Garlow stated: "Sex is God's idea, and second to salvation; it's the best idea He ever had."[7] This danger area involves interactions with the opposite sex that have the potential for an inappropriate sexual and/or emotional relationship.

Discussion

For the Christian, sexual intercourse is proper only when it is between a man and a woman who are married to each other. The Bible is explicit on this standard. Married Christians must be particularly alert to interactions that could lead to inappropriate relations, but this may not be a danger area in the same way for single people who are free to marry. In fact, I would hope there would be no move toward marriage unless both parties feel that "something more" is possible. The discussion of this danger area is limited to situations when one or both people are married to someone else and both are heterosexual in their sexual orientation. Physical relationships between single people are fraught with their own spiritual danger areas. Single people need to decide what is an appropriate level of physical relationship for them when they begin to court a potential spouse, and in casual dating as well. Holding hands may be wrong for some. For others kissing may be okay. After engagement, more intimate physical activity, short of intercourse, may be appropriate. However, the biggest warning here is to decide before you encounter a situation how to recognize it as a danger area and how you are going to deal with it.

With increasing numbers of women in management positions in work organizations, there is more and more interaction between the sexes on routine business matters. If the focus is kept on the business at hand, these interactions should not be spiritual danger areas. So, when does it become a spiritual danger area? As one interviewee stated, "I don't know when you cross that line, but it is too late once the two of you are standing naked in a motel room." Somewhere between a simple business interaction with a person of the opposite sex and "standing naked in a motel room," the Christian has encountered, entered, and succumbed to this spiritual danger.

Examples of the Danger Area

Flirting: Men and women are attracted to each other for a variety of reasons. It is pleasurable emotionally and physically. It may be eye contact or suggestive comments that imply an attraction that leads to the conclusion that you and/or the other party are interested in "something more" than just talking about business.

A Person: A specific person to whom you are attracted and who is married to another person may be a specific danger area to avoid. This is true for a variety of combinations: If a man is married and attracted to a single woman or a man is single and is attracted to a married woman, etc.

Business Trips, Out of Town Conferences and Conventions: A danger area may exist when members of the opposite sex travel together out of town on business.

A Place: President Clinton claimed to be a born-again Christian. However, from all accounts, one of his spiritual danger areas was a windowless hallway that led to the Oval Office. If he could not avoid such a place, he should have never been there with a woman other than his wife. For King David, the roof of his palace became a spiritual danger area for him when Bathsheba was taking a bath on the roof of her house.[1]

Alert Triggers

Alert Trigger 1: You feel the chemistry. The endorphins flow. For males, it is often sexual arousal; for females, it may also be an emotional attraction. When asked to define pornography, Supreme Court Justice Potter Stewart said, "I know it when I see it!"[8] These feelings can occur during business and work encounters. This is normal and natural. It may be okay for single people, although this kind of involvement in the workplace also has its spiritual dangers for them. However, it is a RED ALERT if one or both are married to other people.

Alert Trigger 2: A person "turns you on." As a married Christian, when you see a person to whom you are attracted and vulnerable, you should be alerted that you are walking into a danger area. Keep your guard up!

Alert Trigger 3: Hiding a relationship. Feeling that you need to hide a relationship or encounter with an individual from others should be an alert. The need for a Christian to hide a relationship with someone of the opposite sex is sure evidence that it is not proper and that it is a spiritual danger area.

Alert Trigger 4: Men and women on the same trip. Isolated from the family setting, this can be seductive and subtle.

Protocols for Victorious Action

Protocol 1: Divert the discussion away from the personal to the business. Refer positively to your spouse and family. Find ways to indicate that there is no way that there is going to be "something more" between the two of you.

Protocol 2: Have pictures of your spouse and family in your office. Have a Bible on your desk or bookcase. Let your office environment announce, "No!" Let your office shout to the world that you are taken and not interested in "something more" with anyone other than your spouse. Let your office reflect that your Christian standards are important and inviolate.

Protocol 3: Avoid that specific person to whom you are inappropriately attracted. Have you ever been in a struggle when the opposing forces were overwhelming? When that is the case, retreating is the best strategy if surviving is important to the mission. Armies do it! Smart spiritual warriors do it! This chemistry between men and women can be overwhelming. When that happens, get out of the situation. Run! That is what Joseph did when Potiphar's wife confronted him:

> *One day he (Joseph) went into the house to attend to his duties, and none of the household servants was inside. She caught him by his cloak and said, "Come to bed with me!" But he left his cloak in her hand and ran out of the house* (Genesis 39:11-12 NIV).

(Note to the spiritual warrior: After reading through this first spiritual danger area, do you get the idea? The alert that you are in or entering this danger area is that "feeling" that either of you is interested in something more. That is the red flag, which should trigger an immediate, disciplined, predetermined response.)

Spiritual Danger Area: The Angry Other

Description

In an interaction with another person, the other person is getting angry with you.

Discussion

Day-to-day interactions with other people are not necessarily spiritual danger areas. However, when another person, for whatever reason, becomes angry with you it is a spiritual danger area capable of disrupting your personal relationship with God.

The angry person may be a customer, an employee, a co-worker, or a supervisor. Anyone who requires an interaction in order to do business may become angry with you or the situation. You may not be able to stop the other person's anger, but you can be disciplined in your response. You can respond in such a way that your spiritual self overcomes and is victorious. You can handle it in such a way that your relationship with God directs your response.

<u>Examples of the Danger Area</u>
      Angry Customer: A customer returns an item recently purchased because it unexpectedly broke. The customer is upset when he walks in the door, in part, because his expectations about the product and what you told him about the product were different from his experience. Another example could be in a governmental agency when a staff member followed your directions in handling a transaction but the results were not positive, as you had led the staff member to expect. Many times, anger comes from failed expectations.

<u>Alert Trigger</u>
The other person becomes angry.

<u>Protocol for Victorious Action</u>
Concentrate on treating the other person the way you would want to be treated. This may take the concentration and focus of a wide receiver who has run his pass pattern and gotten hit every time, feet knocked out from under him. Yet, he has to run that pattern again with discipline, knowing that if he does it right, he will be in the right place at the right time when the ball is thrown to him. In spite of abusive language from the other person, perhaps involving unfair and incorrect statements, you must be disciplined in your focus to treat that other person the way you would want to be treated. (Note: becoming angry yourself is as much or more of a spiritual danger area as the "angry other." That is a danger area not developed here, but a spiritual warrior who has a problem with his own anger should investigate it.)

Spiritual Danger Area: Small Things
<u>Description</u>
A small thing is a minor task or event involving values, ethics, or convictions that are performed in isolation, or with little supervision, and that require some judgment.

Discussion

On the day I interviewed the individual who first brought up small things as a danger area, the headlines of the *Tallahassee Democrat* (our local newspaper) announced that a former Speaker of the Florida House of Representatives had been indicted for tax fraud. The interviewee, who had been in a high-level state position, stated that the Speaker's problems did not begin with defrauding the government of taxes. They began with much smaller things. His experience had been that people who show up in high profile crime began by cutting corners on little things a long time before they were caught doing big things wrong. Lack of discipline in little things led to larger infractions.

Examples of the Danger Area

Danger Area #1: Travel Vouchers: Often, there is work-related travel. Every organization has some procedure to authorize travel and reimburse employees for their travel. Amounts are often small, but they can be large if air travel or extended stays in hotels are involved.

In most organizations, the individual initiates the travel reimbursement request. The request for reimbursement is often an opportunity to "fudge." Authorization for certain meals or per diem allowances may require departure times before a given hour. For example, in Florida's state government, a person must leave for a trip before 6:00 AM in order to qualify for full per diem for that day. The spiritual warrior will be completely honest about the departure time, regardless of qualification for per diem. That is a small thing, but it is one the evil forces can use to ambush the true believer.

Danger Area #2: Log of Time Worked: Time worked is reported periodically for purposes of computing one's pay and leave. Most employees keep a log of their time. That is a small thing.

Danger Area #3: Use of Copiers and Faxes for Personal Business: Using copiers and fax machines at work for personal reasons is another small thing that can compromise a Christian's witness and walk with God.

Danger Area #4: Taking Office Supplies for Personal Use: Pencils, pens, paper clips, and pads of paper are examples of small things that can unintentionally find their way home with Christians as well as non-Christian workers.

Alert Trigger

Alert Trigger 1: You may be thinking that this is "no big deal." Each one is a small thing. Key words may also trigger an alert of vulnerability and spiritual danger, such as "travel voucher," "time log," or "no big deal."

Protocol for Victorious Action

Time Logs: Keep a daily time log at your desk or location where you start and end your workday. Record the times in a daily log the first thing when arriving at your desk and the last thing when leaving for the day. Use that time for your time log, not an estimate of the time you arrived in the parking lot.

If you forget to record your leaving time, and remember that you failed to record that time when you get out to your car, write that time down on something you will have with you the next day, such as a day planner. Do not estimate stop and start times. Use actual times. The devil just loves to get Christians to hedge on the truth.

Absolute truth is the Christian's goal - absolute truth about yourself. You have nothing to hide. The dark world of the devil loves deception. The Christian needs to be open and above board in all things. No matter the angle, when the non-Christian world is looking at you, it should see no deception, no chinks in the armor, especially about the small things.

Spiritual Danger Area: Conflict of Interest

Description

A conflict of interest is any decision or action from which you benefit in money, position, and/or influence that results in a negative outcome to the work organization, a colleague, or a customer.

Discussion

Any transaction in the workplace from which you will personally benefit has the potential of being a conflict of interest. Situations that have a conflict of interest are analogous to a zero sum game. That is, in order for you to gain, another party has to lose. Those situations are dangerous to your spiritual wellbeing.

In *Reality Therapy*, Dr. William Glasser defined responsible behavior as behavior in which the individual meets his needs without keeping others from meeting their own needs.[10] According to Glasser, there is an element of irresponsible behavior in decisions and actions that create conflicts of interest. You benefit while others, are harmed.

There is probably a hierarchy of conflicts of interest in work organizations. Conflicts of interest that are experienced by beginning workers, or workers at lower levels in the organization, will often have limited consequences to the well being of the work organization and/or personal benefits to them. However, even the smallest conflict of interest can have a major impact on the spiritual wellbeing of the individuals involved.

Example of the Danger Area:
Your consulting company has a contract to develop a curriculum for a proposed new medical school. In the age of managed care, a modern medical curriculum would be incomplete without some introduction to managed care. This would necessarily include involvement of one of the largest health care organizations in the area in training students or involving students in managed care. However, you have been associated with the Board of Directors of the health care organization from its inception. You and the HMO will benefit by inclusion of the HMO in the medical school curriculum.

Alert Trigger
> *Alert Trigger 1:* I benefit!

Protocol for Victorious Action
Avoid conflicts of interest if possible. If they cannot be avoided, modify the circumstances so that you do not benefit personally. If avoiding or modifying this danger area is not possible, first talk through the situation with a trusted friend who will be objective and will help you see the real conflicts.

Be open about the real conflicts with the significant parties so that there is no appearance that any benefits you may experience are being hidden. Involve all the significant parties in the process to determine if there is indeed a conflict of interest.

For example, in the previous illustration, the "real reason" for including managed care in the potential medical school curriculum may be that it primarily benefits the client (university), and not you or your company, or the HMO. In this particular situation, a meeting was called with the contractor, the president of the university, and medical director of the HMO. After explaining the concern, the president of the university declared that including the HMO in the managed care curriculum for the medical school was not a conflict of interest, but of "mutual interest" to both parties. He approved the inclusion of the HMO in the curriculum. (Note: subsequent revisions of the plan deleted that section of the recommended curriculum.)

Spiritual Danger Area: Transitions
Description
A transition is a significant change in geographical location or organizational position.

Discussion
We only have so much emotional energy available to deal with life. Sometimes we do not realize all that is going on that can deplete that energy and make us spiritually vulnerable. Some of the times when we are most vulnerable are times when we are in transition.

During transition times, we have to deal with many unknowns. We are out of our routine and required to think and deal with many things that we ordinarily do not have to confront. These additional things become distractions, causing us to divert our attention. When we take our eyes off events that have spiritual implications, we become spiritually vulnerable.

Examples of the Danger Area
Danger Area #1 Change in Job: You graduate from college or complete that graduate degree. The period between school and beginning work can be full of energy-demanding surprises. Or your company has reassigned you in the same job to a different location. Or you have been promoted to a new position working with different people and different programs within the same business.

There are often many new experiences during transitions. New experiences are not necessarily bad, but our bodies and emotions do react. Often we interpret these new experiences as bad and go into either the "fight" or "flight" mode, neither of which may be warranted.

Alert Triggers
  Alert Trigger #1: Change of jobs.
  Alert Trigger #2: Change of communities.

Protocol for Victorious Action

During transitions, focus on family relationships. Consciously dwell on and participate in family activities at every opportunity. Encourage growth toward one another. Guard against separations that could undermine family relationships. Those relationships will provide identity and known stability during uncertain periods of transition, when the bedrock of your life seems to be shifting.

Spiritual Danger Area: Spiritual Overconfidence
<u>Description</u>
The determination that as a Christian you do not need to read the Bible, pray regularly, attend worship or Bible study, or tithe are indicators of spiritual overconfidence. If this is true of you, you may be spiritually overconfident.

<u>Discussion</u>
The emerging of spiritual overconfidence is like the process of your eyeglasses getting dirty. You do not realize your glasses are dirty until they are too dirty for you to see through them clearly. Others may notice that your glasses need cleaning before you do. Glasses get dirty gradually; and our vision tends to adjust to this impairment.[1]

Another way to put this is that you have begun to feel comfortable walking through the jungle. You have no sense of danger because you feel you can handle anything that the "authorities, the powers of the dark world and the spiritual forces of evil in the heavenly realms" can throw at you. Do you feel spiritually invincible in the workplace? If you answer "yes," you may be spiritually overconfident.

You may feel more comfortable in the world because you have relaxed your standards. There may be a false sense of overconfidence because you have dumbed down your idea of what it is to be a Christian. Your standard cannot be the Christians around you, but your own maximum relationship with God

<u>Examples of the Danger Area</u>
Danger Area #1 Spiritual Success. You look at other Christians and believe that you are "more Christian" than they are. You have just written a book telling Christians how to be better Christians. That is *prima fascia* evidence that you think you know more about this than others. In that case, you may be wallowing in a spiritual danger area.

138

Alert Trigger
Alert Trigger #1: The feeling of spiritual invincibility or spiritual superiority over other Christians.

Protocol for Victorious Action
Focus on your relationship with God. Acknowledge to God that your relationship to Him is His gift, which you enjoy only by His grace. You have done nothing to earn it. To avoid this danger area, participate in weekly worship and maintain your daily disciplines of Bible study and prayer. This is like cleaning your glasses daily, regardless of whether or not you think they need it.

Spiritual Danger Area: Authority and Power
Description
A position of authority and power in the work organization is one with discretionary authority to direct people and/or resources.

Discussion
There is a difference between authority and power in work organizations. Authority is comprised of legitimate responsibilities that accompany a recognized position on the organizational chart. People may possess power to influence decisions, staff, and resources without necessarily occupying a position of authority.

Power may come from being at the intersection of critical information and the organization. Control of information critical to the work organization may sometimes be in the hands of staff at the lower levels of the organization.

Having authority and/or organizational power is not necessarily bad. It can be used to promote what is good for the organization. What makes possession of authority and/or power a spiritual danger area is that it can be used to influence the organization for events that are bad for the organization. Often individuals are attracted to people who have organizational authority and/or power because of their own self-interest.

Several interviewees stated that some women find authority and power in men to be an aphrodisiac. This is a double danger area, a layering of danger areas one on another. Be doubly vigilant when you find yourself in a double danger area.

Example of the Danger Area

Danger Area #1 Controlling Organizational Resources: You are a manager of staff. In every decision or direction, you can tailor the result so that you will benefit personally. A standard for a manager in decisions affecting resources is to avoid those that result in enhancing your position. I have known managers in state government who never did anything unless they personally got something out of it. People like this are easy to spot and are usually well known within the organization.

That approach to management undermines your testimony as one of God's spiritual warriors. This can also happen with lower level employees who are given new responsibilities that allow them to control resources or teams. They can let this go to their head, get a big head, and take an approach that primarily enhances their position in the organization.

Remember, self-sacrifice was the hallmark of Jesus.

Alert Trigger

Alert Trigger #1: You have the authority to tell others what to do. You have the authority to decide how to spend money. You have organizational power to force others to act or spend the way you direct. You are in a spiritual danger area.

Protocol for Victorious Action

Make decisions or give directions that result in a positive impact for the work organization and the individuals involved, and that have minimal gains to you. The appearance of an ulterior motive may be as bad as the real thing for the spiritual warrior.

Spiritual Danger Area: Fatigue

Description

"Fatigue: a condition of impairment, resulting from prolonged mental or physical activity, or both, usually removable by rest."[2] You know it if you have it. When you are fatigued, you are in a spiritual danger area.

Discussion

Vince Lombardi, the legendary coach of the Green Bay Packers, is reported to have said, "Fatigue makes cowards of us all!" What is it about fatigue that makes us vulnerable to spiritual attack? In my opinion, we become spiritually vulnerable because we lose our focus and concentration. Our reaction time for recognizing spiritual danger is decreased.

Examples of the Danger Area

Danger Area #1 Extending Yourself Beyond Normal Hours of Work: You have often felt this level of fatigue. You know it physically and mentally. You know you are not operating at your peak. Many late night study sessions have made you aware that you can push your body and mind to extraordinary extremes. However, have you always been aware that you are also putting yourself at risk spiritually?

Alert Trigger

Probably the best alert trigger to this danger area is the physiology of fatigue. You feel extremely tired. You feel extremely sleepy. You may also become very "loose" emotionally, finding it easy to cry over things that you would not when rested. Listen to your body. It is telling you that it needs rest. Redefine those feelings to include the spiritual danger you are in.

Protocol for Victorious Action

If you cannot avoid this danger area, then go to great lengths to focus on the spiritual threats that come your way. Obviously, the best protocol is go to bed and be rested!

Chapter Summary

Are the ideas presented here so obvious that they seem trivial and of no interest to the Christian? Some Christians seem to think so. Those Christians seem most likely to trip over the obvious as they walk right into a spiritual ambush. Because they are slow to recognize the spiritual danger area or have no plan to deal with the danger area, they falter, damaging their personal relationship with God and undermining their ministry and testimony in the workplace.

Remember spiritual warrior: a correct response to a spiritual danger area does not require inspiration. It requires discipline!

A spiritual warrior's behavior is driven by his relationship with God. Nothing is more precious to the spiritual warrior than that relationship. He will defend it and protect it to the end. That relationship must be in all that he does. Someone said a watertight ship can sail in any storm on any ocean. For the spiritual warrior, that water tightness comes from his relationship with God.

What the spiritual warrior puts at jeopardy when he enters an unavoidable spiritual danger area is separation from God. The "dark forces of Ephesians 6" cannot sever that relationship, but they can cause separation from God. The protocols describe what the spiritual warrior can do that will result in maintaining his close relationship to God.

Ephesians 6 makes it very plain that the Christian is involved in spiritual warfare. The uninformed, apathetic, undisciplined, uncommitted, and unprepared Christian who blunders into a spiritual danger area is subject to the withering assault of evil forces just as much as the flesh-and-blood soldier who breaks out of the jungle into a danger area and right into an ambush.

Wake Up Spiritual Warrior! Be Alert! Be Prepared! Don't let the unexpected be a surprise!

Look for spiritual danger areas. Avoid danger areas you see ahead. Know your protocols for significant spiritual danger areas you know you will face. That is, know what you are going to do when you find yourself confronted with an unavoidable spiritual danger area. Be disciplined in your response to those in which you find yourself. In so doing, you will not only survive the ambushes in the spiritual jungle of the workplace but also be victorious over each one that challenges you!

Identify your spiritual danger areas in your workplace.

The Next Chapter

The next chapter will help you understand a relatively new ministry focused on helping Christian laymen integrate their faith and their work. This chapter will explain the Churches' need for a course correction to make their ministry more relevant for the layman in the "9 to 5."

Extra Life Insights

(If you can't know great men and women you can know their words!)

"Want to Achieve Your Dreams? Then Never Fall for These Myths:

Myth No. 1: Your Past Determines Your Future

Myth No. 2: Safe Goals Are The Best Goals

Myth No. 3: You Fail if You Fall Short

Myth No. 4: Writing Your Goals Is Unnecessary

Myth No. 5: Specificity Doesn't Really Matter

Failure doesn't mean success is out of reach. It just means we need to change our approach."
—Michael Hyatt
"Sometimes when you're in a dark place you think you've been buried, but actually you've been planted."
–Christine Caine

Notes

1. Airborne and Ranger Training Brigade, U.S. Army Maneuver Center of Excellence, http://www.benning.army.mil/infantry/rtb/ (accessed December 16, 2013).
2. Ranger Class Photo for Class # 66-1, http://www.benning.army.mil/infantry/rtb/Graduates/images/1-66.jpg (accessed December 16, 2013).
3. 20th Special Forces Group (Airborne), http://www.alguard.state.al.us/Units/20thSFG/default.aspx (accessed December 16, 2013).
4. *Ranger Handbook*, SH21-76, July 1992, chapters 4-5.
5. Francis Frangipane, *The Three Battlegrounds* (Cedar Rapids, IA: Arrow Publications: 2006), 17.
6. Beth Moore, *Daniel*, (Nashville, Tennessee: LifeWay Press, 2006), 222.
7. James L. Garlow and Peter Jones, *Cracking DaVinci's Code* (Ease Sussex, England: David C. Cook, 2004), 31.
8. "The Origins of Justice Stewart's 'I Know It When I See It,'" Law Blog, The Wall Street Journal., http://blogs.wsj.com/law/2007/09/27/the-origins-of-justice-stewarts-i-know-it-when-i-see-it/ (accessed December 16, 2013).
9. Nouwen, Henry, GoodReads, https://www.goodreads.com/quotes/179153-you-don-t-think-your-way-into-a-new-kind-of (accessed December 23, 2015).
10. Glasser, William, *Reality Therapy: A New Approach to Psychiatry* (Harper & Rowe: New York, 1965) Kindle Location = 100.

Chapter 6: What Can the Church Do to Help the Spiritual Warrior?

Churches are failing their Christians. Churches focus on reaching the unbeliever and the un-churched and rightly so. However, few adequately prepare their Christians for the Monday morning workplace. Churches can do both. This chapter presents a reorientation of the church as one that launches its Christians into Monday morning.

Hey, spiritual warrior in the workplace, help is on the way!

Many ministers have no clue what their laymen face on Monday morning. Their sermons are well intended but the message regarding daily work life for its members is lost in translation. Most preachers teach evangelism to reach the lost and build the Church. That is important; it is the primary purpose of the Church and the primary message of the New Testament.

Ministers are not hearing this need from their laymen because laymen have never received workplace specific training from their church, and most have never thought this was teaching and training their church could provide. It is as though ministers are casting a broad net for the unbeliever and un-churched, implying that all problems with the unbelieving society can be resolved through evangelism. The implication is that the laymen can resolve the non-Christian problem in the workplace by converting the non-believer. To add perspective to this ministerial, approach it would be the same as telling the soldier when they enter the battlefield that the way to defeat the enemy is to first get them to change their mind. That does not work for the soldier.

If ministers could grasp the reality of what their laymen face on Monday morning they would aggressively lead their church to prepare their Christians for the workplace. The Church can do both: evangelize the world and harden the spiritual warrior for their daily battles with the dark forces of Ephesians 6. As Henry Blackabee has stated, "The Church must follow the Christian into the community." Because Christians are not prepared by their church on Sunday, their defeats on Monday undermine the evangelism message of the Church.

Evangelical laymen are being gobbled up on Monday morning in their workplace by "the roaring lion." The Church needs to provide more explicit training and teaching to help Christians live their Christ-centered values. In my opinion, most churches are failing the layman in this regard, but there are exceptions, such as Redeemer Presbyterian's Center for Faith and Work in New York.

Churches have been slow to respond to the needs of their laymen, so Faith-At-Work ministries outside the walls of the church have sprung up to answer that call.[1]

History of the Faith-At-Work Movement

David W. Miller, Director of the Princeton University Faith & Work Initiative and President of the Avodah Institute, published an excellent book early in 2007 that presents the history and a conceptual structure for describing, analyzing, and understanding the Faith-At-Work movement.

> "The Faith-At-Work movement is a loosely networked group of individual and collective activity, reacting against the church's lack of support for those called to a life in the marketplace, and whose common drive is a deep desire to live a holistic life with particular attention to the integration of faith and work."[2]

Among his insights is that the goal of the Faith-At-Work Movement is to integrate faith and work, to close the Sunday-Monday gap. Miller explains that there have been three waves of effort to integrate faith and work in America.

Miller calls the first wave "The Social Gospel Era" (1890 – 1945).[3] The beginning of this wave was the issuance of a landmark encyclical in 1891 by Pope Leo XIII, "The Condition of Labor." The encyclical stated:

> "The special consideration that must be given to the weak and the poor, the dignity and respect owed to all types of work and workers, and the payment of decent wages, while at the same time rejecting socialism and endorsing the virtues of private ownership."[4]

This was one of the first written documents in which the church took a stand about problems in the workplace.

At the same time, a protestant pastor, Walter Rauschenbusch, began speaking and writing on the economic injustices he saw among inner city and working class populations. Rauschenbusch stated, "Capitalism has generated a spirit of its own which is antagonistic to the spirit of Christianity, a spirit of hardness and cruelty that neutralizes the Christian spirit of love; a spirit that sets material goods above spiritual possessions."

Rauschenbusch also wrote eloquently of his desire to transform business and the hope he held for the constructive role of business in society. It is this hope that resonates with the Faith-At-Work Movement. For instance, in Rauschenbusch's essay "Wanted: A New Kind of Layman," he essentially argued for what in wave two is ministry of the laity and in wave three is Faith-At-Work. Miller states that Joseph H. Oldham (1874-1969), a theologically trained Anglican layperson and one of the movement's key leaders…wrote, "If the Christian faith was to bring about changes in the present and in the future, it could only do so through the working faith of laypeople in the "ordinary affairs of life."[5]

This first wave saw the development of special groups that attempted to address the needs of believers involved in work. Those groups included the Y.M.C.A., Y.W.C.A., The Gideons, etc. Several books contributed to the "popularization of Jesus", such as Charles Sheldon's *In His Steps: What Would Jesus Do?* In 1896, *The Man Nobody Knows* by Bruce Barton, and *Acres of Diamonds* by Russell Conwell.

Miller observes that in the wake of two world wars and the Great Depression, the Social Gospel receded, as did the first wave of Faith-At-Work activity.[6]

The second wave is the Ministry of the Laity Era (c.1946-1985).[7] This wave saw the emergence of more awareness of the role of the layman.

The Vatican II Council that met between 1962 and 1965 brought a lot of attention to the layman and his role in the mission of the Church.

Elton Trueblood wrote during this period: "A minority ought to leave their secular employment in order to engage in full-time work for the promotion of the gospel, but this is not true of most. Most men ought to stay where they are and to make their Christian witness in ordinary work rather than beyond it."[8]

This wave also saw the establishment of many lay organizations that had the purpose of encouraging laypeople to live their faith Monday through Friday. Among those groups were The Full Gospel Business Men's Fellowship International and The Fellowship of Companies for Christ International.

Miller states,

> "By the late 1970s, with a few notable exceptions, most theologians and clergy seemed to think about lay ministry in one of two ways. One limited and misguided way of thinking about lay ministry is to see it merely as a means to increase lay participation in the interior life of the gathered church as opposed to equipping laity for the challenges of life in the scattered Church."

Miller gives several reasons for the receding of the Ministry of the Laity era:

> "Evidence suggests that the church essentially co-opted the energy of the lay ministry movement, directing it to the internal life of the gathered church instead of equipping the laity and unleashing lay ministers into the external life of the scattered church."[9]

The third wave is the Faith-At-Work era (c. 1985 – present). This wave is characterized by the desire of many believers to have a holistic and integrated approach to their faith. They do not want to compartmentalize their church experience from their weekday and work world.

Miller points to many changes in society that have made people more aware of others - the need for social justice, the dismantling of the Berlin Wall and the Soviet Union, the end of apartheid in South Africa, the creation of the Internet and social networking... these and many other events during this period have contributed to changes in believers' attitudes toward church and society. Believers have moved away from denominational loyalty. Miller states:

> "Not content to accept the full range of church teachings and doctrine of their own tradition, baby boomers have become grazers at the spiritual smorgasbord...Many boomers in the Christian tradition have become cafeteria Christians, choosing the beliefs and practices they like and rejecting those that they find disagreeable, outdated or unimportant.[10] In view of this constellation of societal changes, I cannot identify a specific date or a single variable that alone accounts for wave three's emergence in the 1980s and continuation through today. Rather, a rich compendium of significantly altered and still-changing geopolitical, legal, demographic, economic technological, and religious factors, within a historical context, converged to create fertile soil for the Faith-At-Work movement to emerge and flourish."[11]

Os Hillman, one of the leaders of the Faith-At-Work movement states, "Ten years ago we could identify less than twenty-five formal marketplace ministry groups. Today, we have identified more than 1,000 formalized national or international groups and they are growing each day."[12]

Dr. Billy Graham has stated, "I believe one of the next great moves of God is going to be through the believers in the workplace."[13] According to Franklin Graham, "God has begun an evangelistic movement in the workplace that has the potential to transform our society as we know it."[14]

Dr. Henry Blackaby, author of *Experiencing God,* agrees:

> "The people who go out into the workplace are the church. The pastor needs to read his congregation and know his congregation from one end to the other and see where they are spiritually, see where they are physically. Then ask God, 'How do I organize the church to help equip them to function where God has put them in the marketplace?' Most of their time is not spent in the church house. It is spent in the world."[15]

Counterpoints to the Mainstream Faith-At-Work Movement

Because ministers write so much of the Faith-At-Work literature and lead many of the Faith-At-Work programs, there is a need for a course correction to their worldview, which sees all that laymen do as ministry. The following attempts to provide that much-needed realignment of the Faith-At-Work concept to the reality of what laymen face. We will first confront the concepts of the approaches of four "mainstream" ministers and lay leaders, and then present a new church-based orientation for the Faith-At-Work movement.

Rich Marshall

Minister Rich Marshall bases his Faith-At-Work program on Revelation 1:5-6. Marshall states that this verse is a call from God to each Christian to be either a "king" (layman) or "priest" (minister).

> *And from Jesus Christ, the faithful witness, the firstborn from the dead, and the ruler over the kings of the earth. To Him who loved us and washed us from our sins in His own blood, and has made us kings and priests to His God and Father, to Him be glory and dominion forever and ever. Amen* (Revelation 1:5-6 KJV).

Marshall asks," Why not refer to the ones called to business and professions as "kings," and the ones called to church and mission settings as "priests?"[16] Rev. Marshall's church even goes to the effort to ordain the "kings" to make their businesses their ministries.[17]

The problem with Marshall's use of this passage to appoint "kings" and "priests" is that the King James Version gives the wrong impression. The People's New Testament Commentary states:

> "And he made us. Here the Revision must be followed. He made us to be a kingdom; to be priests unto his God. His disciples are constituted a kingdom; a kingdom in which each one is a priest. No disciple needeth a priest to offer incense or sacrifice for him, for he can go directly to the Father through Jesus Christ. Christians are called priests, but are never called kings in a correct translation of the New Testament."[18]

The NIV translation of Revelation 1:5-6 makes Rev. Marshall's erroneous interpretation even more striking,

> *... and from Jesus Christ, who is the faithful witness, the firstborn from the dead, and the ruler of the kings of the earth. To him who loves us and has freed us from our sins by his blood, and has made us to be a kingdom and priests to serve his God and Father—to him be glory and power for ever and ever! Amen* (Revelation 1:5-6 NIV).

Reverend Marshall does have a major positive insight as to God's legitimating of non-church-related professions when he points out that God chose the home of a businessman to give birth and rear His only begotten Son. It might also be pointed out that Jesus chose His disciples from the non-church community. None of the disciples were priests.

There are others who define the jobs/vocations of laymen as ministry and preach that they should approach their jobs as ministry.

Os Hillman

Os Hillman has been at the forefront of the non-church-based workplace ministry in America. Much of the Faith-at-Work movement outside the walls of the church would not exist if it had not been for the work of Os Hillman. Hillman created a new ministry called Marketplace Leaders:

> "Marketplace Leaders' mission is to equip men and women to fulfill God's calling in and through their work life and to raise up change agents who will influence the culture for Jesus Christ."[19]

In 1998, Hillman began to write an online daily devotional that now has 200,000 subscribers. It is called "Marketplace Meditations: Today God Is

First (TGIF)," a daily workplace inspiration.[20]   The Billy Graham Association, New Ventures Division, selected Marketplace Leaders as a ministry it would encourage, and it has helped fund the organization's special events.[21]

With the help of the Association, Os Hillman hosted a conference in March 2003 called, His Presence in the Workplace, "More than 270 workplace leaders, pastors, and non-profit workplace ministries came together to discover what God was doing in the faith and work movement." I was one of the attendees.

Os Hillman has been a leader, cutting new paths for this new ministry. His leadership has been critical in the development of the Faith-At-Work movement outside churches.   However, in my opinion, his approach is flawed. Hillman downplays the importance of the non-ministry aspects of the layman's job by forcing all that the layman does into a ministry format. It is as though he is saying if it is not ministry, it is not important. Hillman gives this perspective in his online bio:

> "Os Hillman is president of Marketplace Leaders, an organization whose purpose is to help men and women discover and fulfill God's complete purposes through their work and **to view their work as ministry**."[22]

In his book *Marketplace Leadership* on "Intercessory Prayer in The Workplace," Hillman states,

> "Imagine if all corporations had a director of corporate intercession as a paid position. I am pleased to tell you that in at least one case, this is already happening. Darlene Maisano is a full-time intercessor for the marketplace and a paid intercessor for several businesses. She is paid as a consultant would be paid. She sits in business meetings, quietly praying and "listening." She has authored the only resource I know of on the subject, "Breaking Open the Door of Success Through Marketplace Intercession."[23]

Hillman also tells of a businessman in Trinidad who hired an individual as an Employee Assistance Officer/Intercessor. This person's job was strategically praying for his optical business.[24] Employee assistance is a common function of personnel offices. It enhances the organization's ability to succeed in its stated mission by enabling its troubled workers to be better able to deal with personal problems that may negatively affect their job performance. Christians are admonished in the Bible always to pray.

> *And pray in the Spirit on all occasions with all kinds of prayers and requests. With this in mind, be alert and always keep on praying for all the Lord's people* (Ephesians 6:18a NIV).

In a business, a chaplain that is an employee of the company often handles this function. However, to use company resources to pay someone to pray for the business seems to cross the line in the same way that doing ministry on company time crosses the line. This certainly would not be allowed in a governmental work organization. The legality of this practice would also be challenged in a publicly traded for-profit organization.

Chuck Ripka

To convey explicitly his vision for the layman viewing his work as ministry, Hillman tells the story of Chuck Ripka:

> "Chuck Ripka lives in Elk River, Minnesota, a community of about 20,000 people 40 miles outside of Minneapolis. Chuck and some business leaders opened a bank in 2003 with the intent to use the bank as a place of ministry. Within the first 18 months of the bank's opening, Chuck and his staff saw more than 70 people accept salvation inside the bank, and there were numerous physical healings. The bank employees offer prayer for their customers in the boardroom and often pray for those who come to the teller windows. There is excitement in the bank each day about what God is going to do."[25]

An article appearing in the New York Times on October 31, 2004, about Ripka and the bank reports, "One tenet listed in the Riverview Community Bank's first annual report is to "use the bank's Christian principles to expand Christianity."[26] Ripka states "Plans for Christianizing the bank expanded as they developed the project."

Chuck Ripka left the bank in 2006 to start his own import/export business. The bank failed and was closed on October 24, 2009. The following is a statement from the FDIC announcement:

> "On Friday, October 23, 2009, Riverview Community Bank, Otsego, MN was closed by the Minnesota

Department of Commerce, and the Federal Deposit Insurance Corporation (FDIC) was named Receiver."[27]

The *Star Tribune* newspaper of Minneapolis-St. Paul had an article on the bank failure: "Ostega Bank Cited for Unsound Practices."[28] Riverview was the 16th bank to fail in Minnesota since early 1998. The reporter did talk to Mr. Ripka, who said he "wasn't sure if the bank had retained its Christian focus."

It is not known if Riverview's religious practices contributed to its failure. There have been 320 banks to fail in the U.S. since October 1, 2000, and 13 were in Minnesota.[29] There are no reports that any of these other failing banks had an overt "Christian ministry orientation." Therefore, it is reasonable that Riverview failed for reasons similar to those other 319 banks.

The Minnesota Department of Commerce stated that Riverview was a state bank that had a "state charter." The charter requires a statement of its purpose. Its stated purpose was that it was a commercial bank providing a full range of commercial bank services. If the charter application had stated that its purpose was to provide a Christian ministry, it would not have been given a bank charter.[30]

If Riverview was going to be operated as a ministry, it should have been a 501(c)(3) not-for-profit organization, as are churches and other religious organizations. It was a for-profit bank. In addition, conversions and requests for prayer are suspect when people are coming in to get loans and other financial services. It would be hard to separate the response of patrons that are based on spiritual need from those responses based on complying with whatever the loan officer asks of the patron in order to receive a loan.

The Riverview Community Bank and its failure constitute an example of the misguided effort to make a for-profit business a ministry.

Rick Warren

In *The Purpose Driven Life*, Rick Warren's list of the five purposes for life given in the Bible are incomplete.[31] The first three should be purposes for all Christians all the time. The last two are purposes for the clergy in their paid jobs and for the ministry laymen provide beyond the job they are paid to do. Warren forces everything a layman does into a ministry format. It appears that for Warren, the lay job the layman is paid for and is called by God to do is not legitimate unless it is approached as a ministry. Here are statements of his five purposes:

1. "Bringing enjoyment to God, living for his pleasure, is the first purpose of your life."[32]
2. "You were formed for God's family. God wants a family and he created you to be a part of it. This is God's second purpose for your life, which he planned before you were born."[33]
3. "You were created to become like Christ. From the very beginning, God's plan has been to make you like his Son, Jesus. This is your destiny and the third purpose of your life."[34]
4. "You were put on earth to make a contribution. You were not created just to consume resources--to eat, breathe, and take up space. God designed you to make a difference with your life…you were created to add to life on earth, not just take from it. God wants you to give something back. This is God's fourth purpose for your life, and it is called your ministry, or service."[35]
5. "Fulfilling your mission in the world is God's fifth purpose for your life. God wants you to have both a ministry in the Body of Christ and a mission in the world. Your ministry is your service to believers, and your mission is your service to unbelievers. You were made for a mission…what is that mission? Introducing people to God![36] The consequences of your mission will last forever, the consequences of your job will not. Nothing else you do will ever matter as much as helping people establish an eternal relationship with God."[37]

"Your call to salvation included your call to service. They are the same. Regardless of your job or career, you are called to full-time Christian service. You are going to give your life for something. What will it be? --a career, a sport, a hobby, fame, wealth? None of these will have lasting significance. Service is the pathway to real significance. It is through ministry that we discover the meaning of our lives."[38]

All five purposes are purposes for ministry for all Christians, but not for all jobs. What about the layman's job, the activity that earns his salary? Purposes 4 and 5 are clearly purposes for a minister's job, the work for which he is paid. However, Warren gives short shrift to the non-ministerial jobs of laymen. Warren states that your God-given mission is to the non-believer. The implication is that non-ministerial jobs must be forced into purposes 4 or 5. It appears that Warren thinks there is no room for non-ministerial work in God's plan, unless it is approached as ministry.

The approaches that see the job of laymen as ministry are not biblical. As stated in Chapter 3, the Bible just does not address the layman's non-ministry work. In Colossians 3:22-25, Paul admonishes slaves to have an attitude about the jobs their masters assign like what they would have if they were working for the Lord. Paul makes no mention of the merit of the tasks themselves.

As quoted earlier, Sherman states, "I think that the workplace is the most strategic arena for Christian thinking and influence today. And second, our greatest need in the workplace right now is for Christians whose lifestyle and workstyle are so unique and so distinctive that coworkers will want to know why."[39]

There is a desperate need for a course correction in the Faith-At-Work movement. This "new" approach needs to be more real, more honest, and more biblical. It needs to teach church members the distinctive lifestyle and workstyle to which Sherman is referring. It needs to recognize and honor the non-ministry work of laymen, the jobs they are being paid to do. The Church needs to teach the laymen the characteristics of the Christian approach to do the "non-ministry" job and what is appropriate ministry to those in the workplace. The Faith-At-Work ministry needs to be developed inside the church and serve alongside the other traditional ministries, such as ministry to college students, ministry to senior adults, ministry to young adults, and ministry to youth.

The Church-Based Faith-At-Work Ministry

We cannot leave this Faith-At-Work ministry to outside not-for-profit organizations like Os Hillman's Marketplace Leadership for one simple reason: the math! Hillman reported that his International Coalition of Workplace Ministries (ICWM) had grown from 10 to 1000 national and international organizations in ten years. However, the Hartford Institute for Religious Studies reported that in 2010 there were 350,000 Christian congregations in the United States, with 64 million attending services the Sunday before the poll was taken in 2010. That is 20.4 percent of the American population. The Gallop poll found double that number.[40]

Os Hillman's Marketplace Leadership is a remarkable organization that is doing great things, and Os Hillman has been a trailblazer, but for the Faith-At-Work ministry to have an impact on the American culture in the workplace, churches need to catch up.

WorkLife
Although developed outside the walls of the church, WorkLife is a ministry that targets a major change of the church to be more focused on the need of the Christian in his workplace. Begun by Doug Spada as His Church at Work, the organization changed its name in 2009 to WorkLife.[41]

Spada offers one of the more vivid and dramatic metaphors for describing the transformation he is trying to bring to churches. Spada says many see the local church as a cruise ship. It is a place for members to come for fellowship, education, relaxation, renewal, and spiritual growth.

Spada asks us to visualize a naval battle group. It is led by two nuclear submarines, followed by an aircraft carrier, which is surrounded by a number of different ships that have different responsibilities in the battle group.[42]

The aircraft carrier has 5,000 crewmembers with a single purpose.

That purpose is to maintain, fuel, arm, and launch fighter aircraft. Spada wants to convert the local church from a cruise ship to an aircraft carrier that reloads, refuels and launches Christians into the workplace every Sunday, just as an aircraft carrier launches its jet fighters. The Christian is fueled, armed, and ready for anything that comes his way, including the "roaring lion."

Spada has an excellent video presentation of this metaphor.
(http://www.youtube.com/watch?v=r-
tDaFcsVdo&list=TLzbRmaH79TMpHUJPI0SOmsvDD40yfCDpC)[43]

WorkLife provides an Internet based course to churches for its members to study the biblical bases of the application of their faith in the workplace. This is called "Maestro." This is available for a fee, based on the number of church members.[44]

WorkLife also offers a broad range of resources for the individual Christian in the workplace, including an assessment tool to determine areas that need further development in applying one's faith in the workplace. Based on the assessment, the individual will receive devotionals Spada calls "WorkLife Coaching Sessions" on Tuesdays and Thursdays. Bible studies, called "Truth Modules," provide "in-depth guidance on work beliefs, skills and relationships." All resources are available to individuals and churches for a minimal fee.

Spada has stated that he thinks all ministries should be self-supporting. He has a business model that includes a fee for service/product. Spada published *The Monday Morning Atheist: Why We Switch God Off at Work and How You Fix It*, in 2012 as a statement for the need for the WorkLife ministry.[45]

Through WorkLife's church consultation services, a number of prominent churches have established Faith-At-Work ministries, including, Discovery Church in Orlando (4,000 members) and Peachtree Presbyterian in Atlanta (6,940).

Redeemer Presbyterian's Center for Faith and Work
The absolute "gold standard" for a church-based Faith-At-Work ministry is Redeemer Presbyterian's Center for Faith and Work in New York City, established in 2003. Under the leadership of pastor Tim Keller and the Center's first director, Katherine Leary Altdorf, this ministry has evolved into several different initiatives.[46]

One initiative is vocation-based fellowships. As of November 2013, there were fifteen vocational groups: Actors, Business, Creative Communications, Educators, Finance, Tech, and others. These are "Vocational Initiatives [that] provide a gospel-centered forum for industry-specific dialogue, community, collaboration, and innovation toward gospel-centered cultural engagement." By 2015 the Vocational Initiatives have evolved into Vocational Intensive and Vocational Courses.

"A Vocational Intensive is a 3-month experience that will allow you an in-depth look at your particular field through the lens of the gospel. Over the course of nine weekly 2-hour meetings and three Saturday sessions, you will learn in community how to apply theological content & biblical truths to your everyday work life, creating a more meaningful & sustainable integration of faith & work."[47]

"A Vocational Course is a 6-8 week program exploring the way the gospel intersects with your calling as a professional in a given field. We deepen our understanding of a Christian worldview of a given industry, discuss the ways in which the gospel challenges common industry idols, explore what Scripture has to say about the tensions inherent in our work, and brainstorm innovative ways to change the way that industry operates."[48]

The Gotham City Fellowship is another program of the Center for Faith and Work:

> "A nine-month program for 42 adults who are employed full-time in New York City and have at least two years of working experience. Our typical class comprises 50% men and 50% women between the ages of 25-35 working in fields including law, finance, education, government, non-profit, design, medicine, and the arts.
>
> The Fellowship begins Labor Day Weekend and finishes Memorial Day Weekend. During these nine months, the Fellows meet two hours a week to discuss the extensive weekly reading of major texts from various eras of church history. Daily devotionals unite the group through guided scriptural and devotional readings. Monthly Saturday gatherings provide in-depth training and city excursions. Three retreats (Labor Day, mid-winter and Memorial Day weekends) focus on personal reflection and spiritual formation.
>
> The Fellows tuition fee of $2500 helps offset program expenses. We are seeking donors who can enable us to provide financial aid, as needed. Applications will be accepted in the spring for cohorts beginning the following September. Fellows will be selected by an admissions committee from applicants who best demonstrate 1) commitment to the City, 2) spiritual maturity, and 3) ability to fulfill the responsibilities of the Program."[49]

The purpose of the Gotham Fellowship is to develop leaders who feed back into the vocational groups.

Among other initiatives, there are lecture series and weekend conferences. For example, "Humanizing Work...Because Work Should Be an Expression of Our Humanity, Not the Source of Our Identity," was offered on November 8-9, 2013.[50]   Dr. Keller and Katherine Leary Altdorf have written a book that discusses the underpinnings of the Center; it is called Every *Good Endeavor: Connecting Your Work to God's Work*.[51]

Nothing captures the philosophy of the Redeemer Center for Faith and Work more than the statement on their home page:

> "FAITH AND WORK. We might see them as
> estranged. But, in truth, they share a crucial aim: to see
> the unseen. Nothing new has been made without faith.
> Nothing unseen has been seen without work. When the
> force of what we do hits why we do it, we wither or we
> flourish. We don't want to just examine that collision.
> We want to live in the intersection where it occurs. To
> celebrate what flies. And to rethink what falls. To map.
> To explore. To create. To risk and to fail better. Not
> just for a nicer 9 to 5. But to serve the city we belong
> to and love. It comes down to one key truth: work
> matters. So do it well."[52]

WorkFaith at First Baptist Church of Tallahassee, Florida

I first heard the term WorkFaith from Dr. Doug Dortch, my pastor at First Baptist of Tallahassee, Florida, in July 2007, after I made a presentation to him and our assistant pastor, Fran Buhler about the need for a Faith-At-Work ministry at our church. He stated that he wanted to call it "WorkFaith."

Soon afterward Dr. Dortch convened a meeting to discuss establishing the new ministry. However, WorkFaith did not materialize as a structured program at First Baptist Church in 2007, in part because the Church was entering into a major building program. I think the delay was good.

Dr. Dortch subsequently appointed a WorkFaith Workgroup in April 2011. After ten months of planning, the WorkFaith ministry began in February 2012. It included a month-long study of R. Paul Stevens' *Taking Your Soul to Work* for adults in the Sunday morning Sunday School hour.[53] Our Minister to Youth preached a sermon series on WorkFaith during the worship service three of the four Sundays in March.

Following this were three monthly weekday lunch meetings, where speakers talked about what they had learned about their faith in the workplace. Speakers included former Florida Secretary of State Kurt Browning, former Executive Director of the Florida Ethics Commission and Secretary of the Florida Department of Professional Regulations Larry Gonzalez, and - via Skype - Nan Futrell, Staff Counsel of the Baptist Joint Committee on Religious Liberty based in Washington, D.C.[54]

A mentoring program was established for individuals who requested it. The Workgroup felt that this had a potential to significantly supplement the counseling load of church staff. A WorkFaith website was created, accessible through the church's website, which allowed individuals to make lunch reservations, request a mentor, and access books and articles on practicing one's faith in the workplace.

The ministry ended when Dr. Dortch left for another church and before a new minister was called. We "ran out of authority" during the interim period.

WorkFaith at First Baptist Church of Tallahassee was a small program with a very limited budget, but it demonstrates what one church can do to address the needs of Christian laymen.

Chapter Summary

This chapter presents the history of the Faith-At-Work ministry. A new orientation for Faith-At-Work is presented, which has laymen taking a Christian approach to their jobs and having a ministry to individuals from the workplace. Examples of "church-based" Faith-At-Work ministries are described. The case is made for every church to establish a Faith-At-Work ministry that is staffed and funded like the traditional ministries, to college students, seniors, etc. Better still, every Church needs to establish a Center for Faith and Work.

Extra Life Insights

(If you can't know great men and women you can know their words!)

"When you are dead, you don't know you are dead. It is difficult only for others. The same is true for stupid."
–Philippe Geluck

"Even idiots occasionally speak the truth accidentally."
–{Lord Peter Wimsey}Dorothy L. Sayers

"Faith is to believe what we do not see, and the reward of the Faith is to see what we believe." -St. Augustine

"The first thing you do when you have a problem is you don't make it worse! –Jerry Sestak

Notes

1. Workplace ministry" is a generic term for the program a church or organization has that promotes the practice of one's faith in the workplace. "Faith-At-Work" is a term used to depict that actual application of one's faith in the workplace. Marketplace Leadership is the Os Hillman ministry. WorkLife is the name of a ministry developed by Doug Spada. WorkFaith is a church-based ministry developed at First Baptist Church of Tallahassee that focuses on the Christian approach to a layman's job.

2. David W. Miller, *God at Work* (New York: Oxford University Press, 2007), 21.

3. Miller, 23.

4. Miller, 26.

5. Miller, 31.

6. Miller, 36.

7. Miller, 39.

8. Miller, 56.

9. Miller, 58.

10. Miller, 63.

11. Miller, 73.

12. "Os' Personal Testimony," Marketplace Leaders, http://www.marketplaceleaders.org/os/testimony/ (accessed December 18, 2013).

13. Hillman, Os, "Are We on the Verge of a Workplace Transformation?" http://www.intheworkplace.com/apps/articles/default.asp?articleid=12780&columnid=1935 (accessed December 23, 2015).

14. Ibid.

15. WorkLife Interviews: Henry Blackaby, http://www.worklife.org/partner/Article_Display_Page/0,,PTID61609_CHID175864_CIID1978542,00.html (accessed December 18,2013).

16. Rich Marshall, *God @ Work* (Shippensburg, PA: Destiny Image, 2000), 7.

17. Marshall, 28.

18. The Revelation of John, Bible Study Tools, http://www.biblestudytools.com/commentaries/peoples-new-testament/revelation/1.html. (accessed December 19, 2013).

19. Hillman, Os, "About Us", Marketplace Leaders, http://www.marketplaceleaders.org/abou%09t-s/ (accessed December 28, 2013).
20. "Today God Is First," Marketplace Leaders, http://www.marketplaceleaders.org/tgif/ (accessed December 18, 2013).
21. Hillman, Os, Ibid.
22. Hillman, Os, "About Us", Ibid.
23. Os Hillman, "Intercessory Prayer in the Workplace.," Marketplace Leaders, http://www.intheworkplace.com/apps/articles/default.asp?articleid=25420&columnid=1935. (accessed December 19, 2013).
24. Os Hillman, "Intercessory Prayer in an Optical Company," "Intercessory Prayer in the Workplace," Marketplace Leadership, http://www.intheworkplace.com/apps/articles/default.asp?articleid=25420&columnid=1935 (accessed December 19, 2013).
25. Ripka Hillman, Os, The 9 to 5 Window, (Revell: Grnd Rapids, Michigan, 2005), Kendal location = 822.
26. Shorto, Russel, "Faith at Work", New York Times, http://www.nytimes.com/2004/10/31/magazine/faith-at-work.html?_r=0 (accessed December 23, 2015).
27. "Failed Bank Information," FDIC Federal Deposit Insurance Corporation, http://www.fdic.gov/bank/individual/failed/riverview-mn.html (accessed December 18, 2013).
28. "Otsego bank cited for unsound practices," StarTribune Business, http://www.startribune.com/business/46_467847.html (accessed December 18, 2013).
29. Ibid.
30. Telephone conversation between the author and a representative of the Minnesota Department of Commerce on May 12, 2012.
31. Rick Warren, The Purpose Driven Life, (Grand Rapids, Michigan: Zondervan, 2002).
32. Warren, 63.
33. Warren, 117.
34. Warren, 171.
35. Warren, 227.
36. Warren, 229.
37. Warren, 282.
38. Warren, 284.

39. Sherman and Hendrix, 51.

40. "Fast Facts about American Religion," Hartford Institute for Religion Research, http://hartfordinstitute.org/research/fastfacts/fast_facts.html#numc ong (accessed December 19, 2013).

41. WorkLife, http://www.worklife.org (accessed December 19, 2013).

42. "Carrier Battle Group," Wikipedia, http://en.wikipedia.org/wiki/Carrier_battle_group (accessed December 2013).

43. Doug Spada, "WorkLife." http://www.youtube.com/watch?v=r-tDaFcsVdo&list=TLzbRmaH79TMpHUJPI0SOmsvDD40yfCDpC (accessed December 19, 2003).

44. Maestro, "WorkLife, "http://www.worklife.org/CC_Content_Page/worklife_products.html (accessed December 19, 2013).

45. Doug Spada, *The Monday Morning Atheist: Why We Switch God Off at Work and How You Fix It,* (Atlanta, GA: WorkFaith Press, 2012).

46. The Center for Faith and Work, Redeemer Presbyterian Church, http://www.faithandwork.org (accessed December 23, 2015).

47. The Center for Faith and Work, Redeemer Presbyterian Church, http://faithandwork.com/programs/2-vocational-intensives (accessed December 23, 2015).

48. The Center for Faith and Work, Redeemer Presbyterian Church, http://faithandwork.com/programs/3-vocational-courses (accessed December 23, 2015).

49. The Center for Faith and Work, Redeemer Presbyterian Church, http://faithandwork.com/programs/1-gotham-fellowship (accessed December 23, 2015).

50. Humanizing Work, http://humanizingwork.org (accessed December 20, 2013).

51. Tim Keller and Katherine Leary Alsdorf, Every *Good Endeavor: Connecting Your Work to God's Work (*New York: Dutton, 2013).

52. The Center for Faith and Work, Ibid.

53. R. Paul Stevens and Alvin Ung, *Taking Your Soul to Work: Overcoming the Nine Deadly Sins of the Workplace* (Grand Rapids, Michigan: William B. Eerdmans Publishing Company, 2010).

54. The Baptist Joint Committee on Religious Freedom, http://www.bjcpa.org (accessed December 20, 2013).

FINAL CONCLUSIONS

The preplanned procedures developed in Chapter 4 to counter the spiritual ambush can be as helpful to the spiritual warrior in the workplace as the action at danger areas developed for the Army Ranger in a hostile jungle. This process helps the spiritual warrior capitalize on the benefits of staying alert for the "dark forces" of Ephesians 6 as the Scriptures admonish.

Some Faith-At-Work organizations are pushing Christian laymen to treat their businesses and their jobs as ministries. This is not scriptural. The word studies in Chapter 2 of the use of "called" and "calling" in the New Testament demonstrate that all but four verses that use these words are, in fact, describing the call to be holy or to come to God, not to some task or job. The four exceptions are the calling of Paul to be an apostle and to go on mission trips. This book encourages the Faith-At-Work movement to view a layman's job and a layman's ministry to those in his workplace as two different things. A layman's ministry to those in his workplace should never be done on company time. A layman's calling to do a non-ministry job is just as legitimate and holy as the calling of a person to the ministry.

The load for teaching laymen about Faith-At-Work has been carried by organizations other than churches. Os Hillman's Marketplace Leadership and Doug Spada's WorkLife have mounted exceptional ministries to Christian laymen. However, because of the math of 350,000 churches and 64 million Christians in America, organizations outside the church do not have the capacity to meet the need.

Churches need to catch up and begin Faith-At-Work ministries. To meet the needs of their laymen beyond training them in evangelism, the Church must develop ministries that prepare their laymen for Monday morning. These ministries must have funding and staffing equal to traditional ministries.

Churches need to morph from being a cruise ship to becoming an aircraft carrier preparing and launching their laymen into Monday morning.

Father, bless the life of the spiritual warrior reading this book! I ask this in the **strong name of Jesus Christ our Lord**! Amen.

Appendix A: Are You a Christian?

"If you don't change your beliefs, your life will be like this forever. Is that good news?"[1] If that is good news, close this book, put it back where you got it, walk away and continue the life your beliefs will lead you to. If that is not good news and you desire a significant change in your life, I invite you to read on.

Listen, what a Christian is, and how to become one, is somewhat complicated and difficult to understand without faith. Faith is what makes all of this work. Faith is defined as "belief or trust: belief in, devotion to, or trust in somebody or something, especially without logical proof."[1] St. Augustine's statement might be helpful: "Faith is to believe what we do not see, and the reward of the Faith is to see what we believe."

I don't have your problem with a distorted worldview. I do not remember when I have not been a Christian. My mother was a daughter of a Baptist preacher. She had me in church from the time I was two weeks old. She taught me the taste of soap when I was eight years old. Because of my dislike of the taste of soap my language and life have been for the most part clean and above board. Christianity was a part of my childhood. It was a part of who I was. It was not until I was an adult and I made a conscious choice based on faith that I really felt I had become a Christian.

I am not a preacher or a minister. I want to explain this to you in down-to-earth, everyday terms, in my own words. I am intentionally going to be very direct and confrontational, because I see this as my one and only chance to talk to you about becoming a Christian.

My urgency in this presentation comes from my concern for you to consider what I believe is absolutely the most important thing you have ever thought about. If my presentation results in helping you "find God," you will find, as have millions through the ages, that your life will never be the same.

First, I think you have to conclude that there is something more to your life, to you, than just skin and bones and blood and all of those things that make you an animal. That "something" is what you are without that body. It is your person. It is your soul!

You have probably seen a dead body at some time in your life. As an adult, you have been to a funeral or visitation at a funeral home. If so, you have probably looked at that body and realized that what that person was has gone. It is not in that body anymore.

Among those things that are no longer a part of that body is what we Christians believe to be the soul. We believe that the soul continues to live beyond the death of the body. We have no proof of this, but based on the teachings of the Bible, we accept on faith that this is true. If you don't believe there is something about you that goes beyond your body, then you will have a difficult time understanding the rest of what I have to say about the definition of a Christian and how you can become one.

You really need to understand how faith works. **Faith does not require proof!** In fact, proof negates faith. If you have proof, you do not need faith. Have you ever come in the house and sat down in a chair? Did you first go through the process of asking whether or not that chair would hold you up when you sat in it? Did you look at the design of the chair and analyze the construction before you released all of your weight on that chair? Probably not! You accepted on faith that the chair would do its job. Faith does not require proof!!

There has to be more to life than bodily functions and human survival. Let us say that, on faith, you accept the idea that you have a soul and that it lives after your body dies. If this soul exists, why? What purpose does the soul serve? We Christians accept that each human being has a soul and that there is a purpose for that soul's existence. To accept this will be your first step of faith.

The next step has to do with an awareness that there is a higher being, a being that is all-powerful and all knowing. We Christians call this being God. Now, there is a need to connect this notion that you have a soul with the notion that there is a higher being. What is that connection?

Read the early chapters of Genesis, and you will see that the original purpose of man's creation was to satisfy God's need for companionship. God has needs, you ask? Yes. God has needs and one of His biggest original needs was for companionship. The early chapters of Genesis tell this story. I like the way the poet, James Weldon Johnson describes the creation of man in his poem "The Creation." It begins with the following verse:

"And God stepped out on space,
And he looked around and said:
I am lonely –
I'll make me a world." [2]

Man was made not only with a capacity for a relationship with his Creator, but also with a programmed need for that relationship. As someone has described it, man was made with a God-shaped space inside his soul that only God can fill. The Bible says that man was made in God's image.

Any interest or desire or spiritual deficit you are experiencing now that brings you to this appendix is the desire to fill that emptiness, and to fill it with God. You may be experiencing an awareness that something is missing in your life. There is something you cannot satisfy, no matter how hard you try. We Christians believe what is missing is a personal relationship with God.

The Bible is very clear that it was God's intent that man would always be in a real and healthy relationship with his Creator. However, God gave man a free will. He did not make us robots, automatons, or clones. He wanted a relationship with a creature that could make choices about his or her life, including the relationship with his or her Creator.

You know the story. Man chose worldly pleasures (the eating of that forbidden fruit) over a relationship with God. The consequence was a break in man's relationship with God and expulsion from the Garden of Eden. Note in your reading of Genesis that it was man who walked away from God. God has always been there, wanting and inviting man back into that original relationship. The rest of the Jewish Bible tells the story of God's progressive revelation of Himself to man. The New Testament tells the story of God's ultimate revelation of Himself, Jesus.

Let me throw in something here that many non-Christians, as well as some Christians, stumble over that I do not want you to stumble over. That is the theory of evolution vs. creationism. For me this "controversy" is not important to my personal relationship with God. There is nothing in the process of coming to a personal relationship with God that requires you to accept one theory or the other. These are only theories, because no one living today was actually there.

The critical element in this controversy is for you to believe that all of creation came from God. Whether He did it in seven 24-hour periods or over eons of time through seven geological periods is not important to your coming into a personal relationship with God. Do not let unanswered questions in your mind stop you from finding and experiencing a personal relationship with God. If you really want an in-depth presentation about the many objections that the world uses to challenge the idea of God and Jesus and faith, read Lee Stroble's, *The Case for Faith.*[3]

Christians believe that God's ultimate revelation to man was in Jesus Christ. God became man so that man could know God. How simple! Jesus was in a pure relationship with God because He is God. Is that confusing to you? It is somewhat confusing to me. However, I accept that God has an element that Christians refer to as "God the Son." That is Jesus.

The second purpose for Jesus was to be *the* way by which all men could once again have a personal relationship with God, just like the one Adam and Eve experienced in the Garden of Eden. That process occurred in the death of Christ on the cross. Christians believe that Christ took on Himself the sin of all men for all time. It was the supreme gift of God that by accepting the death and resurrection of Jesus and asking for forgiveness for his own sins, man could enter into a personal relationship with Christ.

There is also "God the Holy Spirit." That is the element of God that comes into your being when you accept all of this on faith. I once heard a story about the American Indian's concept of conscience. It was described as a box that turns when you do something wrong. When it turns, the corners of the box hurt you inside. The more it turns as a result of our doing and thinking wrongly, the corners wear down until we barely feel it when the box turns. The entry of the Holy Spirit into your life when you become a Christian is like getting a new box. If it has really happened, then you will experience an awareness of a Presence in your life.

To the non-Christian, I know this sounds strange. However, it is true that this simple act can transform your life into one where God as the Holy Spirit enters your soul and establishes a real, personal relationship with you. This is stated in John 3:16: "For God so loved the world that he gave his only begotten Son that whosoever believes in him shall have everlasting life." If you accept that verse on faith, ask God to forgive you of your sins, and ask God to enter your life, then you are a Christian!

Becoming a Christian may or may not be an emotional experience for you. Most people have about as much emotion in their religious experience as they have in the rest of their life. However, the key to this transformation is the faith that it is true and has occurred.

Experiencing God fully comes after your "conversion," after you have accepted God into your life on faith. Think of it in human terms. You meet someone with whom you fall in love. If that has ever happened to you, you know that in every moment thereafter that person is a part of all that you think and do, even when you are not in that person's physical presence.

Getting to know God is kind of like that. It is after you have accepted Him into your life that change will occur in your attitude, thinking, and peace of mind, and you become aware that the emptiness inside you is finally filled.

You do not lose your humanity when you become a Christian. If anything you will become more aware of your humanity, but now there is a new set of parameters. Those parameters or standards are to be found in the

Bible. You need to learn what is expected of a Christian in the Bible and then live it. Don't expect an overwhelming urge to do the "Christian thing" right away. Henry Nouwen has captured the process you need to undergo. "You don't think your way into a new kind of living. You live your way into a new kind of thinking." As you live your new Christian life, your thinking and morality will change to conform to the values you are living.

If you are not at the point of committing to this personal relationship in faith yet, let me suggest that you read the New Testament Book of John. Read it three or four times, and let it really sink into your heart and mind. See if that does not help you understand who and what Jesus is, and what faith does to make all of this work.

Becoming a Christian is hard to understand but easy to do! So "just do it!"

You may also find Billy Graham's presentation on how to become a Christian helpful. Go to http://www.billygraham.org/specialsections/steps-to-peace/steps-to-peace.asp

Another very good presentation on how to become a Christian will be found at http://www.cbn.com/stepstopeace/index.aspx?intcmp=EVAN0015.

I also recommend that you read *Simply Christian: Why Christianity Makes Sense* by N.T. Wright (HarperCollins e-books, 2006) http://www.amazon.com/gp/product/0061920622?keywords=nt%20wright&qid=1452789920&ref_=sr_1_10&sr=8-10.

.

Notes

1. William Somerset Maugham
   http://thinkexist.com/quotation/if_you_don-t_change_your_beliefs-your_life_will/227905.html (Accessed November 6, 2015).

Appendix B: A Review of the Top Ten Best Selling books on Spiritual Warfare on Amazon May 2, 2013

Every person can have an opinion. In order to have an informed opinion, you need to know what others are saying about the subject. I want this presentation to be informed. Therefore, I am following the example Gary Friesen set in his excellent book, *Decision Making and the Will of God.*[1] (Friesen's book is the most scripturally based presentation of how God guides and directs His people that I have ever read.)

Friesen gives a synopsis and critique of fifteen leading books on the subject to show how his presentation agrees and/or differs from recognized authorities in the field. He states:

> "My intention in writing these reviews is constructive examination of biblical truth...the discussion of points of disagreement is a legitimate exercise...I will content myself with pointing out the places where (the views of these authors) diverge from my opinions in my book."[2]

This too is my intention, so that *The Spiritual Ambush* reflects the context of the broader authoritative discussion of spiritual warfare and is not just my opinion, but also my informed opinion and therefore more worthy of your consideration. Unlike Friesen's reviews, most of the content of the following reviews is comprised of direct quotes from the book. The intent is to give the reader a survey of the broader spiritual warfare discussion. Some critiques are added at the end of each review.

To get this additional knowledge about the field of spiritual warfare, I identified the top ten best selling books on Spiritual Warfare on Amazon on May 2, 2013. I read and developed a synopsis and critique of each book, which are included as in this appendix.

Readers need to challenge the credibility of each book by looking at the author's credentials and the publisher's reputation for excellence over time. For example, an author who is the Director of the Southern Baptist International Mission Board, Jerry Rankin, Bestseller #3, carries more authority than an author who is a self-proclaimed "Christian horror writer," Scott Meade, Bestseller #4. In the same way, the history of the publisher brings credibility to a book. A book like Bestseller #10 published by Thomas Nelson Publishers, with its heritage that goes back to 1798 in Scotland, has more credibility than Demon Hunters Publishing, a self-publishing entity with a very limited record of accomplishment, which published Bestseller #4.

Just because words are printed in a book does not make them legitimate, believable, or of value for consideration. A reader needs to be discriminating in his judgment of what is written - including, I might add, the words in *The Spiritual Ambush.*

Besides giving the credentials of the author and publisher, I rate each book on the following four attributes:

> 1. The Model of Deliverance Ministry: Which of the four models described in *Understanding Spiritual Warfare*, discussed in Chapter 1 and reviewed in Appendix B, and discussed in Chapter 1, best describes this author's approach to spiritual warfare?
> 2. Demon Possession: Does the author believe a demon can live inside an individual?
> 3. Staying Alert: Does the author address the importance of staying alert as a part of the Christian's spiritual warfare strategy?
> 4. Translation of Isaiah 14:12: Only the KJV translates "shining morning star" as "Lucifer." In the time of the translation of the KJV, "Lucifer" was a name given to Venus, the brightest star.[3] The Hebrew Bible translates this as "O day-star, son of the morning!"[4] Bible scholars have determined the verse is not referring to Satan but to the King of Babylon. Using the KJV version of Isaiah 14:12 to enumerate characteristics of Satan undermines the author's credibility in exposition of other Scriptures.

The books are listed in order of their ranking as to the number of sales on Amazon on May 2, 2013.

Number 1 Bestseller: Payne, *Spiritual Warfare: Christians,*
Demonization and Deliverance
Karl Payne
(WND Books: New York, 2011)

Author: Dr. Karl Payne is the Pastor of Leadership Development at
Antioch Bible Church in Redmond, Washington, and chaplain for the
Seattle Seahawks. Dr. Payne has a Masters of Divinity and Doctorate of
Ministry from Western Seminary.

Number of Pages = 230

Important Points Regarding:
Model of Deliverance Ministry: Ground-Level.
Demon Possession: Never-believers can be demon-possessed; Christians
can be "demonized" but not possessed.
Staying Alert: Does not address alertness.
Translation of Isaiah 14:12-14: Does not use the name Lucifer.

Synopsis
Dr. Payne's presentation is of the ground-level model of "deliverance
spiritual warfare." He includes case studies of his efforts to deliver
individuals from demons. He has worked with "demonized Christians"
since 1982. "The book provides clear, simple transferable materials on
spiritual warfare that anyone willing to do his homework and apply it can
confidently utilize."

Dr. Payne sees spiritual warfare as a three-pronged attack by "the
world, the flesh, and the devil." Spiritual warfare confronts these prongs.
Each is capable of destroying "our testimony for the Lord Jesus Christ."
The world, the flesh, and the devil are each real, and each represents one-
third of the spiritual warfare pie that Christians must learn to recognize and
confront. Demonic or supernatural warfare represents only one third of the
battle we face as soldiers of Christ.

Our enemies--the world, the flesh, and the devil (sociological,
physiological and supernatural opposition) represent every possible
combination of spiritual warfare we will encounter in this life. We must
learn how to recognize all three enemies and not focus on one at the expense
of the others.

It is critical to lay down ground rules when dealing with an individual who is "possessed or oppressed by demons." Dr. Payne makes the individual and the "demon(s)" understand the ground rules.

What are the ground rules? The statement, "In the name of the Lord Jesus Christ" precedes all the ground rules. The Lord Jesus Christ is our authority, not a rabbit's foot. The purpose of repeating His name is to make it clear to the demons involved that we understand the Lord Jesus Christ is the reason the Christian will win this conflict.

A. In the name of the Lord Jesus Christ, we bind the strong man.

B. In the name of the Lord Jesus Christ, there will be one-way traffic only.

C. In the name of the Lord Jesus Christ, you may speak only that which can be used against you.

D. In the name of the Lord Jesus Christ, the answers you give must stand as truth before the white throne of God.

E. In the name of the Lord Jesus Christ, there will be no profanity.

F. In the name of the Lord Jesus Christ, (name of person) is to have complete and full control of his tongue, mind and body.

G. In the name of the Lord Jesus Christ, I will give commands stating, "We command," because this is (name of person)'s fight.

H. In the name of the Lord Jesus Christ, when I give commands you will give clear, concise, complete answers in (name of person)'s mind to the questions addressed to you.

I. When I give commands in the name of the Lord Jesus Christ, you will clearly give your answers to (name of person).

J. In the name of the Lord Jesus Christ, there will be no hiding, duplicating, or changing of authority and rank. We bind you by the authority structure you now have, and that structure will only be altered if we choose to change it.

K. In the name of the Lord Jesus Christ, when I give commands for you to answer, you will give your answers to (name of person).

L. Lastly, In the name of the Lord Jesus Christ, we ask the Holy Spirit of God to enforce all of the ground rules and to punish severely any demons that attempt to step outside of the ground rule box.

Dr. Payne declares that it is possible for Satan to "totally dominate and control a non-Christian" but that Satan cannot possess a "true Christian." However, Satan can oppress both. Deliverance is required to free the individual from each.

Dr. Payne states that the Christian mind is a primary battlefield of demonic attack. "Win in your mind, and you will win in your life. Lose in your mind, and you will lose in your life. "Remember that Spiritual warfare is primarily mental.

Critiques

Critique #1 Traditional "deliverance spiritual warfare" described by Dr. Payne is directed toward demons, not the individual possessed or oppressed by the demon.

Critique #2 Since Satan cannot possess a Christian but can possess a non-Christian, it would appear that one approach not taken by Dr. Payne would be to work toward having the non-believer become a Christian. Dr. Payne's approach requires that the individual be free of the demon before he becomes a Christian. It would appear that traditional deliverance ministry sees ridding a person of his demons as easier than having him embrace Christ.

Critique #3 Dr. Payne states that the mind is the place of spiritual warfare. If you can get your mind aligned with God, then you can repel demons. Theology is the key to getting your mind right with God. This is Freudian psychology; in essence, change in emotion (thinking) comes before change in behavior. However, behaviorists would agree with Henri Nouwan: "You don't **think** your way into a new way of living; you **live** your way into a new way of thinking" (emphasis added). Changing one's behavior can lead to a change in one's thinking and emotions.

178

Number 2 Bestseller: Prince, *Spiritual Warfare*
Derek Prince
(Whitaker House: New Kensington, PA, 1987)

Author: Peter Derek Vaughan Prince (1915-2003) was born in Bangalore, India, into a British military family. He was educated at Eaton College and Cambridge University (B.A. and M.A.) and later at Hebrew University, Israel. As a student, he was a philosopher and self-proclaimed atheist. While in the British Medical Corp during World War II, Prince began to study the Bible as a philosophical work. As a result, he became a Christian. He migrated to the United States in 1963 and became an international Bible teacher. His daily radio program *Derek Prince Legacy Radio* (presently hosted by author Stephen Mansfield) broadcasts to half the population of the world in various languages.

Publisher: Robert E. Whitaker Sr. started Whitaker House in 1970. http://www.whitakerhouse.com

Number of Pages = 138

Important Points Regarding:
Model of Deliverance Ministry: Classical Model.
Demon Possession: Does not discuss.
Staying Alert: Does not address alertness.
Translation of Isaiah 14:12-14: Does not use the name Lucifer.

Synopsis
"Paul took it for granted that, as Christians, we are involved in a war for which we need the appropriate armor, and that our adversary is the Devil Himself."

Prince declares that although there is no established doctrine regarding how many heavens there are, he believes there are three:
1. The visible and natural heaven with the sun, the moon, and the stars that we see with our eyes.
2. Intermediate heaven, where Satan's headquarters are located.
3. God's dwelling place as reported in 2 Corinthians 12.

Prince believes that chapter 10 of Daniel reveals a lot about the war between Satan and his dark kingdom and God. The length of Daniel's prayer for help, 21 days, implies that the good angel sent to help Daniel was delayed by "the King of Persia" (Satan), but archangel Michael saved the day.

We absolutely must understand that the battleground is in the realm of the mind. Satan deliberately and systematically builds strongholds in people's minds.

Two common strongholds in people's minds are prejudices and preconceptions.

> "The great essential fact is this: Christ has already defeated Satan and all his evil powers and authorities totally and forever. Satan's primary weapon against us is guilt. Rev 12:10. Satan accuses us to make us feel guilty. Guilt is the key to our defeat, and righteousness is the key to our victory."

Prince states that the spiritual weapons Paul lists in Ephesians 6 are defensive weapons. Prince points out that there is no protection for the back; therefore, the Christian should not take on the devil alone. We need fellow Christians, the Church, to protect our back.

A general once stated, "The army that wins is the one that advances." Prince believes this is true in spiritual warfare. Prince states Christians have four primary offensive weapons: Prayer, Praise, Preaching and Testimony (being a witness).

Critiques

Critique #1: Not all biblical scholars believe that "the King of Persia" was Satan.

Number 3 Bestseller: Rankin, *Spiritual Warfare*
Jerry Rankin
(B & H Publishing: Nashville, Tennessee, 2009)

Author: Jerry Rankin is the President of the Southern Baptist International Mission Board. He was a missionary to Asia for 23 years.

Publisher: B&H Publishing Group, a division of LifeWay Christian Resources, is "a non-profit publisher made up of people who are passionate about   taking   God's   Word   to   the   world." http://www.bhpublishinggroup.com

Number of Pages = 286

Important Points Regarding:
Model of Deliverance Ministry: Classical and strategic level.
Demon Possession: "When one encounters a person who is apparently demon possessed, it's not important to determine if they are possessed or mentally ill. It is obvious that they are afflicted and need to be made whole."
Staying Alert: "Decisions should be made ahead of time regarding activities entertainment, and relationships, avoiding anything that is inappropriate."
Translation of Isaiah 14: The reference in Isaiah 14:12-14 is usually considered an analogy to this event (Satan's fall from heaven). Rankin does not use this verse to list attributes of Satan but hedges on its interpretation.

Synopsis
Rankin is a man of substance and extensive experience in missions. His 23 years as a missionary, and then his work as president and CEO of the Southern Baptist International Mission Board, give his observations about spiritual warfare extreme credibility. He found that the dark force of demons was present where he served, countering his efforts to bring Christ to southeast Asia. However, he brings balance and perspective to the discussion with the following statement: "Spiritual warfare is not so much about demon possession, territorial spirits, or generational bondage as it is overcoming Satan's lies and deceits in our own life."

Rankin states, "We have a Trinitarian enemy. The devil is opposing us. The world around us is distracting us. The flesh-that old, sinful nature-is within us, seeking to defile us. They are all conspiring to defeat us, collaborating, and working together to rob God of His glory in our life. The battlefield is our life, our soul."

The Devil Rankin describes the first of the "Trinitarian enemy" as the devil. The Bible tells us of the nature of Satan: "So the great dragon was thrown out-the ancient serpent who is called the Devil and Satan, the one who deceives the whole world. He was thrown to earth and his angels with him" (Revelation 12:9). Basically, Satan is a deceiver.

Rankin tells of many experiences where he observed the dark forces of Satan on the mission field: "Christ is not known, where He is not acknowledged as Lord, where the cultures and nations and peoples of the world are the kingdoms of Satan, under dominion to the powers of darkness."

Although Satan is behind every temptation, blaming him does not absolve us of any responsibility for sin and doing that which is contrary to God's will.

The Bible (1 John 2:15-17) reveals three basic categories of temptation: The lust of the flesh; the lust of the eyes, which is the appeal to our aesthetic nature and leads to covetousness; and pride of life, appealing to our innate desire not only to be liked but also to be the center of attention.

In summary, Rankin states four characteristics of our enemy as revealed in Scripture:
1. Adversary
2. Deceiver
3. Tempter
4. Hinderer

The World The second aspect of our tripartite enemy in spiritual warfare is the world. The world is the domain in which we live and in which Satan works. In order not to be corrupted by the world "decisions should be made ahead of time regarding activities entertainment, and relationships, avoiding anything that is inappropriate."

Rankin quotes John 17:15: "I am not praying that You take them out of the world but that You protect them from the evil one." He states that one of the most helpful protections from the evil one is to be in an accountability relationship. That is why God gave us the Church. Your relationship with Church members is a source of those accountability relationships.

<u>The Flesh</u> "The flesh is self-serving and is susceptible to Satan's temptation because it is totally self-centered...Love is a key to walking in victory because it is the antithesis of the self-centered nature of the flesh."

Rankin offers five practical keys to victory over the flesh:

1. Believe Christ has conquered sin for us.
2. Set your mind on things of the Spirit.
3. Counter self-centeredness with love.
4. Be led by the Holy Spirit.
5. Make no provision for the flesh.

It hurts to deny the flesh. "Suffering is the natural consequence of walking in the Spirit in this world. It is a given for us just as it was for Christ." Victory over the flesh requires daily decisions.

Fasting is an example of denying the flesh. "We fast not to obligate God to do something, but because our hunger for Him exceeds our desire for food."

"Satan is against us, seeking to defeat us; the flesh is within us, seeking to defile us; and the world is around us, seeking to distract us." Some of Satan's "favorite fiery darts (flaming arrows) are: unforgiveness, anger, doubt, pride, unholy living and creating dissension."

We will face adversity "because we live in a fallen, imperfect world in which accidents, illnesses, tragedies, and natural disasters occur." Rankin gives many accounts of adversity missionaries have faced. "Adversity is Satan's favorite weapon because it is common to everyone and causes us to focus on ourselves and doubt God." No, God does not cause hard times, but Christians can get through them if "we praise God for who He is and thank Him in those circumstances."

Rankin laments the lack of interest by today's Christians in holiness and "a ministry characterized by spiritual anointing...The Bible doesn't teach a second blessing and a subsequent experience of receiving the Holy Spirit after we have received Jesus Christ as Lord and Savior. But we should experience a yearning to appropriate the power over sin and a desire for a victorious life that God has already provided through His Spirit's presence within us."

Rankin states that, like many missionaries, he has been in places around the world where he has seen "manifestations of the powers of darkness I could not explain." He concludes, "When one encounters a person who is apparently demon possessed, it's not important to determine if they are possessed or mentally ill. It is obvious that they are afflicted and need to be made whole."

Faith is the element in the Christian life to counter the world, the flesh, and the devil. So, how do we get faith? Romans 10:17 gives us the answer: "So faith comes from what is heard, and what is heard comes through the message about Christ. Having a foundation of faith and believing God, the next step is renewing the mind.... do not be conformed to this age, but be transformed by the renewing of your mind, so that you may discern what is the good, pleasing, and perfect will of God" (Romans 12:1-2). "The best way to resist the thoughts that Satan places in our minds is to think God's thoughts. That is what it means to renew the mind."

Of all that we are in Christ, none of this "frees us from making decisions acting on our free will. Those decisions are not automatically godly." Praying at all times helps in appropriating what God has provided us to make holy decisions.

Obedience in observing a Sabbath is a key to living a holy, sanctified life. Observing a Sabbath rest is another practical, biblical discipline that reflects one's heart for God.

There are six practical disciplines in claiming the victory:
1. Feeding on God's Word
2. Praying at all times
3. Praising the Lord in all things
4. Denying the flesh in fasting
5. Being accountable to others
6. Observing a Sabbath

Finally, how does the Bible sum up obedience, righteousness, and fulfilling the law? It is in one word, as we saw in Gal. 5:13: love. Love is other--centered. It is an antidote to Satan's attacks because it is the antithesis of the self-centered nature of the flesh. Only love will give us a desire to go all the way in a life of sacrifice.

Critiques

Critique #1: Rankin states, "Decisions should be made ahead of time regarding activities, entertainment, and relationships, avoiding anything that is inappropriate." This is consistent with Chapter 4 of *The Spiritual Ambush*, which recommends that Christians identify spiritual danger areas and their response before they enter them.

Critique #2: Rankin states, "We work in the marketplace to support our families and to provide for our physical and material needs in this world. But we must remember that we live to serve God and bring glory to Him, even in the secular workplace." This is an example of how preachers and the Christian Church have distorted this for the layman. What the layman does "in the secular world" is important and critical aside from ministry. His selection of and approach to his "secular" work are godly things and should not be put down by the clergy. Many pastors and the Church just do not get it. A minister's work in the Kingdom is not superior to the work of the Christian layman, including the "non-ministry" part of his work life. To continue this position is to reject 90% of the life of the congregation. It is sad! Pastors need to wake up if they want to reach the world.

Critique #3: "Flesh" embodies the new nature as well. It is not all bad. When God created the flesh, he said it was "very, very good."

Number 4 Bestseller: Meade, *Spiritual Warfare: Fighting Demons*
Scott Meade
(Demon Hunter Publishing Company, 2010)

ALERT: THIS BOOK IS FICTION!

Author: Scott Meade

Publisher: Self-published by Demon Hunter Publishing Company

Number of Pages = 59

Important Points Regarding:
Model of Deliverance Ministry: N/A
Demon Possession: N/A
Staying Alert: N/A
Translation of Isaiah 14:12-14: N/A

Synopsis
In this book, Meade is committed to illuminating the role of demons in spiritual warfare. After quoting Ephesians 6:12-13, he asks the question; "If we do not wrestle against flesh and blood, then who or what do we wrestle against?"

Contrary to the statements of a number of theologians writing on spiritual warfare, Meade declares, "Demons can and will possess Christians if given the chance." Meade claims that he has "the gift to sense the presence of an evil spirit (and) can easily discern the spirits.... I am sometimes able to catch a glimpse of an evil spirit when it enters a room. The latter is usually in the form of small, twinkling lights or a dark shadow, shifting somewhere around me. Both move swiftly. How swiftly?" He then writes about how demons travel and how fast they travel: "There is very strong evidence in favor of the belief that they travel through what is called the astral plane, or the ether." Meade declares that he can feel the presence of demons by pressure in his heart and back when he is standing in a spot occupied by a demon.

Today's demons are the remnants of those created when angels mated with human females that gave birth to giants, called "Nephilim". (Genesis 6:1-8).

Meade then gives some personal experiences. He states he had a dream where he was sitting in a chair, and a demon with long arms came up behind him and began to rub up and down his body. When he jerked free, he woke up but felt someone pressing his neck, and he saw a tall figure. He stated, "In the name of Yeshua, I command you to leave my home. I do not believe that it was around to hear me, but it is not a good idea to intimidate them."

When Meade is involved with deliverance of a demon from a person, he simply says, "In the name of Yeshua, I command you to come out of this person and go to the abyss! Done! Our Messiah is our Intercessor. Nuff said." Ministers involved in deliverance ministries report that statement does not always work for them.

Meade reports that after he was baptized when he encountered people that opposed him or his Christianity, he "noticed that their eyes were different than most people's eyes. Their eyes were filled with blackness, as if they had enlarged pupils, covering the entire iris (the colored part of the eye)."

Meade became aware of "twinkling lights and shifting shadows." He believes this was God's way to warn him that a demon was present. "I have asked for this ability to be enhanced so that I would always know for certain when evil is close by, and I received it."

Meade announces an underlying truth about his view of spiritual warfare: "Evil cannot do anything against us unless God allows it."

In chapter seven, his last chapter, Meade summarizes all of his findings.

Note about the author: Scott Meade has published one novel, *Twisted Christian*, a Christian "horror" story. He considers himself a "Christian horror writer." Meade's Amazon author's page states, "His studies have led him away from the mainstream teachings of traditional churches. He is now known as the 'demon hunter.'"

Critiques

Critique #1: Scott Meade is not an educated theologian. He is a novelist. He is also a heavy metal musician and computer repairperson. His first book, *Twisted Christian*, was a "Christian horror" story. In my opinion, this book is more fiction than non-fiction, in the same vein as Dan Brown's *The DaVinci Code* and Jonathan Cahn's *The Harbinger*.

Critique #2: Meade uses the Hebrew throughout the narrative without explanation:

hasatan (Hebrew for Satan), B'rit Hadashah (New Testament), Yeshua (Jesus), Nephilim (Sons of God).

Critique #3: The book is lacking a professional presentation; i.e., there is no Table of Contents. It appears to be self-published by Demon Hunter Publishing Company.

Critique #4: The front and back covers feature original color paintings by a friend of Meade, which may be the most attractive element of the book and may be a major reason for its best-selling status on Amazon.

Number 5 Bestseller: Sherman, *Spiritual Warfare for Every Christian: How to Live in Victory and Retake the Land*
Dean Sherman
(YWAM Publishing: Seattle, Washington, 1995)

Author: Dean Sherman is Dean of the College of Christian Ministries at Youth with A Mission's University of the Nations.

Publisher: YWAM Publishing began in 1972. See history at: http://www.ywampublishing.com/t-about.aspx

Number of Pages = 211

Important Points Regarding:
Model of Deliverance Ministry: Advocate for all four models.
Demon Possession: Spiritual warfare deals with two levels: the big or cosmic level, and the individual, personal level. In dealing with the kingdom of darkness, we stand against the rulers, principalities, and powers in nations, in people groups, and in authority structures. In addition, we must bring freedom from bondage to individuals through prayer, intercession, and personal ministry.
Staying Alert: Staying alert is mentioned ten times. Spiritual warfare demands alertness, a constant vigilance toward the enemy's activities. This alertness is much like spiritual radar.
Translation of Isaiah 14:12-14: Declares that Isaiah 14 is about Lucifer/Satan.

Synopsis
     Sherman relates his experience with demons and the dark forces he had as an YWAM missionary in Port Moresby, Papua New Guinea in 1970. The church members believed in Christ, but they also believed in witchcraft. Sherman's team went to an outlying village that church members said had a curse from the local shaman. The team leader got inexplicably ill unto death. He did not get better until Sherman prayed that the demon causing the illness leave him. In spite of this "real world experience" with demons, Sherman cautions, "Christians need balance in their life and not see demons in every situation and behavior."

"The only reliable source of information concerning powers of darkness is the Bible. Our beliefs and doctrines concerning the devil should never be based on our experiences or on the testimony of demons. When it come to spiritual warfare, if it's not in the Bible, be careful."

Sherman states that Satan is real and is a threat to the Christian. We must be alert and aware 24/7. He strikes at the Christian's weakness. There are "three strategic battlegrounds: the mind, the heart, and the mouth."

"Most spiritual warfare takes place in the human mind. It involves recognizing when a thought is not righteous, or when it does not agree with God's truth. Not all evil thoughts are from Satan, but he will exploit them and add to them."

The battlefield of the heart lies in attitudes and emotions. Satan's three main avenues of attack are pride, unbelief, and fear. None should ever be a part of a Christian's thinking.

"Spiritual warfare is like wrestling in that it demands constant alertness."

The principal inhabitants of the unseen world are angels. There are three kinds of angels: (warriors, messengers, and worshiping angels. Michael is the chief warrior angel, Gabriel is the chief messenger angel. Worshiping angels that do nothing but worship God, i.e., "Worthy is the Lamb," Rev. 5:11-12).

Satan attacks the world with "three prongs": rulers, principalities, and powers. Rulers are spirit beings that hold office within Satan's hierarchy. They rule by "exerting opinion or will over others. Principalities (territorial spirits) are simply beings with broad areas of influence in Satan's kingdom. Satan deploys his forces according to a map of the world. Satan has a particular battle plans for each geographic area and for each group of people." Powers "refers to kinds (strongholds) of evil and the demons assigned to those sins."

"Satan is working through mankind to do his business on the planet. And God is working through mankind to defeat the enemy."

Sherman declares that the presence of evil on earth is because God prizes the free will of man above the absence of evil. God could have created earth without sin or evil, but it would have eliminated man's free will. He wants the love of humans to be their choice.

We cannot blame our sin on God or others. Temptation does not come from God: "But each one is tempted when he is carried away and enticed by his own lust" (James 1:13-15). Satan attacks Christian throughs our infirmities, reproaches, distresses, persecutions, and difficulties. We are going to experience all of these. Just as He did with the Hebrews, God can use our difficulties to hone us into strong spiritual warriors.

"There is a battle going on. It is fierce and hot. The theater of this war is we. We are the battlefield." Prayer is our principal weapon, because God answers our prayers. We need to be "stubborn" prayers, particularly for others (intercessory prayer).

"Spiritual warfare is not just a prayer prayed or a demon rebuked – it is a life lived."

Regarding the model of deliverance ministry needed, Sherman states, "Some think spiritual warfare is only deliverance. Others emphasize pulling down strongholds in the heavenlies. Still others say spiritual warfare is doing the work of Jesus: preaching, teaching, and living the truth. Yet another group claims all this is impractical. They claim we should focus on feeding the hungry, resisting racism, and speaking out against social injustice. I believe we have to do it all."

Sherman states that the winner will be the one who does not give up. "It is this weapon of endurance that finally convinces the devil that he has to give up. Spiritual warfare is a life lived. It is embracing the truth and living daily, aware of the enemy and committed to God. It is knowing that God has left it up to us. To be a Christian is to be a spiritual warrior. To be a spiritual warrior is to walk consistently and victoriously through life, with Christ at our side."

Critiques

Critique # 1: Key teaching point: "The only reliable source of information concerning powers of darkness is the Bible. Our beliefs and doctrines concerning the devil should never be based on our experiences or on the testimony of demons. When it comes to spiritual warfare, if it's not in the Bible, be careful."

Critique # 2: Sharman advocates for all four models of deliverance ministry.

Critique # 3: Sherman states that the spiritual battlefield is inside of us. I think that is an incomplete assessment. Many Christians are "squared away" regarding their holiness, thinking, and feelings. These Christians need help combating the outside dark forces of Ephesians 6, particularly the spiritual ambush.

Number 6 Bestseller: Ingram, *The Invisible War: What every Believer Needs to Know About Satan, Demons, and Spiritual Warfare*
Chip Ingram
(Baker Books: Grand Rapids, Michigan, 2006)

Author: Chip Ingram serves as senior pastor of Venture Christian Church in Los Gatos, California, and is President of Living on the Edge, an international teaching and discipleship ministry. Over the past twenty-five years, Chip has pastored churches ranging from 500 to 5,000 and served as President of Walk Through the Bible. Chip holds an M.S. from West Virginia University and a Th.M. from Dallas Theological Seminary.

Publisher: Herman Baker founded Baker Books in 1939 in Grand Rapids, Michigan. It has six divisions (imprints): Bethany House, Revell, Baker Books, Baker Academic, Chosen, and Brazos Press.

Number of Pages = 190

Important Points Regarding:
Model of Deliverance Ministry: Ground-level and strategic-level.
Demon Possession: "Personally, I don't believe a Christian can actually be possessed by a demon. But there may be levels of influence and control that can simulate those symptoms."
Staying Alert: Guerrilla fighting all around...our alert signals should always be on "code red."
Translation of Isaiah 14:12 "Satan's names reveal his tactics...Lucifer (son of the morning Isaiah 14:12.) The two core Old Testament passages about Satan are Ezekiel 28 and Isaiah 14", Kindle location = 684.

Synopsis
 The author presents his material as a curriculum on Satan, demons, and spiritual warfare, as "Spiritual Warfare (SW) 101 – 401." Ingram quotes C.S. Lewis to emphasize the challenge of his presentation: "There are two equal and opposite errors into which our race can fall about the devils. One is to disbelieve in their existence. The other is to believe, and to feel an excessive and unhealthy interest in them."
 Ingram strives to reach a balance between those extremes. He has "heard people get much more detailed about demonic activity than the Bible

ever does...these are...only speculations; Scripture doesn't spell these things out for us."

Ingram became a pastor of a church in Santa Cruz, California. This city, which had more occult bookstores than Boulder, Colorado, was reputed to be a renowned center of occult activity.

He had personal encounters with demonic spirits: "It's terrifying to have physical manifestations of evil in your home. Audio manifestations were not uncommon."

In SW 101 Ingram establishes what every believer needs to know about spiritual warfare.

> Basic Truth #1: There is an invisible world (Eph. 6:12).
> "Satan and his demons are behind unbelief, deception, fear, false religions and persecution."
> Basic Truth #2: We are involved in an invisible war.
> "Most of it is between our ears. Our minds, our belief systems, our worldviews--this is where the enemy aims."
> Basic Truth #3: Our foe is formidable.
> Jesus certainly thought Satan was real. He referred to Satan 25 times and had a personal encounter with him in Mat. 4:1-11. Satan is of the highest class of evil angels. Satan attempts to destroy all that is good and God-ordained.
> Basic Truth #4: We must respect our foe but not fear him.
> "Anger, pride, worry, self-reliance, discouragement, worldliness, lying and immorality are all his inspiration. One of Satan's biggest lies = life is a playground. Our primary goal is to be happy."
> Basic Truth #5: We do not fight for victory; we fight from victory.
> "In Christ's power we are invincible."

SW 201 is "How to Prepare Yourself for Spiritual Battle." "The great majority of spiritual warfare need never go beyond the regular practice of living out our position in Christ by faith. There are times, when we must move beyond 'standing firm' and engage the enemy in actual combat."

Satan's major approach to the Christian is deception. We can counter his deceptive tactics by girding ourselves with the belt of truth and the breastplate of righteousness. Righteousness means "uprightness, right living, integrity in one's lifestyle and character."

By applying truth and righteousness to our daily life, we can defeat Satan's attacks of deception.

SW 301 teaches the Christian how to do battle with Satan and win. Ingram considers this level to be advanced training. "There are times, however, when we must move beyond standing firm and engage the enemy in actual combat." Ingram experienced an "evil presence" in his bedroom at night while he was a pastor in Santa Cruz. He concluded the only way to combat that "evil presence" was through spiritual warfare.

The Christian can expect Satan's attacks in five specific situations, when the Christian is:

1. Taking significant steps of faith for spiritual growth.
2. Invading enemy territory.
3. Exposing Satan for who he really is.
4. Repenting and makes a clean break with the world.
5. Is being prepared by God for a great work for His glory.

Satan starts his pattern of temptation with a disguise that causes us to focus on our own identity and worth, there by offering an appealing, immediate lust of the flesh, lust of the eyes, and pride. The Christian can counter this attack by trusting God's character, promises, program, and timing. Ingram states, "In the cosmic conflict, the front lines are between your ears. Human thinking is ground zero in the war."

The Christian's main weapon in spiritual warfare is God's Word, the sword of the Spirit (Eph. 6:17). Jesus quoting Scripture during the temptations in the wilderness is Ingram's proof.

SW 401 states that the strongest and most powerful tool Christians have for spiritual warfare is intercessory prayer. Ingram believes that the missing ingredient in most Christian's lives is prayer. He relates the story of a missionary who camped alone in the jungle after a visit to a village. Men from the jungle came to his campsite to rob and kill him. They later told him, after becoming Christians, that what stopped them were the 26 guards around his camp. The missionary laughed and said he was alone. The native said no, there were many men with him. They all saw the guards and counted them.

The missionary did not think much about the story until he returned to his home church in the United States. At one service he attended, a member told him that he'd had a strong urge to pray for the missionary on the exact same night that the missionary had camped alone in the jungle. His urgency was so great he'd called other men at the church to come and pray with him for the missionary. The church member then asked all of the men who'd come and prayed that night to stand. Twenty-six men stood.

Ingram states that prayer needs to be consistent, intense, and strategic. "Prayer isn't a sport. It is work. Prayer is no game."

Ingram states that most of the advice about conducting spiritual warfare focuses on prevention. However, if Satan is already in the person, the Christian must be involved in deliverance. "There are a lot of problems with the practice of deliverance." Christians involved in deliverance ministry "forget the part of the equation that says we live in a fallen world and bad things happen. As people created with free will, there is also the matter of personal responsibility. ...Negative consequences of choices are not demonic. Satan is not behind everything. But it's a fallen world, and sometimes we simply reap the results of fallenness."

Ingram identifies 10 steps of deliverance:
1. Accept Christ.
2. Repent of known sin.
3. Renounce the works of the devil.
4. Destroy occult objects.
5. Break unholy friendships.
6. Rest in Christ's deliverance.
7. Resist the devil.
8. Renew your mind.
9. Pray with others.
10. If necessary, exorcise-it is a
    New Testament practice.

Critiques

Critique #1: Ingram leans on Isaiah 14:12 for attributes of Satan. However, only the King James Version translates the Hebrew for "son of the morning" (NIV) or "son of dawn" (RSV) as "Lucifer". The name Lucifer does not appear in any other translation. Bible scholars believe that this verse refers to the King of Babylon.

Number 7 Bestseller: Phillips, *Everyone's Guide to Demons & Spiritual Warfare*
Ron Phillips
(Charisma House: Lake Mary, Florida, 2010)

Author: Ron Phillips is senior pastor of Abba's House (Central Baptist Church) in Chattanooga, Tennessee. He is author of 20 books, including *Our Invisible Allies*.

Publisher: Charisma House, A Strang Company. Established in 2006

Publisher's Description of the Book:
"*Everyone's Guide to Demons and Spiritual Warfare* is a basic training manual for anyone who wants to understand spiritual warfare principles and know how to stand against satanic attacks. By incorporating demon-defying principles in our daily spiritual lives, we can learn to put the enemy to flight and move from bondage into freedom. The author also identifies several specific demonic spirits that attack God's people, and provides strategies for overcoming evil in our lives."

Number of Pages = 278

Important Points Regarding:
Model of Deliverance Ministry: Ground-level Deliverance Model.
Staying Alert: Not emphasized.
Demon Possession: Non-Christians can be possessed. "In the New Testament there is no such phrase (as possession); rather the term demonization is used. No Christian can be totally taken over by demons, but every Christian can be oppressed, harassed, and dominated by the enemy's activity."
Translation of Isaiah 14:12: Uses name Lucifer.

Synopsis:
Pastor Ron Phillips has developed six essays about our enemy Satan and how we can deal with him. The first four essays tell about who Satan is. The last two explain how the Christian gain have and maintain victory over Satan.

Section I: Facing the Reality of Your Enemy (Chapters 1-6)

Satan will make the Christian's life a battleground with trouble in his home, his church, and his personal life. "The Church must rediscover spiritual warfare." It does that by studying the Bible. Revelation 5 "is the centerpiece of human struggles." It is the record of Satan's war against humanity and the purposes of God.

"Today many Christians are deceived to the point they do not believe in the power of Satan and the awful influence of the demonic."

We must come to the rescue of those captured by the enemy. Colossians 1:13 speaks of salvation as being "delivered from the power of darkness."

The Church must become a "spiritual armory" providing serious training for spiritual warfare. David is our example of a serious spiritual warrior. He trained and he worshiped God.

Pastor Phillips lists five essentials for the warrior:
1. Get under authority -- submission
2. Get on fire for the cause -- passion
3. Be prepared for warfare -- discipline
4. Believe you can win -- vision
5. Know your weapons -- power

Section II: Tracing the History of Your Enemy (Chapters 5-10)

Pastor Phillips quotes the ancient Chinese military philosopher Sun Tzu (544 BCE – 496 BCE) to emphasize the importance of knowing our enemy the devil: "If you know the enemy and know yourself, you need not fear the result of a hundred battles. If you know yourself but not the enemy, for every victory gained you will also suffer the defeat. If you know neither the enemy nor yourself, you will succumb in every battle."

Pastor Phillips then introduces the reader to Satan. Satan, once known as Lucifer, was an angel who rebelled against God, resulting in his expulsion from heaven along with one-third of all of the angels. These fallen angels are now the demons we face. Satan's downfall is recorded in Isaiah 14:12-15 (see Critique 1). Satan's fall occurred between Genesis 1:1 and Genesis 1:2.

Lucifer ruled from the Garden of Eden, which we now call Jerusalem. Genesis 10:25 tells of the time the continental plates of Africa, Europe, and Asia collided -- 101 years after the flood. "Eber had two sons. One was named Peleg, for during his days the earth was divided." (See Critique 2.)

Satan was already in the Garden of Eden before God placed man there. "I believe Satan planted the tree of the knowledge of good and evil! I believe this because God had already given Adam and Eve permission to eat everything except from that tree. This resulted in man being driven out of the garden east of Eden near what came to be Jericho." "It is my firm belief that the Garden of Gethsemane is Old Eden."

Satan's war on man began in the Garden of Eden, when the serpent deceived Eve and Adam made the "free will" decision to knowingly disobey God. Pastor Phillips documents Satan's numerous attacks on the line of David, ending with the appearance of Jesus, ("the second Adam") who defeated Satan on the Cross.

Revelation reveals Satan's war on the Church. The demonic strongholds that can be found in the Church include the spirit of religion, intimidation, compromise, control (Jezebel), traditionalism, inferiority, and pride.

Section III: Understanding the Dynasty of Your Enemy (Chapters 11-15)
The first mention of Satan in biblical history is found in Job 1 and 2, when he attacks and accuses Job. Job's response and subsequent victory silence Satan for centuries. The next time Satan appears in the Bible is when he provokes David to count his men instead of trusting God to deliver the victory.

Satan leads the forces of darkness. His former name was Lucifer, "bearer of light." Lucifer became Satan the "accuser" or "adversary." Satan's "army of hell" is organized into three groups:
1. Principalities are top-ranking demonic beings.
2. Powers are the next level down of demonic beings. They seem to operate invisibly in governmental centers such as national governments.
3. Rulers of darkness "want to take over the offices of government, the legislatures, and the courts." These lower-level spirits are the ones we deal with daily.

Demons cannot possess Christians but can possess non-believers. However, a believer can be "demonized, which means he is controlled but not owned." Demons can effect Christians most when they have unconfessed, habitual sin. Satan uses deception to lead Christians away from God. One of the most effective tools is "accusations," a tool he effectively used against Job.

All mental illness is not the result of demonic attacks, but Philips lists fourteen that are, including suicide, addictive behavior, abnormal sexual behavior, speech difficulties, and doctrinal error.

Section IV: Knowing The Strategies of Your Enemy (Chapters 16 – 26)

Pastor Phillips discusses the different strategies of Satan. These include: fear, depression, affliction, error, perversion, confusion, bitterness, death, pressure, poverty and legalism.

Section V: Enforcing the Victory over Your Enemy (Chapters 25-32)

At Calvary, Jesus disarmed and defeated Satan. Victory over Satan will occur if the battle plan is based on Jesus' Crucifixion, our own salvation and the work of the Holy Spirit in each Christian. The Holy Spirit will make our prayers effective, give us an understanding of the Bible, and gives us power in the use of the Bible in this battle.

We can draw on God for effectiveness through prayer, fasting, praise, and worship.

We must arm ourselves for victory by putting on the equipment Paul describes in Ephesians 6. To maintain victory over Satan, the Christian must avoid the strongholds of "wrong thinking that can harbor a demonic entity." These strongholds include the spirit of infirmity, fear, sexual immorality, pride, perversion, the Antichrist, depression, lying, jealousy, and stupor.

Pastor Phillips offers eight steps to remove a stronghold:
1. Confess Jesus Christ as your Lord and Savior.
2. Realize only God can remove a stronghold.
3. Identify the stronghold.
4. Confess sins related to the stronghold.
5. Thank God for forgiveness.
6. Visualize the destruction.
7. Ask God to free you from the demonic force of the stronghold.
8. Make restitution.

Section VI: Maintaining the Victory over Your Enemy (Chapters 33-40)

The way we maintain our victory over Satan is to submit to God and resist the devil (James 4:7). We can repel Satan with prayer and God's Word. Pastor Phillips offers 10 proclamations the Christian can use to repel Satan. We can repulse Satan by worshiping God and loving others unconditionally.

In the Christian life, we face a threefold enemy: the world, the flesh, and the devil.

To maintain our victory over Satan, we need not succumb to curses. "A curse can also be called habits." We can rid ourselves of a curse by confessing aloud that we yield to God, renouncing the curse, receiving the deliverance, and praising God. There are "hedges" we can build around ourselves through prayer, spiritual leadership, and unity with other Christians, angelic protection, and revival.

Critiques

Critique 1: In Section II, Pastor Phillips's attempt to integrate science and theology undermines his theology. For example, the Holman Christian Standard Bible states "Exactly what is meant by 'the earth was divided' is uncertain. It may be a reference to the Tower of Babylon event, a devastating earthquake, a large Mesopotamian canal project or a political division."[1]

Critique 2: In Section II, Pastor Phillips interprets Isaiah 12 as the casting out of Satan from heaven. The Holman Christian Standard Bible rejects Pastor Phillips's assertion: "The context seems clear that the one fallen from the heavens is not Satan, even though the KJV translated 'shining morning star' as 'Lucifer,' but is instead the Babylonian king."[2] No other translation uses the name Lucifer in Isaiah 14:12.

Notes

1. The Holman Christian Standard Bible, (Holman Bible Publishers: Nashville, Tennessee, 2010), 28.
2. Ibid. 1150.

Number 8 Bestseller: Frangipane, *The Three Battlegrounds: An In-Depth View of the Three Arenas of Spiritual Warfare: The Mind, the Church and the Heavenly Places*
Francis Frangipane
(Arrow Publications: Cedar Rapids, IA, 2006)

Author: Francis Frangipane is the founder of River of Life Ministries in Cedar Rapids and the author of 14 books.

Publisher: Established in 2003 and incorporated in Iowa, current estimates show Arrow Publications has annual revenue of $1 to $2.5 million, and employs a staff of approximately five to nine. The owner is Francis Frangipane.

Number of Pages = 171

Important Points Regarding:
Model of Deliverance Ministry: Classical Model
Demon Possession: This author does not believe that a Christian can be possessed...but does believe you can have a demon if you refuse to repent of your sympathetic thoughts toward evil.
Staying Alert: Does not address alertness.
Translation of Isaiah 14:12-14: Does not use the name Lucifer.

Synopsis
Frangipane cautions students of spiritual warfare to follow the counsel of Proverbs 20:18 and "Prepare plans by consultation, and make war by wise guidance." He encourages students to read books and consult others, "Wisdom is better than strength...wisdom is better than weapons of war" (Ecclesiastes 9:16, 18).

Unlike many books on spiritual warfare that state that the spiritual battlegrounds are "the world, the flesh, and demons," Frangipane makes the case that the battlegrounds are the mind, the Church, and the spiritual realm he labels as "Heavenly Places."

The Battleground of the Mind: Satan is in the darkness of this world, including the darkness of man's heart and soul. Our humanness, what other spiritual warfare writers label "flesh," is always a path for Satan's attack. The counterattack by the Christian can be his humility. Frangipane defines humility as "the surrender of the soul to the Lord, and the devil is terrified of Jesus Christ." The challenge for the Christian is to determine if the attack is coming from the devil or from the flesh.

Frangipane states,

> "A demon (Satan) can't possess a Christian in the same way as does the Holy Spirit, but a demon can oppress a Christian. The way the Christian can counter Satan is to pull down his strongholds" (2 Cor. 10:3-5). A principal stronghold is "carnal thought systems."

Christians are not perfect. There are still many strongholds within the Christian after conversion, including "unbelief, cold love, fear, pride, unforgiveness, lust, greed, or any combination of these, as well as the possibility of many others." Frangipane reminds us, "As (a man) thinketh in his heart, so is he (Prov. 23:7)."

The strongholds within the Christian come from three sources: first is the world into which we are born, which gives us our initial worldview. Second are our life experiences. These modify our worldview. The third "comes from false church doctrines and teachings." The solution to Satan's strongholds in our mind is to cultivate the peace that comes from becoming Christ like. This peace will counter Satan-produced "fear, worry, doubt, and self-pity."

The Battleground of the Church: The Church is important in the war against Satan. There is a spiritual war going on in the Church and for the Church. Therefore, Christians must find ways to do Church right.

One thing Frangipane encourages within the Church is "oneness" of the fellowship. Oneness of the Church is the result of love. "Bitterness...is the lack of love. This cold love is a demonic stronghold" within the Church.

Members of the Church need to avoid "false discernment." That is, we need to make accurate judgments about what we see and experience (John 7:24). "Righteous judgment is the direct result of love." Having righteous judgment will let Christians make good decisions and act in the best interest of furthering the Church.

The Church must be a community of worshipers of God. "No one can do warfare who is not first a worshiper of God."

It helps the Church to know where Satan is. Hebrews 12 and the Book of Revelation indicate that Satan is not in heaven. "Where then is Satan? Jude tells us that the devil and his demons are imprisoned, spiritually chained with 'eternal bonds' to darkness for judgment (Jude 6)." Frangipane explains Scripture that says the devil is in heaven (Ephesians 6:12; Revelation 12:12; and Luke 10:18), and heaven is the spiritual "territory" from which Satan seeks to control the world. "It would be foolish to assume we know more than we do about this dimension, but we know this: it is from here that Satan releases his war against the Church."

The Battleground of the Heavenly Places: Frangipane sees the real struggle in the spiritual realm, the "Heavenly Places," to be the struggle over who defines reality. Will it be the Word of God or the world without God (Satan)? It is a battle of displacement, with Christ filling the spiritual territories once held by Satan. "All spiritual warfare is waged over one essential question: Who will control reality on earth; heaven or hell?

To win the battles of the mind, Christians must know Scripture. Frangipane lists verses every spiritual warrior must memorize.

To prevail, we must resist and fight the "antichrist." The "antichrist" is all that opposes Christ. "This principality uses the power-demons of Jealousy, Fear, Unforgiveness, and Ambition – whatever is necessary to keep independent, local churches from becoming the 'armed and dangerous,' united body of Christ. It is anti-love, anti-forgiveness, anti-reconciliation!"

Another threat to the spiritual warrior is "the spirit of Jezebel." Jezebel was the Phoenician wife of Ahab, the king of Israel (874-853 BCE.) "When we speak of Jezebel, we are identifying the source in our society of obsessive sensuality, unbridled witchcraft, and hatred for male authority." Jezebel tried to destroy all of God's prophets and install worship of Baal and Asherah (1 Kings 18:4). After Elijah proved these prophets false, Jezebel threatened to kill Elijah. Elijah ran for his life. The name Jezebel has come to convey wickedness and sexual immorality.

Frangipane speaks of the "spirit of Jezebel" but does not characterize it as an entity, a standalone personality that some spiritual warfare writers would call a demon. It is more a set of ideas that are in man's mind that undermine and defeat the spiritual warrior. "We cannot be successful in the heavenly war if we are not victorious in the battlefield of our minds. There is only one realm of final victory against the enemy: Christ likeness."

Another spiritual threat is the "spirit of Babylon." This term comes from the Hebrew exile to Babylon, where they thrived by compromising their faith in God. "The spirit of Babylon epitomizes self-exaltation, and self-exaltation is the source of compromise. To discern the spirit of Babylon, look first for pride."

Frangipane states, "It is very important to not charge ahead, attacking principalities in warfare without having strategies and without people praying for the protection of those doing warfare."

Frangipane recommends that Churches train teams of spiritual warriors that have targeted prayer support before they attack Satan's strongholds in the Church, community, and individuals.

Number 9 Bestseller: Warner, *Spiritual Warfare: Victory Over the Powers of This Dark World*
Timothy M. Warner
(Crossway Books: Wheaton, Illinois, 1991)

Author

Dr. Timothy Warner is currently the Senior Vice President for International Ministries of Freedom with the organization Christ Ministries of La Habra, California. In this capacity, he conducts seminars and teaches college and graduate-level courses in the area of spiritual warfare. This ministry has taken him to Latin America, Europe, Asia, and Africa, as well as Canada and the United States.

He is a graduate of Taylor University (B.A., 1950), New York Theological Seminary (M.Div.,1953), New York University (M.A., 1955), and Indiana University (Ed.D., 1967). Taylor University recognized his life of ministry with an honorary Doctor of Letters degree in 1990.

Dr. Warner and his wife, Eleanor, served as missionaries in a tribal village in West Africa from 1953 to 1959, and for twenty-three years he ministered at Fort Wayne Bible College in a variety of capacities, including Chairman of the Missions Department and, from 1971-80, President. He then became a member of the faculty at Trinity Evangelical Divinity School in Deerfield, Illinois, teaching in the area of missions and directing professional doctoral programs. He retired from Trinity in 1992 and has ministered with Freedom in Christ Ministries since that time.

He is the author of *Spiritual Warfare: Victory over the Powers of This Dark World* and *Beginner's Guide to Spiritual Warfare*.   (Christianbook.com)

Publisher

Clyde Dennis began a tract publishing business in 1938. In 1978, Crossway began a book publishing division under the leadership of Clyde's son Dr. Lane Dennis.

Number of Pages = 160

Important Points Regarding:

Model of Deliverance Ministry: Ground-level and strategic level
Staying Alert: Does not mention staying alert.

<u>Demon Possession:</u> Ministered to "demon-possessed" people in a tribal village in West Africa.

<u>Translation of Isaiah 14:12-14:</u> Does not talk about Lucifer.

Synopsis

Dr. Warner and his wife served as missionaries in a tribal village in West Africa. He dealt with people who were demon-possessed. He found that non-Western cultures were open to the presences of demons. Warner states that there is a conflict in worldviews. The animistic worldview dominates non-Western societies, where everything shares the same kind of spiritual power. "In this worldview the physical and spiritual are inseparable."

The Western worldview has two discrete, functional realms: the supernatural and the natural realm.

The biblical worldview accepts three orders of beings: The Deity, angels, and human beings, which are in "constant, functional contact. We are not given a full-blown theology of angels in the Scriptures, but we are told enough to assume that God uses angels to carry out His purposes in the world."

The Old Testament model emphasizes the glory of God, which He reveals through acts of power. God's intervention was always based on Israel's faith and obedience.

Warner states, "Satan cannot begin to compete with God on the level of glory. But he does have power to manipulate that which God has created."

Warner laments that missionaries with a Western worldview take with them a dysfunctional syncretism. (Syncretism is the combination of different forms of belief or practice.) Western missionaries fail to take their belief in spiritual power and spirit beings when they go to the mission field. They ignore the presence of spirits in the life of Jesus. One-third of all of His healings involved casting out of demons.

Satan's aim is to neutralize us in terms of effective witness. Our position in the battle will need to be defensive as well as offensive. "

Some Christians see Satan and demons in everything. Warner says we need balance in our worldview. He quotes C.S. Lewis:

"There are two equal and opposite extremes into which our race can fall about the devils (demons). One is to disbelieve in their existence. The other is to believe, and to feel an excessive and unhealthy interest in them.

They themselves are equally pleased by both errors and
hail a materialist or a magician with the same delight."

"We have defined the primary combatants in this conflict as God,
the holy angels, and believers on one side and Satan, the fallen angels, and
unbelievers on the other." Warner states if battle is truly against spiritual
forces, they will be brought down by spiritual weapons, not by weapons of
the world. In this battle, the Christian faces the world, the flesh, and the
Devil. There is some of each of these three elements in each spiritual battle
the Christian faces.

This spiritual battle was won at the Cross. Revelation 12 describes
Satan's defeat in heaven. Satan has never been outside the control of God.

Warner relates the story of a missionary to China who had an
encounter with a demon-possessed woman. The demon left the woman
after the missionary demanded the demon leave her in the name of Jesus
Christ. Warner discusses the authority all believers have to demand demons
depart. This "authority is delegated power. No one is competent to exercise
authority until he has first learned to live under authority."

Warner states that the "Bible does not make any clear, didactic
statement on demon possession. Nor on the trinity." He states that a
Christian cannot be demon-possessed because it implies ownership.

"The more aggressive a Christian becomes in his offensive
initiatives against Satan the more Satan counterattacks." Warner gives an
account that a missionary's child was infected by a demon after playing in
a sandbox by a "demon-possessed tree." After the missionaries determined
this had happened, they demanded the demon depart the tree and their
property "in Jesus' name" and the demon did depart.

Satan can counterattack by attacking the body, food and sex
appetites, and physical objects and places.

"All spiritual warfare is a matter of spiritual effectiveness or
ineffectiveness." "Satan's ultimate aim is always to get us to doubt the
character of God and to reject His authority in our lives." Satan often
attacks the mind of the believer with ungodly thoughts. This is another
reason to read and meditate on the Bible, in order to create a "biblical filter
in the mind."

Attacks can come from curses from practitioners of the black arts.
Warner describes the effect and resolution of a curse put on a missionary
family by a witch doctor.

Warner does not believe that all problems believers face is due to
attacks by Satan.

The success of the Israelites against their enemies never depended on the size of their army but on their reliance on the Lord. "It was spiritual power that determined who won."

Warner introduces the idea of "power encounter." This is a term first introduced by Alan Tippett in 1969 in *Verdict Theology*. Tippett does not give a definition but states, "The Scriptures leave us with a clear picture of a battle being fought, of a conflict of powers, with a verdict of victory or defeat for man's soul." Some believe that "power encounters" must be a part of all missionary or evangelistic ministry. Warner states he is somewhere in the middle with his "balanced" approach to spiritual warfare.

Warner declares, "Open demonic activity is on the increase."

On his mission field, conversion involved "aggressively challenging the devil's claim on an individual. In the baptismal service, there was acknowledgement of a change of loyalties from Satan to God."

Another type of power encounter is open confrontation with practitioners of occult arts. Warner relates that a missionary confronted demonic forces when natives lifted their spears to throw them and kill him. God froze their arms so that the natives could not through their spears.

Efforts were made to destroy all symbols of the occult.

When demons were driven out of individuals and places, people were set free to follow God. Driving demons out was so effective in evangelism that the authorities in China passed laws in Henan Province for churches demanding, "Do not pray for the sick or exorcise demons."

Prayer is the key to spiritual warfare. It is not a rear-echelon support activity. Prayer is in fact spiritual warfare. Unless a church has a strong, organized prayer ministry, it is just on a "treadmill."

Warner quotes Peter Wagner in his belief that demons can inhabit locations. The demons in locations must be bound before they can be defeated. Warner tells of "the amazing revival in Argentina." He laments that we seldom claim a whole nation, as did John Knox: "Give me Scotland or I die!"

When we pray intercessory prayers, we can expect counterattacks from Satan.

Number 10 Bestseller: Murphy, *The Handbook for Spiritual Warfare (Revised and Updated)*
Dr. Ed Murphy
(Thomas Nelson Publishers: Nashville, Tennessee, 2003)

Author: Dr. Ed Murphy
Publisher: Thomas Nelson

Number of Pages = 626

Important Points Regarding:
Model of Deliverance Ministry: Ground Level.
Staying Alert : Does not discuss.
Demon Possession: Does not believe a Christian can be demon possessed but believe Christians can be demonized. Non-Christians can be demon possessed.
Translation of Isaiah 14:12-14 "Lucifer...While there is reason to doubt the validity of this traditional secondary interpretation (all agree the primary interpretation has to do with the king of Babylon and the leader of Tyre), it is consistent with the biblical picture of Satan and his fallen angels."

Section 1: The Origin and Scope of Spiritual Warfare
Dr. Murphy presents the concept of world view as "one's basic assumptions about reality." He compares the traditional world view with the western world view. The Traditional world view does not separate spirits, devil and evil from their view of every day life. The Western world view does make this separation and does not imbue situations, events and things with the spiritual component as does the Traditional world view. He states that "Effective ministry in our day demands that we must recover the knowledge and experience of the spirit world that the early church possessed. We must relearn the forgotten art of spiritual warfare." Demonic influence is evident in the lives of individuals. A Christian can never be possessed by the Devil because even a bad Christian belongs to God.

Chapter 3 of Genesis is the most important Spiritual Warfare passage in the Old Testament (woman encounters Satan, eats and shares the fruit of the forbidden tree and all suffer the consequences).

Dr. Murphy is involved in the deliverance ministry and tells of several occasions in which he was able to rid and individual of the devil.

He cautions individuals that they should not use Mark 16:17-18 as proof that today's Christians have the words of Jesus to support their involvement in casting out demons because Mark 16: 9-20 was not in the original manuscripts.

Section 2: The Normal Christian Life

The "normal Christian life" is one of sanctification. God wants us to live a holy life. That holy living is in conflict with our sinful nature, so spiritual warfare is on going.

Dr. Murphy is involved in delivering individuals from demons. Demon deliverance is often gradual, it is progressive, not all at once. Dr. Murphy describes on intervention that includes his statement that "demons came into manifestation while we were talking on the phone."

Two most powerful verses of testimony of victory in spiritual warfare found anywhere in Scripture are Romans 8:38-39

> *For I am convinced that neither death nor life, neither angels nor demons, neither the present nor the future, nor any powers, neither height nor depth, nor anything else in all creation, will be able to separate us from the love of God that is in Christ Jesus our Lord* (NIV)

Dr. Murphy states, "it is important to understand the spiritual warfare is a multidimensional sin issue that plaques all believers. As Christian Soldiers, we continually combat evil on three fronts: the flesh, the world and the Devil."

It is imperative that believers recognize the sin war in which they are engaged has nothing to do with salvation, only with sanctification. Dr. Murphy quotes Ray Stedman: After reviewing Ephesians 6:10-13 Stedman says it is clear that Paul's view of the basic characteristics of life can be put in one word struggles. Life, he says, "is a conflict, a combat, a continual wrestling." Murphy concludes, "there is only one enemy, the devil, as Paul brings out in Ephesians 6. But the channels of his indirect approach to men are through the world and the flesh."

Section 3: The Believer's Warfare With the Flesh

"My own definition of the flesh is our defective humanness inclined towards self centeredness, with its center in our sinful bodies which includes our mind, emotions and will." Dr. Murphy states, "the real battleground is the mind, the imagination, the fantasy realm." Pornography is a mind-imagination-fantasy game. Man needs discipline in the sexual area just as he needs discipline to be a success in life. He states, "I realized that my thought life desperately needed changing. He quotes Philippians for our guidance:

> Finally, brothers and sisters, whatever is true, whatever
> is noble, whatever is right, whatever is pure, whatever
> is lovely, whatever is admirable—if anything is
> excellent or praiseworthy—think about such things
> (Philippians 4:8 NIV).

Dr. Murphy states: "Sexual sin is always premeditated." To sin or not sin is a choice.

"Gender is like language," says Johns Hopkins University Medical Psychologist John Money: "Genetics ordains only that language can develop, not whether it will be Nahuatl, Arabic or English."

There is a lot of scripture that establishes that homosexuality in any form is sinful. The Southern Baptist has been successful in rejecting the ordination of homosexuals.

Dr. Murphy labels masturbation as "auto-self-stimulation." He gives seven reasons it should be resisted by Christians:

1. It is not necessary.
2. Masturbation does not decrease sexual tension; it only increases it.
3. Usually involves sexual sin and lust in the fantasy realm.
4. Fixates on one's own sexual organs and sexual desires.
5. It is habit forming.
6. plays a central part in promiscuity.
7. There can be a definite demonic dimension to
     uncontrolled masturbation.

He states the so called Gay Rights Movement is a demonic movement. Maintaining a truly moral life in today's sexually saturated culture is really spiritual warfare.

The worst sins of God's people were idolatry and idolatrous **syncretism**, that is combining the worship of Yahweh with elements of paganism.

Section 4: The Believer's Warfare with the World

Syncretism is defined by the Oxford Dictionary as : "the amalgamation or attempted amalgamation of different religions, cultures, or schools of thought." Dr. Murphy states "The church of Africa is like a river a mile wide but only an inch deep. Syncretism was a constant battle. He states, "I was compelled to teach over and over again ...to make the decision whom they were going to serve, the true God or the no-gods." Syncretism is one of the major barriers to world evangelism facing the church today.

Dr. Murphy quotes Chuck Colson: "many in the world have adopted the worldview of Donahumism. This TV talk-show view of reality says, "Do whatever is right for you, and you are being faithful to whatever is true for you. The key idea, says Colson, is "that you, and only you, should decide what you want. No one else has a right to tell you what to do." The result? Philosophical nihilism: Humans thus exist without a purpose besides the purpose they invent for themselves. Colson states that pragmatism is the only philosophical system made in America. With this philosophy, Does it work? has replaced is it right? What are some of the natural consequences of this view? Abortion on demand, no-fault divorce, flight from ethics in business, disregard for the law. In summary, Colson writes, The 1960's adage, "if it feels good, do it" has been updated for the 1990's "if it works, do it." This is pragmatism at its worst.

Dr. Murphy, "Love of the Father and love for the world are mutually exclusive. The battle of the Christian is with the world. Dr. Murphy quotes General Omar Bradley: "We have grasped the mystery of the atom, but we have rejected the Sermon on the Mount. The world has achieved brilliance without wisdom, power without conscience. Ours is a world of nuclear giants, but we are ethical infants. We know more about war than we do about peace, more about killing than living."

To win over the world: " ...we detach ourselves from this world, we ignore it. We win over the world by learning what it means to be in the world, but not of it."

Section 5 - Part Three: A Survey of Biblical Teaching Old Testament

The primary purpose of Genesis is to provide the beginning of the history of God's Elect nation, Israel. Dr. Murphy calls Genesis historical symbolism. He tells us that there is a war in heaven before Geneses. It is not revealed in Genesis but in the rest of the Bible. Adam and Eve are the first casualties of this spiritual warfare.

Dr. Murphy states that from Genesis we learn of two great drives that are built into man. The first is his need for a relationship with God, and the second his need for a relationship to the opposite sex.

The most important verse in the fall of man is Genesis 3:15:

> And I will put enmity between you and the woman,
> and between your offspring and hers; he will crush

your head, and you will strike his heel" (Genesis 3:15 NIV).

In Genesis 3:15 we have the first prophesy of the coming of Christ.

Dr. Murphy sees a lot in the struggle of Cain and Able. It is the first episode of evil against good. "Abel did as he was taught, but Cain did as he thought." Cain's problem came not from the world but from within Cain. "The World has never been at peace since."

God gave the human race a new beginning with Noah the human heart was still the same. The warfare with the flesh and the world and the Devil continued.

The tower of Babel story is the last great judgment that befell mankind in primeval times.

Building the tower was man's attempt to make himself God or equal to God.

Dr. Murphy says we have the anatomy of a power encounter in the relationship of the Pharaoh and Moses: "This is the only record of a power encounter in all Scripture where the servants of the no-gods are allowed to duplicate the power demonstrations of the servants of God for a period of time."

All the nations of the biblical world are traced to the 3 lines of these 3 sons of Noah: Shem, Ham and Japheth (Genesis 10). The Israelites are descendants of Shem:

> This is the account of Shem's family line. Two years
> after the flood, when Shem was 100 years old, he
> became the father of Arphaxad (Genesis 11: 10 NIV).

The entire story of Exodus 3-12 must be seen as an encounter, a contest between God and the gods of Egypt. So Moses, Jethro, and God himself saw the entire Exodus story as a series of power encounters.

W.S. Lasor says there were 39 gods and goddesses widely worshipped in Egypt.

The Israelites were in Egyptian bondage 400 years and Babylon bondage for 70 years. They returned from Babylon in about 457-440 BCE.

Satan and his demons are fully developed personalities with mind, emotions, and will, like the men they inspire towards evil.

The most horrible dimension of demonic religious activity among Israel's neighbors, the practice of child sacrifice. Israel fell into the darkness of this horrible practice. There are dozens of references to child sacrifice to the gods in the OT. There are none in the New Testament.

The first mention of the subject of human sacrifice in the Bible is in Gen 22.

> *Then God said, "Take your son, your only son, whom*
> *you love—Isaac—and go to the region of Moriah.*
> *Sacrifice him there as a burnt offering on a mountain I*
> *will show you" (Genesis 22:2 NIV).*

In Leviticus 18:21, God forbids child sacrifice, equating it with profanation of His name.

> *"Do not give any of your children to be sacrificed to*
> *Molek, for you must not profane the name of your God.*
> *I am the LORD" (Leviticus 18:21 NIV).*

Saul become demonized by his pride and rebellion in his jealousy of David.

The climax is reached with the spirit of the Lord departs from Saul, and an evil spirit from the Lord terrorizes him. Saul's is a most unusual case. Saul's demonization seems to move through progressively worsening stages. Saul dies as a severally demonized believer. He is truly a mystery man.

We are reminded again of the 4 Ps that plaque many Christian and especially Christian leaders: power, position, pleasure, and possessions. All are evidences of the sin of pride.

Dr. Murphey then talks about King Ahab of Israel and his evil wife Jezebel. God says, Ahab did more to provoke the Lord God of Israel than all the Kings of Israel before him:

> *Ahab son of Omri did more evil in the eyes of the*
> *LORD than any of those before him. He not only*
> *considered it trivial to commit the sins of Jeroboam*
> *son of Nebat, but he also married Jezebel daughter of*
> *Ethbaal king of the Sidonians, and began to serve Baal*
> *and worship him. He set up an altar for Baal in the*
> *temple of Baal that he built in Samaria (1 Kings 16:30-*
> *32 NIV).*

First Kings 18 records the most famous power encounter in all of the Scripture, that between the prophet Elijah and 450 prophets of Ball and 400 prophets of Asherah.

Section 6 - Part Four: A Survey of Biblical Teaching: New Testament: Jesus Encounters the Devil and Demons

The Hebrew of the concept of the devil developed gradually. It was not till the "intertestamental period that Satan really comes forth as a very powerful and independent personality."It is in the New Testament that Satanology and demonology develops more fully.

Dr. Murphy surveys the New Testament passages that deal with demons.

In the "temptations of Jesus" we are face-to-face with spiritual warfare of the most intense magnitude. Jesus, the Son of God, meets the Devil. Jesus if victorious: "The Second Adam has not fallen and will not fall."

Mark 1:23-27 records first encounter with demons: demonized man in the synagogue of Capernaum.

Jesus did not hunt down demons. He only dealt with them when their victims came for help or the demons tried to impede His redemptive ministry.

The fact that confronts us in all demonization is that demons are in control of the demonized person.

In Mark 5 Jesus is confronted by the man from the cemetery that argued with Jesus. This is the only occasion in the Gospels in which demons do not immediately obey Jesus. In all other cases, "He cast out the spirits with a word." Jesus cast out the legion of demons into a herd of pigs that ran down a bank and drowned in the lake.

Section 7 - The Apostolic Church Encounters Demons

It seems evident that the emphasis on the spirit world in general and demons in particular is so different in the Acts, Epistles, and Revelation, it is as if the disciples ministered in a different world after Pentecost.

We see then that a deliverance ministry was an essential part of the apostolic commission to mission.

The enemy we face is the singular Devil. All our other enemies are but extensions of his evil power.

The Bible does not explain why there are few teachings about demons and demon deliverance in Acts and the Epistles.

The case of Ananiases and Sapphiras demonstrates Satan can gain partial control over the hearts of believers who willfully sin.

A recurring motif in Acts of the conflict between Christianity and the magical practices which were so prevalent in the Greco-Roman world of the first century.

Dr. Murphy describes Paul's encounter with the demonized slave girl of Philippi in Acts 16:16-18. The girl was controlled by a spirit of divination practiced fortune telling. She was indwelt by the spirit of the Greek god Apollo. Her deliverance was instantaneous.

Paul had no encounters with demons in Athens but a lot with idolatry.

When we are willing to admit that all this formed the universal socio-cultural context of the NT world, we will begin to understand that **power encounter** of the spirit world was going on all the time. Most Western Christians need to learn that the demonic is not as remote as some of them would wish to believe.

Dr. Murphy defines power encounter: "power encounter is a crisis point of encounter in the on-going spiritual warfare between the 2 supernatural kingdoms, the goal of which is the glory of God or of a no-god and the obedience of men to God or to the no-god." Spiritual warfare and power encounter are not synonymous. Power Encounter must be something special or unique. Evangelism always involves spiritual warfare and occasionally it involves power encounter.

Paul's ministry in Ephesus (Acts 19:11-20) included at least three power encounters. Metzger: "Of all ancient Greco-Roman cities, Ephesus, the 3rd largest city in the Empire, was by far the m most hospitable to magicians, sorcerers, and charlatans of all sorts."

The syncretism of those days was simply incredible.

Section 8 - Spiritual Warfare in the Epistles and Revelation

The Epistles do not contain close-up descriptions of evil spirits being cast out or of disobedient believers being slain by the Holy Spirit. Nowhere do the Epistles directly discuss any teaching on the possibility of the demonization of Christians or their deliverance.

In the OT God's enemies are portrayed primarily as men and nations, while in the NT they are seen as the hostile spiritual powers who work through men and nations opposing God, his kingdom and his people. Paul's first reference to Satan is found in 1 Thessalonians 2:18. This epistle is the only book in the Bible whose focus is primarily in Satan's future final efforts to control, deceive, and rule mankind through his own "christ," the Antichrist, "the man of lawlessness." While we must look at Satan and his demons as Paul does here, they are not the focus of Scripture.

Paul had a realistic view of human sexuality. We must walk carefully in such a sensual world, always practicing Philippians 4:8.

In Corinthians the target of Satan's warfare is deception, described as "strongholds." "Strongholds" are ways of thinking and evaluating that are false, arrogant, and destructively disobedient. The ultimate source for all such deception is Satan.

No pastor is automatically protected from the Wormwoods just because the Holy Spirit is in the life. The Holy Spirit is not a spiritual vacuum cleaner, automatically sucking up and expelling all the evil and evil spirits which may co-inhabit the person.

Dr. Murphy states we should "also understand that, in spite of their incredible might, these evil cosmic powers have been totally defeated by Christ in our behalf."

In Ephesians 6 Paul is not writing about demonization but about warfare between the power of the Devil and power of God in the life of believers.

Paul's repetition of "stand firm" 3 times strengthens the view that it is the central command around which all else flows.

Walter Wink is the champion of this more socio-cultural institutional view of spirit evil. Wink continues saying that it is the "supra-human dimension of power in institutions and the cosmos which must be fought, not the mere human agent. Dr. Murphy states, "While favorably responding from the depths of my being to Wink's words, I most emphasize the strong personal supernatural dimension to this warfare motif as well as the social. In fact, the personal-spiritual dimension seems to be Paul's primary focus in Ephesians 6:10-20."

"The purpose of the divine death was 2 fold: to abolish the Devil and to remove the fearful power death hold over the lives of God's children."

Next to the gospel of Matthew there are more references to the work of evil supernaturalism in Revelation than anywhere else in the NT.

If there exists one single key to victory in the spiritual warfare, this is it: God, in our behalf, has already totally defeated Satan and his demonic hosts through the Lord Jesus Christ.

Section 9 - Part Five Practical Considerations - On the Demonization of Christians

Dr. Murphy states, "the possible demonization of true Christians is the single most controversial area of spiritual warfare today." Dr. Murphy observes, "neither Jesus, his apostles, nor the early church ever cast out demons from a believer." Dr. Murphy's position is that true believers can be demonized. "I am not affirming that true believers can be demon possessed. They cannot be."

Dr. Murphy believe under "unusual conditions of sin, true believers can become demonized. These sin areas do not automatically lead to demonization.

1. Generational sin.
2. Child abuse.
3. Anger, bitterness, rage, rejection and rebellion.
4. Sexual sins.
5. Curses in the spirit world
6. Ocult practices.

Section 10 - Demonization and Child Abuse

Evil spirits, therefore are always directly or indirectly involved in child abuse.

Dr. Murphy states, "I have taken dozens of them through deliverance from demons which entered their lives as children. The did not leave at conversion or ordination. They left only through putting into practice the deliverance procedures revealed in God's Word."

Major causes seem to be the breakdown of traditional Judeo-Christian ethical standards, the breakdown of the home, and the general sexual looseness which permeates our culture. "All serious pedophiles that I have dealt with were demonized."

Many cases of demonization are traceable to times of trauma. I have concluded that in the U.S., at least sexual abuse after occult involvement is the number one cause of demonization."

Second to Satan's hatred of God is his hatred for humanity made in the image of God. Child abuse becomes a spiritual warfare issue.

Demons are power beings. People who seek power, even for healing, generally find it first from demons.

Section 11 - Demonization and Mental Health Issues

Dr. Murphy presents the detailed case study of Carman, a demonized person with multiple personalities.

Christians can suffer from depressive illnesses and even more serious brain disorders like schizophrenia without involving demons.

Dr. Murphy cautions, "we should never make diagnoses about our counselees that go beyond our range of experience and knowledge. We cannot cast out non-existent demons!"

In 1983 Dr. Murphy had a break down. His friends said he needed a psychiatrist. He went to one, Dr. Basil Jackson. Dr. Jackson told Dr.

Murphy, "No, it is not demonic. It is a biological-brain malfunction called endogenous or clinical unipolar depression. Demons have nothing to do with it."

Dr. Murphy cautions preachers not to label all behavior they see as demonic.

Section 12 – New Age, Victory and Dangers of Spiritual Warfare

Dr. Murphy states: "The New Age movement is so dangerous because it seems so right for modern man. It denies the objective reality of evil centered in an evil being called Satan. It seems so obviously Christian in its focus on God, Christ, good, world order, full human and earthly happiness."

The New Age movement is a satanic movement of self-deification diametrically opposed to Christianity.

God permits all of us to suffer demonic affliction. Though it hurts, it is good for us. James 4:1-8 is one of the most complete "how-to-passages" on spiritual warfare in Scripture. It is the only passage that deals with all three dimensions of the believer's multidimensional sin problem, the flesh, the world, and evil supernaturalism.

Dr. Murphy states that his experience with his deliverance ministry is "45-10-45." 45% of time in pre-deliverance counseling, 45% of time in post-deliverance counseling, 10% of time in actual deliverance.

Dr. Murphy states: "None of us lives 100 percent of the time perfectly obedient to the lordship of Christ over every area of our life." We can resist the Devil if we follow three scriptural commands:

Command One: "Submit Therefore to God;"
Command Two: Resist the Devil;"
Command Three: "Draw Near to God."

Dr. Murphy names 10 pitfalls in Spiritual Warfare:
Pitfall One: Not Dealing Adequately with Sin;
Pitfall Two: Inadequate Pre-Deliverance Counseling;
Pitfall Three: Inadequate Post-deliverance;
Pitfall Four Incorrect Diagnosis;
Pitfall Five: Overestimating Satan's;
Pitfall Six: Underestimating Satan's Power;
Pitfall Seven: Evil People in Our Midst;
Pitfall Eight: The Pitfall of Blended Gifts (gift of tongues);
Pitfall Nine: The Pitfall of unbalanced Emphasis of
        Specific Manifestations of the Holy;
Pitfall Ten: Ministry Outside the Area of Our Faith and Experience.

Dr. Murphy states there are at least four steps for effective Spiritual Warfare:

1.   To neutralize and defeat this type of evil force, we need to start with long range, united intercessory ministries,   accompanied by widespread repentance on the part of believers and the practice of a godly kingdom lifestyle by the believers in churches of the area;
2.   The believers need spiritual book camp training;
3.   We should join with other more experienced believers;
4.   We must all be in subjection to and in fellowship with mature believers.

WE ARE AT WAR!

Notes

1. Garry Friesen, *Decision Making and the Will of God* (Colorado Springs, CO: Multnomah Books, 2004)
2. Friesen, 425.
3. Mormonism and the LDS Church. Accessed December 24, 2013. http://www.lds-mormon.com/lucifer.shtml.
4. Mechon Mamre, Isaiah 14. Accessed December 24, 2013. http://www.mechon-mamre.org/e/et/et1014.htm

Appendix C: Number 37 on Amazon Bestsellers List
Understanding Spiritual Warfare: Four Views
James K. Beilby (Editor) and Paul Rhodes Eddy (Editor)
Published by: Baker Publishing Group, Grand Rapids, MI, 2012

Editors and Authors

The editors are both Ph. D. graduates of Marquette University and faculty at Bethel University in St. Paul, Minnesota. Dr. Beilby is Professor of Systematic and Philosophical Theology. Dr. Eddy is Professor of Biblical and Theological Studies.

The essay on the World Systems Model was written by Dr. Walter Wink (1935-2012) who is a "groundbreaking figure" in the field of New Testament theology. He was Professor Emeritus of Biblical Interpretation at Auburn Theological Seminary in New York City.

Dr. David Powlison wrote the essay on the Classical Model. He teaches pastoral counseling at Christian Counseling and Educational Foundation, as well as Westminster Seminary. He edits and writes for the *Journal of Biblical Counseling*.

Gregory Boyd, senior pastor of Woodland Hills Church in St. Paul, Minnesota, wrote the essay on the Ground-Level Deliverance Model.

Dr. C. Peter Wagner and Rebecca Greenwood wrote the essay on the Strategic-Level Deliverance Model. Among their accomplishments, Dr. Wagner was Professor of Church Growth at Fuller Theological Seminary for thirty years. Rebecca Greenwood is the founding president of Christian Harvest International and on the faculty at Wagner Leadership Institute.

Publisher:

Baker Academic is one of seven imprints of the Baker Publishing Group, which includes Revell. Revell was started in 1888 by D.L. Moody and his brother-in-law, Fleming H. Revell, when they "saw the need for practical books that would help bring the Christian faith to everyday life."

Number of Pages = 230

Important Points Regarding:

This book presents a typology of approaches to spiritual warfare, to include: The World Systems Model, The Classical Model, The Ground-Level Deliverance Model, The Strategic-Level Deliverance Model

Synopsis
A contemporary proponent presents each approach in an essay, followed by comments of the other writers. The credentials of the writers are given below. This typology helps the reader of spiritual warfare literature have a frame of reference for the variety of books on the subject. Before the essays are presented, the editors' introduction frames the discussion in terms of issues that have arisen about spiritual warfare.

Introduction
Christians need to be careful not to bring military and warfare terminology into the concept of evangelism. "Ultimately, no fellow human is recognized as 'enemy' when viewed from a kingdom perspective."

In the Old Testament, the Hebrews saw the struggle as interwoven between man and the spirit world. Jesus and His disciples saw the struggle, not with man, but with Satan.

Three of the writers see Satan as a free agent active in human events. Walter Wink presents the idea that evil is not embodied in the free, acting person of the devil but bound with earthly, human institutions and structures. "Thus, in Wink's view, these spiritual powers cannot exist apart from their corresponding human institutions and structures."

Much of the spiritual warfare literature focus on one or more of three threats to the Christian: the world, the flesh, and the devil. This "triumvirate" can be found throughout the Bible, but it appears to have been joined together in the Book of Common Prayer in 1546, where the Lord is asked to spare His people from "all the deceits of the world, the flesh, and the devil." The editors state, "These three foci themselves are not mutually exclusive."

One overlay that may be applied to all spiritual warfare literature is the Calvinist tradition that sees all that happens as God's doing, even the bad activities of Satan. The Armenian view is that "angels and humans were created by God with libertarian freedom...that allowed Satan and the demonic to choose a path of evil and rebellion that God never intended for them."

Many proponents of the "Deliverance Model" of spiritual warfare do believe that non-Christians can be possessed by a demon. However, they believe that a Christian cannot be possessed but can be oppressed by a demon, thus also having a need to be delivered from the demon.

Chapter 1
The World Systems Model
Walter Wink

Wink sees Satan in the Bible, not as evil, but as a faithful servant of Yahweh. Although many see Satan's presence throughout the Old Testament, he only shows up by name on three occasions: 1 Chronicles 21:1, Job, and Zechariah 3:1-5. Satan acts as a prosecutor. Even into the New Testament, he appears as a helper for God. Jesus describes Satan as a "sifter," as in sifting the wheat from the chaff, when he describes Peter's denial experience.

In I Corinthians 5, Paul describes a situation in the Church where a man is sleeping with his stepmother, and the Church accepts this man's behavior. "Paul does not say that Satan enticed this man to sin; rather, Satan is the means of his deliverance! This understanding of Satan has little in common with the irremediably evil Satan of popular Christian thought."

Wink continues to demonstrate that Satan helps God, a role contrary to the common wisdom of today's Christians that Satan is an enemy of God. Wink does this by questioning the role of Satan in the temptations of Jesus. "The Spirit leads Jesus out into the wilderness 'to be tempted by the devil' (Matt. 4:1 RSV). What kind of collusion is this? Why if he (Jesus) needs testing, does the Spirit not provide it? Why place him in ultimate jeopardy by throwing him into the hands of Satan? It makes no sense at all if Satan is evil personified. But if he is the heavenly sifter, the setter of choice, then we have a different story altogether."

Wink does concede that Satan does "fall. We know that anyone born of God does not continue to sin; the one who was born of God keeps him safe, and the evil one cannot harm him. We know that we are children of God, and that the whole world is under the control of the evil one" I John 5:18-19 (NIV).

Wink declares that "Satan becomes the symbol of the spirit of an entire society alienated from God, the great system of mutual support in evil, the spirit of persistent self-deification blown large, the image of unredeemed humanity's collective life."

> "There is a concentration of evil in a directional pull counter to the will of God."

One of Wink's mantras is, "History belongs to the intercessors, who believe the future into being." Wink recommends that the Christian must pray aggressively. He points to numerous incidents in the Bible that show "it pays to haggle with God." Wink quotes Rudolf Bultmann: "Prayer is not to bring the petitioner's will into submission to the unchanging will of God, but prayer is to move God to do something which he otherwise would not do."

To summarize Wink's essay, Wink does see Satan not as a standalone entity exercising discretion and independence from God, but only as evil and worldliness expressed in societal institutions. The Christian can counter these forces through intercessory prayer.

Wagner and Greenwood are adamant in their reaction to Wink's "relative interest in a metaphysical Satan" by declaring that they are "intensely interested in the metaphysical question, to which we would answer with an unequivocal yes, there is a Satan."

One of the tenants of their approach to spiritual warfare is "know your enemy."

Chapter 2
The Classical Model
David Powlison

The "Classical Model" of spiritual warfare is that described by Paul in Ephesians 6:10-20. Powlison emphasizes that Satan is not some "metaphor for human darkness, reducible to psychological or sociocultural forces." He is a person. "The devil is a purposeful, intelligent, malevolent personal agent." Powlison gets his identity of the devil as a person in part from the first time the Bible mentions the "evil one." The Bible "carefully underscores creatureliness: "the serpent...more crafty than any other beast of the field...the Lord God made" (Gen. 3:1).

"The phrase 'spiritual warfare' never appears in the Bible. It is a pastoral, theological term for describing the moral conflict of the Christian life. It is a metaphor for our lifelong struggle with our lies and other liars, our lust and other tempters, our sins and other evildoers, the present darkness that continually unsettles us..."

The Church has always accepted that Ephesians 6 is the way God intends for Christians to deal with Satan. Paul's reference to the "breastplate of righteousness" in verse 14 and "helmet of salvation" in verse 17 come from Isaiah 59:17: "He put on righteousness as his breastplate, and the helmet of salvation on his head."

Powlison states that we can know the biblical view of spiritual warfare by observing how Jesus fought. Jesus fought the Ephesians 6 way, by bringing light to darkness. Jesus and the disciples were never concerned about why a person had demons. Knowing why had nothing to do with releasing the individual from demons. Demon possession was just another malady, like blindness, lameness, or leprosy.

Powlison states, "Deliverance from the sin of pursuing the occult never includes any sort of deliverance from inhabiting spirits."

In summary, Powlison believes that Satan is an independent entity working his evil. He is not limited to institutional and societal manifestations as Wink suggests. He is not embodied in demons that can be cast out of individuals and territories.

Chapter 3
The Ground-Level Deliverance Model
Gregory Boyd

Boyd gives a very methodical presentation of the appearance of Satan/the devil/demons in the biblical narrative. From his survey of the Scriptures, Boyd concludes that the "dark powers" are "agents, each of whom possesses something like a mind and a will over against humans." The Scripture provides his precedent for establishing a ministry to deliver individuals from these agents.

He follows up his biblical documentation with accounts of his personal experience with demons through a "balanced" deliverance ministry __ one that is not too focused on demons and not too focused on psychological counseling, but including both.

For those who have difficulty accepting the existence of demons, Boyd states, "I, for one, have never understood the logic that affirms faith in a personal God but finds belief in a personal devil, powers, or demons to be incredible."

The world we live in looks like a war zone because the world is a war zone.

Wagner and Greenwood state, "We are afflicted by the world, the flesh and the devil, and we believe that the struggle for a godly lifestyle usually involves more confrontation with the world and the flesh than the devil. However, when the devil or his demons do enter the picture, deliverance is needed. What Boyd does: We call this ground-level spiritual warfare, and we consider it closer to the primary way of doing spiritual warfare than just living good individual lifestyles."

Chapter 4
The Strategic-Level Deliverance Model
C. Peter Wagner and Rebecca Greenwood

"Spiritual warfare" is an invisible battle in the spiritual realm involving a power confrontation between the kingdom of God and the kingdom of darkness. Spiritual warfare occurs on three different levels: ground level, occult level, and strategic level. They are helpful terms. They are not three separate worlds, but only one invisible world of darkness.

Ground-level spiritual warfare is the practice of deliverance ministry that involves breaking demonic influences in an individual. It occurs on a personal level.

Occult-level spiritual warfare involves resistance to a more ordered level of demonic authority. Warfare at this level deals with witchcraft, Satanism, freemasonry, New Age beliefs, Eastern religion, and many other forms of spiritual practices that glorify Satan and his dark army.

Strategic-level spiritual warfare (SLSW) requires power confrontations with high-ranking principalities and powers, as described in Ephesians 6:12. These demonic entities are assigned to geographical territories and social networks. They are also referred to as territorial spirits. Their assignment is to keep large numbers of humans, networked through cities or any other form of social institutions, in spiritual captivity.

Spiritual mapping is the practice of identifying the spiritual conditions at work in a given community, city, or nation. By gathering objective information (including key historical facts such as foundational history, locations of bloodshed, idolatrous practices...and combining it with spiritual impressions (prophecy, revelation, words of knowledge, dreams, and visions), believers can prayerfully combine all of this information and draw a map that identifies the open doors between the spirit world and the material world.

Prayer walking is a technique of SLSW. It is just what it sounds like: walking while praying. In addition, it is defined as "praying on-site with insight."

The other authors soundly criticize SLSW. Gregory Boyd states, "I grow concerned, however, when practices for which there are no biblical precedents take center stage in anyone's theology and ministry," and continues that they "place too much confidence in, and too much importance on, personal revelations on confronting individual powers."

Critique #1: It is not surprising that Paul would pull from Isaiah the description of the armor. Preachers have always used "proof texts" from their Bibles to make their point. That is what Paul has done here by quoting from the Hebrew Bible.

Critique #2: Powlison's presentation of the classical model from Ephesians 6 highlights the armament and prayer as a Christian's tools for spiritual warfare, but it fails to focus on a key vulnerability caused by surprise when Paul cautions, "Stay alert," in verse 18b. This and other verses advising alertness and vigilance are what led to this book on the spiritual ambush (I Peter 5:8).

Critique #3: Granted, the classical commentaries on Acts do not address the issue of possible SLSW in these passages. The existence of such things as "territorial spirits" had not entered the minds of many of those biblical scholars. Wagner states, "I will not hesitate to admit that I do not have airtight arguments for my thoughts on these matters. "

Critique #4: Wagner claims scriptural basis for SLSW in Paul's encounter with a demon-oppressed slave girl. "When the owners discovered that their hope of profit was gone, they caught hold of Paul and Silas and dragged them before the authorities...". Wagner claims that the disposed demon caused the upset of the town. That is contrary to Acts 16:19 ("And when her masters saw that the hope of their gains was gone, they caught Paul and Silas, and drew [them] into the marketplace unto the rulers").

It was not the devil that upset the community; it was the slave owners motivated by the loss of revenue. Wagner's scriptural basis of SLSW is a stretch of the biblical truth.

Appendix D: Characteristics of the Nine Best Sellers on Spiritual

Author	Model of Deliverance	Demon Possession	Staying Alert	Isaiah 14:12 Lucifer
1. Payne	ground level	Yes non-believer	no	no
2. Prince	classical	n/a	no	no
3. Rankin	classical model	no	yes	no
5. Sherman	all	no	yes	yes
4.	—	—	—	—
6. Ingram	Ground and strategic levels	no	9 times red alert	yes
7. Phillips	ground level	yes (non-believers)	no	yes
8. Frangipane	classical	no	no	no

Author	Model of Deliverance	Demon Possession	Staying Alert	Isaiah 14:12 Lucifer
9. Warner	ground and strategic levels	no	no	no
10. Murphy	ground level	yes	no	no

Appendix E: How to Become a Confident Christian

The spiritual warrior must have a real relationship with a real God. He needs to know where he stands with God. The real spiritual warrior gets real with the Scripture, God, and his personal salvation.

Am I saved? Have you ever asked that question? Have you ever doubted your salvation? The warrior needs to certify his salvation so that question will never come up again. That is the beginning of the confidence required of a spiritual warrior. Nothing is worse for a warrior entering a battle than a lack of confidence in who he is and what he is doing.

How to Remove All Doubt about Your Conversion

After I became a Christian, I prayed many times that God would reveal Himself to me in some real, physical, undeniable way, so that I would be propelled into a dynamic ministry based on a dynamic revelation of God. I prayed that prayer because many times I doubted my conversion experience, because I did not "feel" different. I wanted a "Damascus Road experience," just like the Apostle Paul (Acts 9:3).

I became a Christian in 1948, when I was nine years old, during Vacation Bible School at the First Baptist Church in Birmingham, Alabama. I recall being very aware that God had "saved" me and understanding the meaning of baptism and joining the church. I grew up as a "goody-goody" kid, largely thanks to my mom, who was the daughter of a Baptist preacher. Her father was Joseph Edward Lowry, pastor of the 12th Street Baptist Church in Gadsden, Alabama, in the 1920s.

During my childhood, Mom made sure I went to Sunday school and church. When I was seven, my mom taught me the taste of soap because of the bad words that came out of my mouth. All of this led to my growing up without a lot of "sinful" behavior.

It was in my thinking that some of Paul's reaction to his "Damascus Road Experience" had to be related to the very bad life he led before his conversion. The difference in his behavior after his conversion was dynamic and undeniable, as clearly different as night is from day. Oh, how I wanted that kind of a real encounter with God. It was my constant prayer, often when I was alone and at night.

One of my duties as the part-time music and youth director for my home church, Birmingham's Ninth Avenue Baptist Church, was to do the Sunday-morning bulletin. In those days before computers, 1958 - 1962, preparing the bulletin involved typing the words on a stencil, putting the stencil on the mimeograph machine, and running the bulletin paper through the machine. Being a young, single college student who was very much interested in finding one of those Howard College girls to marry, it was not unusual for me to go by the church after my Saturday-night date to do the bulletins. It was often midnight or later before I got around to doing that task.

Ninth Avenue was a church in an old, but adequate, building for our congregation, with an attendance of about 200 in Sunday School each Sunday. The only door that had an outside lock was the front door of the sanctuary. However, the light switch for the sanctuary lights was back by the baptismal pool behind the pulpit. The church office was behind the sanctuary in the "educational wing." So, after finishing the bulletin, I would have to turn the lights off and walk through the dark sanctuary to the front door, so I could lock the door to the church as I left.

Early one Sunday morning, at about 1:00 AM, I turned out the lights and entered the dark sanctuary. As I often did, I was praying that God would reveal Himself to me in some physical and undeniable way. Just after I prayed that prayer and turned to walk down the center aisle of the sanctuary, my hand brushed something "physical and undeniable" right there in the middle of the aisle at the front of the church. I swung around and knelt, convinced that God had appeared in response to my prayer. As I knelt there, speaking to God, my eyes gradually adjusted to the dark. I began to see that it was not God I had touched, but rather a lectern someone had left in the middle of the aisle. Relieved that I had not had a heart attack when I had believed I was face-to-face with God but disappointed that my longed-for "real, dynamic, physical encounter with God" had not occurred, I stood and proceeded through the dark sanctuary.

I believe that honesty must come with conversion, particularly being honest with yourself. Although I had been a Christian for quite some time, I still did not understand the dynamics of faith when it came to my conversion, because truthfully there were times I did not feel saved. While living a Christian life the best I knew how, I continued to pray for a Damascus Road experience. This desire lasted throughout college and after graduation, as I began working for the welfare department in Birmingham while serving part-time as the music and youth director at the First Baptist Church in Ashland, Alabama. A year later, when I entered the Army, I was still praying for that undeniable encounter with God.

In Korea in 1965-66, there was a shortage of chaplains because at that time virtually everything and everyone was going to Vietnam, including Army chaplains. Missionaries were our chaplains. A Navigator[5] missionary was assigned to my unit, the 1st Brigade of the 2nd Infantry Division. I got involved in the Navigator Bible studies. I learned a lot from the Navigators but continued to desire that "real encounter with God."

When I returned to the states, I was stationed at Ft. Benning in Columbus, Georgia. I was assigned as the custodian of the Youth Activities Club. All of the dependent children's activities came under my shop.

I moved into the Navigator home in Columbus. I became very active in the Navigator Ministry, including participating in their Bible studies.[4] I remember one Bible study that was about the relationship of the disciples to Jesus. During the study, I commented that I found it very interesting that Judas had experienced the same encounter with Jesus as the other disciples, but "it had not taken." Judas' contact had been real, but it had not changed his life.

After the Bible study, one of the Navigator staff complimented me on a very meaningful insight. I then told him I still struggled with a desire to have a "real undeniable encounter with God," a Damascus Road encounter like Paul. I told him that I felt such an experience would remove the doubt I sometimes had about whether conversion had "taken." I wanted an encounter that would erase all my doubt and compel me never to question my salvation again.

My Navigator friend suggested that in order to remove that doubt, I should pray the "sinner's prayer." I was to pray that God would forgive me of my sins and enter my heart (Romans 10:9). After I prayed that prayer, I should then observe my life objectively. If there was no change in my life, then I should accept on faith that my conversion had been genuine and that my relationship with God was real.

I prayed that prayer. There was no change in my behavior, thinking or spiritual experience. I concluded that my original conversion was real. I was a Christian with a real relationship with God. I accepted that on faith. Since then, I have never again prayed that prayer for a Damascus Road experience. Since then, there has never been a single instance of self-doubt of my conversion.

I recommend this process to you. If you have ever questioned your salvation and desired a "Damascus Road Experience" like Paul's to validate your conversion, I challenge you to pray the "sinner's prayer" on faith and watch what happens in your life. You will either confirm your previous experience, or you will have a real encounter with God. The bottom line is that it means no more doubts regarding your conversion.

Appendix F: Verses in the New Testament (NIV) that Include the Word "Calling" Occurs in 21 Verses in the New Testament (NIV)

#	Definition	VERSE
1	Shouting	**Mat 3:3** - This is he who was spoken of through the prophet Isaiah: "A voice of one **calling** in the wilderness, 'Prepare the way for the Lord, make straight paths for him.' "
2	Shouting	**Mat 9:27** - As Jesus went on from there, two blind men followed him, **calling** out, "Have mercy on us, Son of David!"
3	Summon	**Mat 11:16** - "To what can I compare this generation? They are like children sitting in the marketplaces and **calling** out to others:
4	Summon	**Mat 27:47** - When some of those standing there heard this, they said, "He's **calling** Elijah."
5	Shouting	**Mar 1:3** - "a voice of one **calling** in the wilderness, 'Prepare the way for the Lord, make straight paths for him.' "
6	Summon	**Mar 6:7** - **Calling** the Twelve to him, he began to send them out two by two and gave them authority over impure spirits.
7	Summon	**Mar 10:49** - Jesus stopped and said, "Call him." So they called to the blind man, "Cheer up! On your feet! He's **calling** you."
8	Summon	**Mar 12:43** - **Calling** his disciples to him, Jesus said, "Truly I tell you, this poor widow has put more into the treasury than all the others.

9	Summon	**Mar 15:35** - When some of those standing near heard this, they said, "Listen, he's **calling** Elijah."
10	Shouting	**Luk 3:4** - As it is written in the book of the words of Isaiah the prophet: "A voice of one **calling** in the wilderness, 'Prepare the way for the Lord, make straight paths for him.
11	Summon	**Luk 7:18** - John's disciples told him about all these things. **Calling** two of them,
12	Shouting	**Luk 7:32** - They are like children sitting in the marketplace and **calling** out to each other: " 'We played the pipe for you, and you did not dance; we sang a dirge, and you did not cry.'
13	Shouting	**Jhn 1:23** - John replied in the words of Isaiah the prophet, "I am the voice of one **calling** in the wilderness, 'Make straight the way for the Lord.' "
14	Labeling	**Jhn 5:18** - For this reason they tried all the more to kill him; not only was he breaking the Sabbath, but he was even **calling** God his own Father, making himself equal with God.
15	Requesting	**Act 22:16** - And now what are you waiting for? Get up, be baptized and wash your sins away, **calling** on his name.'
16	Summoned To God	**Eph 4:1** - As a prisoner for the Lord, then, I urge you to live a life worthy of the **calling** you have received.
17	Summoned To God	**2Th 1:11** - With this in mind, we constantly pray for you, that our God may make you worthy of his **calling**, and that by his power he may bring to fruition your every desire for goodness and your every deed prompted by faith.
18	Summon	**Heb 3:1** - Therefore, holy brothers and sisters, who

		share in the heavenly **calling**, fix your thoughts on Jesus, whom we acknowledge as our apostle and high priest.
19	Labeling	**Heb 4:7** - God again set a certain day, **calling** it "Today." This he did when a long time later he spoke through David, as in the passage already quoted: "Today, if you hear his voice, do not harden your hearts."
20	Labeling	**Heb 8:13** - By **calling** this covenant "new," he has made the first one obsolete; and what is obsolete and outdated will soon disappear.
21	Summoned To God	**2Pe 1:10** - Therefore, my brothers and sisters, make every effort to confirm your **calling** and election. For if you do these things, you will never stumble,

Notes

"NIV Search Results for "calling"." Blue Letter Bible. Accessed 27 Oct, 2015.
http://www.blueletterbible.orghttps://www.blueletterbible.org/search/searc
h.cfm

Appendix G: Verses in the New Testament (NIV) That Include the Word "Called." Occurs in 202 Verses in the New Testament (NIV).

#	Definition	VERSE
1	Named	**Mat 1:16** - and Jacob the father of Joseph, the husband of Mary, and Mary was the mother of Jesus who is **called** the Messiah.
2	Summoned	**Mat 2:4** - When he had **called** together all the people's chief priests and teachers of the law, he asked them where the Messiah was to be born.
3	Summoned	**Mat 2:7** - Then Herod **called** the Magi secretly and found out from them the exact time the star had appeared.
4	Summoned	**Mat 2:15** - where he stayed until the death of Herod. And so was fulfilled what the Lord had said through the prophet: "Out of Egypt I **called** my son."
5	Named	**Mat 2:23** - and he went and lived in a town **called** Nazareth. So was fulfilled what was said through the prophets, that he would be **called** a Nazarene.
6	Named	**Mat 4:18** - As Jesus was walking beside the Sea of Galilee, he saw two brothers, Simon **called** Peter and his brother Andrew. They were casting a net into the lake, for they were fishermen.
7	Summoned	**Mat 4:21** - Going on from there, he saw two other brothers, James son of Zebedee and his brother John. They were in a boat with their father Zebedee, preparing their nets. Jesus **called** them,
8	Labeled	**Mat 5:9** - Blessed are the peacemakers, for they will be **called** children of God.

9	Labeled	**Mat 5:19** - Therefore anyone who sets aside one of the least of these commands and teaches others accordingly will be **called** least in the kingdom of heaven, but whoever practices and teaches these commands will be **called** great in the kingdom of heaven.
10	Summoned	**Mat 10:1** - Jesus **called** his twelve disciples to him and gave them authority to drive out impure spirits and to heal every disease and sickness.
11	Named	**Mat 10:2** NIV - These are the names of the twelve apostles: first, Simon (who is **called** Peter) and his brother Andrew; James son of Zebedee, and his brother John;
12	Labeled	**Mat 10:25** - It is enough for students to be like their teachers, and servants like their masters. If the head of the house has been **called** Beelzebul, how much more the members of his household!
13	Summoned	**Mat 15:10** - Jesus **called** the crowd to him and said, "Listen and understand.
14	Summoned	**Mat 15:32** - Jesus **called** his disciples to him and said, "I have compassion for these people; they have already been with me three days and have nothing to eat. I do not want to send them away hungry, or they may collapse on the way."
15	Summoned	**Mat 18:2** - He **called** a little child to him, and placed the child among them.
16	Summoned	**Mat 18:32** - "Then the master **called** the servant in. 'You wicked servant,' he said, 'I canceled all that debt of yours because you begged me to.

17	Summoned	**Mat 20:25** - Jesus **called** them together and said, "You know that the rulers of the Gentiles lord it over them, and their high officials exercise authority over them.
18	Spoke	**Mat 20:32** - Jesus stopped and **called** them. "What do you want me to do for you?" he asked.
19	Labeled	**Mat 21:13** - "It is written," he said to them, " 'My house will be **called** a house of prayer,' but you are making it 'a den of robbers.'"
20	Spoke	**Mat 21:16** - "Do you hear what these children are saying?" they asked him. "Yes," replied Jesus, "have you never read, " 'From the lips of children and infants you, Lord, have **called** forth your praise'?"
21	Labeled	**Mat 23:7** - they love to be greeted with respect in the marketplaces and to be **called** 'Rabbi' by others.
22	Labeled	**Mat 23:8** - "But you are not to be **called** 'Rabbi,' for you have one Teacher, and you are all brothers.
23	Labeled	**Mat 23:10** - Nor are you to be **called** instructors, for you have one Instructor, the Messiah.
24	Summoned	**Mat 25:14** - "Again, it will be like a man going on a journey, who **called** his servants and entrusted his wealth to them.
25	Named	**Mat 26:14** - Then one of the Twelve--the one **called** Judas Iscariot--went to the chief priests
26	Named	**Mat 26:36** - Then Jesus went with his disciples to a place **called** Gethsemane, and he said to them, "Sit here while I go over there and pray."
27	Named	**Mat 27:8** - That is why it has been **called** the Field of Blood to this day.

28	Labeled	**Mat 27:17** - So when the crowd had gathered, Pilate asked them, "Which one do you want me to release to you: Jesus Barabbas, or Jesus who is **called** the Messiah?"
29	Labeled	**Mat 27:22** - "What shall I do, then, with Jesus who is **called** the Messiah?" Pilate asked. They all answered, "Crucify him!"
30	Named	**Mat 27:33** - They came to a place **called** Golgotha (which means "the place of the skull").
31	Summoned	**Mar 1:20** - Without delay he **called** them, and they left their father Zebedee in the boat with the hired men and followed him.
32	Summoned	**Mar 3:13** - Jesus went up on a mountainside and **called** to him those he wanted, and they came to him.
33	Summoned	**Mar 3:23** - So Jesus **called** them over to him and began to speak to them in parables: "How can Satan drive out Satan?
34	Summoned	**Mar 7:14** - Again Jesus **called** the crowd to him and said, "Listen to me, everyone, and understand this.
35	Summoned	**Mar 8:1** - During those days another large crowd gathered. Since they had nothing to eat, Jesus **called** his disciples to him and said,
36	Summoned	**Mar 8:34** - Then he **called** the crowd to him along with his disciples and said: "Whoever wants to be my disciple must deny themselves and take up their cross and follow me.
37	Summoned	**Mar 9:35** - Sitting down, Jesus **called** the Twelve and said, "Anyone who wants to be first must be the very last, and the servant of all."

38	Summoned	**Mar 10:42** - Jesus **called** them together and said, "You know that those who are regarded as rulers of the Gentiles lord it over them, and their high officials exercise authority over them.
39	Spoke	**Mar 10:49** - Jesus stopped and said, "Call him." So they **called** to the blind man, "Cheer up! On your feet! He's calling you."
40	Labeled	**Mar 11:17** - And as he taught them, he said, "Is it not written: 'My house will be **called** a house of prayer for all nations'? But you have made it 'a den of robbers.'"
41	Named	**Mar 14:32** - They went to a place **called** Gethsemane, and Jesus said to his disciples, "Sit here while I pray."
42	Named	**Mar 15:7** - A man **called** Barabbas was in prison with the insurrectionists who had committed murder in the uprising.
43	Summoned	**Mar 15:16** - The soldiers led Jesus away into the palace (that is, the Praetorium) and **called** together the whole company of soldiers.
44	Named	**Mar 15:22** - They brought Jesus to the place **called** Golgotha (which means "the place of the skull").
45	Labeled	**Luk 1:32** - He will be great and will be **called** the Son of the Most High. The Lord God will give him the throne of his father David,
46	Labeled	**Luk 1:35** - The angel answered, "The Holy Spirit will come on you, and the power of the Most High will overshadow you. So the holy one to be born will be **called** the Son of God.

47	Named	**Luk 1:60** - but his mother spoke up and said, "No! He is to be **called** John."
48	Labeled	**Luk 1:76** - And you, my child, will be **called** a prophet of the Most High; for you will go on before the Lord to prepare the way for him,
49	Named	**Luk 2:25** - Now there was a man in Jerusalem **called** Simeon, who was righteous and devout. He was waiting for the consolation of Israel, and the Holy Spirit was on him.
50	Summoned	**Luk 6:13** - When morning came, he **called** his disciples to him and chose twelve of them, whom he also designated apostles:
51	Labeled	**Luk 6:15** - Matthew, Thomas, James son of Alphaeus, Simon who was **called** the Zealot,
52	Named	**Luk 7:11** - Soon afterward, Jesus went to a town **called** Nain, and his disciples and a large crowd went along with him.
53	Named	**Luk 8:2** - and also some women who had been cured of evil spirits and diseases: Mary (**called** Magdalene) from whom seven demons had come out;
54	Shouted	**Luk 8:8** - Still other seed fell on good soil. It came up and yielded a crop, a hundred times more than was sown." When he said this, he **called** out, "Whoever has ears to hear, let them hear."
55	Summoned	**Luk 9:1** - When Jesus had **called** the Twelve together, he gave them power and authority to drive out all demons and to cure diseases,
56	Named	**Luk 9:10** - When the apostles returned, they reported to Jesus what they had done. Then he took them with

		him and they withdrew by themselves to a town **called** Bethsaida,
57	Shouted	**Luk 9:38** - A man in the crowd **called** out, "Teacher, I beg you to look at my son, for he is my only child.
58	Named	**Luk 10:39** - She had a sister **called** Mary, who sat at the Lord's feet listening to what he said.
59	Shouted	**Luk 11:27** - As Jesus was saying these things, a woman in the crowd **called** out, "Blessed is the mother who gave you birth and nursed you."
60	Summoned	**Luk 13:12** - When Jesus saw her, he **called** her forward and said to her, "Woman, you are set free from your infirmity."
61	Labeled	**Luk 15:19** - I am no longer worthy to be **called** your son; make me like one of your hired servants.'
62	Labeled	**Luk 15:21** - "The son said to him, 'Father, I have sinned against heaven and against you. I am no longer worthy to be **called** your son.'
63	Summoned	**Luk 15:26** - So he **called** one of the servants and asked him what was going on.
64	Summoned	**Luk 16:2** - So he **called** him in and asked him, 'What is this I hear about you? Give an account of your management, because you cannot be manager any longer.'
65	Summoned	**Luk 16:5** - "So he **called** in each one of his master's debtors. He asked the first, 'How much do you owe my master?'
66	Spoke	**Luk 16:24** - So he **called** to him, 'Father Abraham, have pity on me and send Lazarus to dip the tip of his

finger in water and cool my tongue, because I am in agony in this fire.'

67	Shouted	**Luk 17:13** - and **called** out in a loud voice, "Jesus, Master, have pity on us!"
68	Summoned	**Luk 18:16** - But Jesus **called** the children to him and said, "Let the little children come to me, and do not hinder them, for the kingdom of God belongs to such as these.
69	Shouted	**Luk 18:38** - He **called** out, "Jesus, Son of David, have mercy on me!"
70	Summoned	**Luk 19:13** - So he **called** ten of his servants and gave them ten minas. 'Put this money to work,' he said, 'until I come back.'
71	Named	**Luk 19:29** - As he approached Bethphage and Bethany at the hill **called** the Mount of Olives, he sent two of his disciples, saying to them,
72	Named	**Luk 21:37** - Each day Jesus was teaching at the temple, and each evening he went out to spend the night on the hill **called** the Mount of Olives,
73	Named	**Luk 22:1** - Now the Festival of Unleavened Bread, **called** the Passover, was approaching,
74	Named	**Luk 22:3** - Then Satan entered Judas, **called** Iscariot, one of the Twelve.
75	Named	**Luk 22:47** - While he was still speaking a crowd came up, and the man who was **called** Judas, one of the Twelve, was leading them. He approached Jesus to kiss him,
76	Summoned	**Luk 23:13** - Pilate **called** together the chief priests, the rulers and the people,

77	Named	**Luk 23:33** - When they came to the place **called** the Skull, they crucified him there, along with the criminals--one on his right, the other on his left.
78	Shouted	**Luk 23:46** - Jesus **called** out with a loud voice, "Father, into your hands I commit my spirit." When he had said this, he breathed his last.
79	Named	**Luk 24:13** - Now that same day two of them were going to a village **called** Emmaus, about seven miles from Jerusalem.
80	Named	**Jhn 1:42** - And he brought him to Jesus. Jesus looked at him and said, "You are Simon son of John. You will be **called** Cephas" (which, when translated, is Peter).
81	Summoned	**Jhn 1:48** - "How do you know me?" Nathanael asked. Jesus answered, "I saw you while you were still under the fig tree before Philip **called** you."
82	Summoned	**Jhn 2:9** - and the master of the banquet tasted the water that had been turned into wine. He did not realize where it had come from, though the servants who had drawn the water knew. Then he **called** the bridegroom aside
83	Named	**Jhn 4:5** - So he came to a town in Samaria **called** Sychar, near the plot of ground Jacob had given to his son Joseph.
84	Labeled	**Jhn 4:25** - The woman said, "I know that Messiah" (**called** Christ) "is coming. When he comes, he will explain everything to us."
85	Named	**Jhn 5:2** - Now there is in Jerusalem near the Sheep Gate a pool, which in Aramaic is **called** Bethesda and which is surrounded by five covered colonnades.

86	Labeled	**Jhn 10:35** - If he **called** them 'gods,' to whom the word of God came--and Scripture cannot be set aside—
87	Summoned	**Jhn 11:28** - After she had said this, she went back and **called** her sister Mary aside. "The Teacher is here," she said, "and is asking for you."
88	Shouted	**Jhn 11:43** - When he had said this, Jesus **called** in a loud voice, "Lazarus, come out!"
89	Summoned	**Jhn 11:47** - Then the chief priests and the Pharisees **called** a meeting of the Sanhedrin. "What are we accomplishing?" they asked. "Here is this man performing many signs.
90	Named	**Jhn 11:54** - Therefore Jesus no longer moved about publicly among the people of Judea. Instead he withdrew to a region near the wilderness, to a village **called** Ephraim, where he stayed with his disciples.
91	Summoned	**Jhn 12:17** - Now the crowd that was with him when he **called** Lazarus from the tomb and raised him from the dead continued to spread the word.
92	Labeled	**Jhn 15:15** - I no longer call you servants, because a servant does not know his master's business. Instead, I have **called** you friends, for everything that I learned from my Father I have made known to you.
93	Named	**Jhn 19:17** - Carrying his own cross, he went out to the place of the Skull (which in Aramaic is **called** Golgotha).
94	Shouted	**Jhn 21:5** - He **called** out to them, "Friends, haven't you any fish?" "No," they answered.

95	Named	**Act 1:12** - Then the apostles returned to Jerusalem from the hill **called** the Mount of Olives, a Sabbath day's walk from the city.
96	Named	**Act 1:19** - Everyone in Jerusalem heard about this, so they **called** that field in their language Akeldama, that is, Field of Blood.)
97	Named	**Act 1:23** - So they nominated two men: Joseph **called** Barsabbas (also known as Justus) and Matthias.
98	Named	**Act 3:2** - Now a man who was lame from birth was being carried to the temple gate **called** Beautiful, where he was put every day to beg from those going into the temple courts.
99	Named	**Act 3:10** - they recognized him as the same man who used to sit begging at the temple gate **called** Beautiful, and they were filled with wonder and amazement at what had happened to him.
100	Named	**Act 3:11** - While the man held on to Peter and John, all the people were astonished and came running to them in the place **called** Solomon's Colonnade.
101	Summoned	**Act 4:9** - If we are being **called** to account today for an act of kindness shown to a man who was lame and are being asked how he was healed,
102	Summoned	**Act 4:18** - Then they **called** them in again and commanded them not to speak or teach at all in the name of Jesus.
103	Named	**Act 4:36** - Joseph, a Levite from Cyprus, whom the apostles **called** Barnabas (which means "son of encouragement"),

104	Summoned	**Act 5:21** - At daybreak they entered the temple courts, as they had been told, and began to teach the people. When the high priest and his associates arrived, they **called** together the Sanhedrin--the full assembly of the elders of Israel--and sent to the jail for the apostles.
105	Summoned	**Act 5:40** - His speech persuaded them. They **called** the apostles in and had them flogged. Then they ordered them not to speak in the name of Jesus, and let them go.
106	Named	**Act 6:9** - Opposition arose, however, from members of the Synagogue of the Freedmen (as it was **called**)--Jews of Cyrene and Alexandria as well as the provinces of Cilicia and Asia--who began to argue with Stephen.
107	Labeled	**Act 8:10** - and all the people, both high and low, gave him their attention and exclaimed, "This man is rightly **called** the Great Power of God."
108	Spoke	**Act 9:10** - In Damascus there was a disciple named Ananias. The Lord **called** to him in a vision, "Ananias!" "Yes, Lord," he answered.
109	Summoned	**Act 9:41** - He took her by the hand and helped her to her feet. Then he **called** for the believers, especially the widows, and presented her to them alive.
110	Named	**Act 10:5** - Now send men to Joppa to bring back a man named Simon who is **called** Peter.
111	Summoned	**Act 10:7** - When the angel who spoke to him had gone, Cornelius **called** two of his servants and a devout soldier who was one of his attendants.
112	Shouted	**Act 10:18** - They **called** out, asking if Simon who was known as Peter was staying there.

113	Summoned	**Act 10:24** - The following day he arrived in Caesarea. Cornelius was expecting them and had **called** together his relatives and close friends.
114	Named	**Act 10:32** - Send to Joppa for Simon who is **called** Peter. He is a guest in the home of Simon the tanner, who lives by the sea.'
115	Named	**Act 11:13** - He told us how he had seen an angel appear in his house and say, 'Send to Joppa for Simon who is **called** Peter.
116	Labeled	**Act 11:26** - and when he found him, he brought him to Antioch. So for a whole year Barnabas and Saul met with the church and taught great numbers of people. The disciples were **called** Christians first at Antioch.
117	Named	**Act 12:12** - When this had dawned on him, he went to the house of Mary the mother of John, also **called** Mark, where many people had gathered and were praying.
118	Named	**Act 12:25** - When Barnabas and Saul had finished their mission, they returned from Jerusalem, taking with them John, also **called** Mark.
119	Named	**Act 13:1** - Now in the church at Antioch there were prophets and teachers: Barnabas, Simeon **called** Niger, Lucius of Cyrene, Manaen (who had been brought up with Herod the tetrarch) and Saul.
120	***Called to Do A Task**	**Act 13:2** - While they were worshiping the Lord and fasting, the Holy Spirit said, "Set apart for me Barnabas and Saul for the work to which I have **called** them."

121	Named	**Act 13:9** - Then Saul, who was also **called** Paul, filled with the Holy Spirit, looked straight at Elymas and said,
122	Shouted	**Act 14:10** - and **called** out, "Stand up on your feet!" At that, the man jumped up and began to walk.
123	Named	**Act 14:12** - Barnabas they called Zeus, and Paul they **called** Hermes because he was the chief speaker.
124	Named	**Act 15:22** - Then the apostles and elders, with the whole church, decided to choose some of their own men and send them to Antioch with Paul and Barnabas. They chose Judas (**called** Barsabbas) and Silas, men who were leaders among the believers.
125	Named	**Act 15:37** - Barnabas wanted to take John, also **called** Mark, with them,
126	***Called to Do A Task**	**Act 16:10** - After Paul had seen the vision, we got ready at once to leave for Macedonia, concluding that God had **called** us to preach the gospel to them.
127	Shouted	**Act 16:29** - The jailer **called** for lights, rushed in and fell trembling before Paul and Silas.
128	Named	**Act 17:7** - and Jason has welcomed them into his house. They are all defying Caesar's decrees, saying that there is another king, one **called** Jesus."
129	Summoned	**Act 19:25** - He **called** them together, along with the workers in related trades, and said: "You know, my friends, that we receive a good income from this business.
130	Shouted	**Act 23:6** - Then Paul, knowing that some of them were Sadducees and the others Pharisees, **called** out in the Sanhedrin, "My brothers, I am a Pharisee,

		descended from Pharisees. I stand on trial because of the hope of the resurrection of the dead."
131	Spoke	**Act 23:17** - Then Paul **called** one of the centurions and said, "Take this young man to the commander; he has something to tell him."
132	Named	**Act 23:23** - Then he **called** two of his centurions and ordered them, "Get ready a detachment of two hundred soldiers, seventy horsemen and two hundred spearmen to go to Caesarea at nine tonight.
133	Summoned	**Act 24:2** - When Paul was **called** in, Tertullus presented his case before Felix: "We have enjoyed a long period of peace under you, and your foresight has brought about reforms in this nation.
134	Named	**Act 27:8** - We moved along the coast with difficulty and came to a place **called** Fair Havens, near the town of Lasea.
135	Named	**Act 27:14** - Before very long, a wind of hurricane force, **called** the Northeaster, swept down from the island.
136	Named	**Act 27:16** - As we passed to the lee of a small island **called** Cauda, we were hardly able to make the lifeboat secure,
137	Named	**Act 28:1** - Once safely on shore, we found out that the island was **called** Malta.
138	Summoned	**Act 28:17** - Three days later he **called** together the local Jewish leaders. When they had assembled, Paul said to them: "My brothers, although I have done nothing against our people or against the customs of our ancestors, I was arrested in Jerusalem and handed over to the Romans.

139	*Called to Do A Task	Rom 1:1 - Paul, a servant of Christ Jesus, **called** to be an apostle and set apart for the gospel of God—
140	Summoned	Rom 1:6 - And you also are among those Gentiles who are **called** to belong to Jesus Christ.
141	Summoned	Rom 1:7 - To all in Rome who are loved by God and **called** to be his holy people: Grace and peace to you from God our Father and from the Lord Jesus Christ.
142	Labeled	Rom 7:3 - So then, if she has sexual relations with another man while her husband is still alive, she is **called** an adulteress. But if her husband dies, she is released from that law and is not an adulteress if she marries another man.
143	Summoned	Rom 8:28 - And we know that in all things God works for the good of those who love him, who have been **called** according to his purpose.
144	Summoned	Rom 8:30 - And those he predestined, he also **called**; those he **called**, he also justified; those he justified, he also glorified.
145	Summoned	Rom 9:24 - even us, whom he also **called**, not only from the Jews but also from the Gentiles?
146	Labeled	Rom 9:26 - and, "In the very place where it was said to them, 'You are not my people,' there they will be **called** 'children of the living God.' "
147	*Called to Do A Task	1Co 1:1 - Paul, **called** to be an apostle of Christ Jesus by the will of God, and our brother Sosthenes,
148	Summoned	1Co 1:2 - To the church of God in Corinth, to those sanctified in Christ Jesus and **called** to be his holy people, together with all those everywhere who call on the name of our Lord Jesus Christ--their Lord and ours:

149	Summoned	**1Co 1:9** - God is faithful, who has **called** you into fellowship with his Son, Jesus Christ our Lord.
150	Summoned	**1Co 1:24** - but to those whom God has **called**, both Jews and Greeks, Christ the power of God and the wisdom of God.
151	Summoned	**1Co 1:26** - Brothers and sisters, think of what you were when you were **called**. Not many of you were wise by human standards; not many were influential; not many were of noble birth.
152	Summoned	**1Co 7:15** - But if the unbeliever leaves, let it be so. The brother or the sister is not bound in such circumstances; God has **called** us to live in peace.
153	Summoned	**1Co 7:17** - Nevertheless, each person should live as a believer in whatever situation the Lord has assigned to them, just as God has **called** them. This is the rule I lay down in all the churches.
154	Summoned	**1Co 7:18** - Was a man already circumcised when he was **called**? He should not become uncircumcised. Was a man uncircumcised when he was called? He should not be circumcised.
155	Summoned	**1Co 7:20** - Each person should remain in the situation they were in when God **called** them.
156	Summoned	**1Co 7:21** - Were you a slave when you were **called**? Don't let it trouble you--although if you can gain your freedom, do so.
157	Summoned	**1Co 7:22** - For the one who was a slave when **called** to faith in the Lord is the Lord's freed person; similarly, the one who was free when **called** is Christ's slave.

158	Summoned	**1Co 7:24** - Brothers and sisters, each person, as responsible to God, should remain in the situation they were in when God **called** them.
159	Labeled	**1Co 8:5** - For even if there are so-**called** gods, whether in heaven or on earth (as indeed there are many "gods" and many "lords"),
160	Labeled	**1Co 15:9** - For I am the least of the apostles and do not even deserve to be **called** an apostle, because I persecuted the church of God.
161	Summoned	**Gal 1:6** - I am astonished that you are so quickly deserting the one who **called** you to live in the grace of Christ and are turning to a different gospel--
162	Summoned	**Gal 1:15** - But when God, who set me apart from my mother's womb and **called** me by his grace, was pleased
163	Summoned	**Gal 5:13** - You, my brothers and sisters, were **called** to be free. But do not use your freedom to indulge the flesh; rather, serve one another humbly in love.
164	Summoned	**Eph 1:18** - I pray that the eyes of your heart may be enlightened in order that you may know the hope to which he has **called** you, the riches of his glorious inheritance in his holy people,
165	Labeled	**Eph 2:11**- Therefore, remember that formerly you who are Gentiles by birth and **called** "uncircumcised" by those who call themselves "the circumcision" (which is done in the body by human hands)--
166	Summoned	**Eph 4:4** - There is one body and one Spirit, just as you were called to one hope when you were **called**;

167	Summoned	**Phl 3:14** - I press on toward the goal to win the prize for which God has **called** me heavenward in Christ Jesus.
168	Summoned	**Col 3:15** - Let the peace of Christ rule in your hearts, since as members of one body you were **called** to peace. And be thankful.
169	Named	**Col 4:11** - Jesus, who is **called** Justus, also sends greetings. These are the only Jews among my co-workers for the kingdom of God, and they have proved a comfort to me.
170	Labeled	**2Th 2:4** - He will oppose and will exalt himself over everything that is **called** God or is worshiped, so that he sets himself up in God's temple, proclaiming himself to be God.
171	Summoned	**2Th 2:14** - He **called** you to this through our gospel, that you might share in the glory of our Lord Jesus Christ.
172	Summoned	**1Ti 6:12** - Fight the good fight of the faith. Take hold of the eternal life to which you were **called** when you made your good confession in the presence of many witnesses.
173	Labeled	**1Ti 6:20** - Timothy, guard what has been entrusted to your care. Turn away from godless chatter and the opposing ideas of what is falsely **called** knowledge,
174	Summoned	**2Ti 1:9** - He has saved us and **called** us to a holy life--not because of anything we have done but because of his own purpose and grace. This grace was given us in Christ Jesus before the beginning of time,
175	Labeled	**Heb 3:13** - But encourage one another daily, as long as it is **called** "Today," so that none of you may be hardened by sin's deceitfulness.

176	Summoned	**Heb 5:4** - And no one takes this honor on himself, but he receives it when **called** by God, just as Aaron was.
177	Labeled	**Heb 9:2** - A tabernacle was set up. In its first room were the lampstand and the table with its consecrated bread; this was **called** the Holy Place.
178	Labeled	**Heb 9:3** - Behind the second curtain was a room **called** the Most Holy Place,
179	Summoned	**Heb 9:15** - For this reason Christ is the mediator of a new covenant, that those who are **called** may receive the promised eternal inheritance--now that he has died as a ransom to set them free from the sins committed under the first covenant.
180	Summoned	**Heb 11:8** - By faith Abraham, when **called** to go to a place he would later receive as his inheritance, obeyed and went, even though he did not know where he was going.
181	Labeled	**Heb 11:16** - Instead, they were longing for a better country--a heavenly one. Therefore God is not ashamed to be **called** their God, for he has prepared a city for them.
182	Labeled	**Jas 2:23** - And the scripture was fulfilled that says, "Abraham believed God, and it was credited to him as righteousness," and he was **called** God's friend.
183	Summoned	**1Pe 1:15** - But just as he who **called** you is holy, so be holy in all you do;
184	Summoned	**1Pe 2:9** - But you are a chosen people, a royal priesthood, a holy nation, God's special possession, that you may declare the praises of him who **called** you out of darkness into his wonderful light.

185	Summoned	**1Pe 2:21** - To this you were **called**, because Christ suffered for you, leaving you an example, that you should follow in his steps.
186	Labeled	**1Pe 3:6** - like Sarah, who obeyed Abraham and **called** him her lord. You are her daughters if you do what is right and do not give way to fear.
187	Summoned	**1Pe 3:9** - Do not repay evil with evil or insult with insult. On the contrary, repay evil with blessing, because to this you were **called** so that you may inherit a blessing.
188	Summoned	**1Pe 5:10** - And the God of all grace, who **called** you to his eternal glory in Christ, after you have suffered a little while, will himself restore you and make you strong, firm and steadfast.
189	Summoned	**2Pe 1:3** - His divine power has given us everything we need for a godly life through our knowledge of him who **called** us by his own glory and goodness.
190	Labeled	**1Jo 3:1** - See what great love the Father has lavished on us, that we should be **called** children of God! And that is what we are! The reason the world does not know us is that it did not know him.
191	Summoned	**Jde 1:1** - Jude, a servant of Jesus Christ and a brother of James, To those who have been **called**, who are loved in God the Father and kept for Jesus Christ:
192	Labeled	**Rev 2:24** - Now I say to the rest of you in Thyatira, to you who do not hold to her teaching and have not learned Satan's so-**called** deep secrets, 'I will not impose any other burden on you,

193	Shouted	**Rev 6:10** - They **called** out in a loud voice, "How long, Sovereign Lord, holy and true, until you judge the inhabitants of the earth and avenge our blood?"
194	Shouted	**Rev 6:16** - They **called** to the mountains and the rocks, "Fall on us and hide us from the face of him who sits on the throne and from the wrath of the Lamb!
195	Shouted	**Rev 7:2** - Then I saw another angel coming up from the east, having the seal of the living God. He **called** out in a loud voice to the four angels who had been given power to harm the land and the sea:
196	Named	**Rev 11:8** - Their bodies will lie in the public square of the great city--which is figuratively **called** Sodom and Egypt--where also their Lord was crucified.
197	Named	**Rev 12:9** - The great dragon was hurled down--that ancient serpent **called** the devil, or Satan, who leads the whole world astray. He was hurled to the earth, and his angels with him.
198	Shouted	**Rev 14:15** - Then another angel came out of the temple and **called** in a loud voice to him who was sitting on the cloud, "Take your sickle and reap, because the time to reap has come, for the harvest of the earth is ripe."
199	Shouted	**Rev 14:18** - Still another angel, who had charge of the fire, came from the altar and **called** in a loud voice to him who had the sharp sickle, "Take your sharp sickle and gather the clusters of grapes from the earth's vine, because its grapes are ripe."
200	Named	**Rev 16:16** - Then they gathered the kings together to the place that in Hebrew is **called** Armageddon.

| 201 | Labeled | **Rev 17:14** - They will wage war against the Lamb, but the Lamb will triumph over them because he is Lord of lords and King of kings--and with him will be his **called**, chosen and faithful followers." |
| 202 | Labeled | **Rev 19:11** - I saw heaven standing open and there before me was a white horse, whose rider is **called** Faithful and True. With justice he judges and wages war. |

* Four verses where "called" was used to call to do a task.

Notes

"NIV Search Results for "called"." Blue Letter Bible.
Accessed 27 Oct, 2015
http://www.blueletterbible.orghttps://www.blueletterbible.org/search/search.cfm

Appendix H: Russell's Letter

(Note: Russell was a successful engineer and longtime employee of South Central Bell and ATT. He died in 2011.)

December 1, 2009

Jim,

Thanks for the follow up on our conversation. I am excited about the name "Work Faith" instead of "Work Place Ministry." "Work Faith" appears to me a goal, which I would very much like to achieve.

I believe anything brought to the workplace should be work-related. Living God's Word on the job is to be totally job and not church or religion. Is it not written, "True religion is to visit the widows and keep unspotted from the world?" Which has nothing to do with most jobs.

Jesus paid a great price to live God's Word. I know to live God's Word a Christian must also pay a price continuously according to the level of knowledge and commitment exercised. The cost is flesh control, which involves self-denial. A Christian must ignore his or her desires and thoughts, and submit to the direction of God's Word.

One major area I had to deal with this is humility. A few years ago, I was presented an opportune situation to live humbly on the job. I was involved in a project to move some 50,000 working telephone lines from an old switch machine to a new one minimizing service outage to only a few minutes. Part of the plans consisted of removing a few hundred software configurations and replacing new ones in one of the supporting switch equipment units. It would take several people several hours to remove and re-type these software changes one at a time, so I pre-typed the commands for all the numbers in a batch file that could process all changes in a couple of minutes and be initiated remotely from my desk.

My manager asked me and a colleague to go to the equipment located in the central office two blocks away and learn how to manually initiate the batch file directly at the equipment in case the remote attempt failed. There were about seven or eight technicians in the central office that I worked with daily. I had a good working relationship with all but one, David, who made it known he did not like me. We were graciously met at the guard station by one of the technicians and taken to the li8ocation of the equipment we were looking for. While this technician explained the access I would need to the equipment, David walked up to me and informed me that I was not supposed to be in this central office and he would have to escort me out of the building.

My first reaction on the inside of me was to find his manager, put this person in his place, and continue my job as planned. My second reaction involved thoughts and words of response not necessary to explain. My third reaction came from my spirit inside and, thank God, I responded to this reaction only. From inside there was a very soft and gentle urge to say, "We have just finished. That will be fine". David escorted us past the guards and held the door open for us to leave. During the walk back to my office, my colleague said David was extremely ugly and rude. I said, "I have seen ugly and rude and David was not." He was just doing what he felt he should do. After arriving at my office, the phone was ringing. One of the technicians from the central office was calling to say that not everyone in the office shared David's way of handling the situation. David's manager called my manager and me to apologize. This may sound like it is an easy thing to be spirit-led on the job; however, I can assure any Christian it's not easy or simple and cannot be achieved spontaneously.

Another major way I have to deal with myself is in the area of pride. Over the years, God has literally blessed everything I have been associated with at work. People are always complimenting me on a good job. I have to constantly fight pride because I know it is not because I am smart or knowledgeable, but because God has chosen to bless the work of my hands. I have actually responded at times, "God just bails me out every day." Again, this sounds easy, but not so.

I cannot believe you're still reading my rambling. I know God will bless your efforts to lead and assist Christians to live God's Word on the job through "Work Faith" I would like to hear how it progresses.

Russell

Appendix I: Apocrypha Books and the Christian Bible in Which They Appear

Name of Book	Roman Cath	Greek Orth	Russ Orth	Latin Vulg Apend	Greek Apend	Protest Anglican Apoc
Tobit	*	*	*			*
Judith	*	*	*			*
Additions to Esther	*	*	*			*
Wisdom of Solomon	*	*	*			*
Ecclesiasticu (Sirach)	*	*	*			*
Baruch	*	*	*			*
Letter of Jeremiah	*	*	*			*
Additions to Daniel	*	*	*			*
1 Maccabees	*	*	*			*
2 Maccabees	*	*	*			*
1Esdras		*	*	*		*
Prayer of Manasseh		*	*	*		*
Psalm 151		*	*			

Name of Book	Rom Cath	Greek Orth	Russ Orth	Vulg Apend	Greek Apend
3 Maccabees		*	*		
2 Esdras			*	*	
4 Maccabees					*

Appendix J: Parallel Passages in New Testament Quoted from Old Testament

http://www.blueletterbible.org/study/misc/quotes01.cfm
Accessed on 6/2/15

1	Mat 1:23	Isa 7:14
2	Mat 2:6	Mic 5:2
3	Mat 2:15	Hsa 11:1
4	Mat 2:18	Jer 31:15
5	Mat 3:3	Isa 40:3
6	Mat 4:4	Deu 8:3
7	Mat 4:6	Psa 91:11, 12
8	Mat 4:7	Deu 6:16
9	Mat 4:10	Deu 6:13
10	Mat 4:10	Deu 10:20
11	Mat 4:15, 16	Isa 9:1, 2
12	Mat 4:15, 16	Isa 42:7
13	Mat 5:21	Deu 5:17
14	Mat 5:27	Deu 5:18
15	Mat 5:38	Deu 19:21
16	Mat 5:48	Gen 17:1
17	Mat 7:23	Psa 6:8
18	Mat 8:17	Isa 53:4
19	Mat 9:13	Hsa 6:6
20	Mat 11:10	Mal 3:1
21	Mat 12:7	Hsa 6:6
22	Mat 12:18	Isa 42:1
23	Mat 12:18-21	Isa 42:1-4
24	Mat 13:14	Isa 6:9, 10
25	Mat 13:35	Psa 78:2
26	Mat 15:4	Exd 20:12
27	Mat 15:4	Deu 5:16
28	Mat 15:4	Exd 21:17
29	Mat 15:8, 9	Isa 29:13
30	Mat 19:5	Gen 2:24

31	Mat 19:18	Exd 20:12 &c
32	Mat 19:19	Lev 19:18
33	Mat 21:5	Zec 9:9
34	Mat 21:9	Psa 118:26
35	Mat 21:13	Isa 56:7
36	Mat 21:13	Jer 7:11
37	Mat 21:16	Psa 8:2
38	Mat 21:42	Psa 118:22, 23
39	Mat 22:24	Deu 25:5
40	Mat 22:32	Exd 3:6
41	Mat 22:37	Deu 6:5
42	Mat 22:39	Lev 19:18
43	Mat 22:44	Psa 110:1
44	Mat 24:21	Jer 30:7
45	Mat 25:41	Psa 6:8
46	Mat 26:31	Zec 13:7
47	Mat 27:9, 10	Zec 11:13
48	Mat 27:35	Psa 22:18
49	Mat 27:46	Psa 22:1
50	Mar 1:2, 3	Mal 3:1
51	Mar 1:2, 3	Isa 40:3
52	Mar 4:12	Isa 6:9
53	Mar 7:6, 7	Isa 29:13
54	Mar 7:10	Exd 20:12
55	Mar 7:10	Deu 5:16
56	Mar 7:10	Exd 21:17
57	Mar 7:10	Pro 20:20
58	Mar 10:6	Gen 1:27
59	Mar 10:7	Gen 2:24
60	Mar 10:19	Exd 20:12, 13, 14
61	Mar 11:9	Psa 118:26
62	Mar 11:17	Isa 56:7
63	Mar 11:17	Jer 7:11
64	Mar 12:10, 11	Psa 118:22, 23
65	Mar 12:19	Deu 25:5

66	Mar 12:26	Exd 3:6
67	Mar 12:29, 30	Deu 6:4, 5
68	Mar 12:31	Lev 19:18
69	Mar 12:36	Psa 110:1
70	Mar 14:27	Zec 13:7
71	Mar 15:28	Isa 53:12
72	Mar 15:34	Psa 22:1
73	Luk 1:17	Mal 4:5, 6
74	Luk 2:23	Exd 13:2
75	Luk 2:24	Lev 12:8
76	Luk 3:4, 5, 6	Isa 40:3, 4, 5
77	Luk 4:4	Deu 8:3
78	Luk 4:8	Deu 6:13
79	Luk 4:8	Deu 10:20
80	Luk 4:10, 11	Psa 91:11, 12
81	Luk 4:12	Deu 6:16
82	Luk 4:18, 19	Isa 61:1, 2
83	Luk 7:27	Mal 3:1
84	Luk 8:10	Isa 6:9
85	Luk 10:27	Deu 6:5
86	Luk 10:27	Lev 19:18
87	Luk 13:27	Psa 6:8
88	Luk 18:20	Exd 20:12
89	Luk 18:20	Deu 5:17, 18 &c
90	Luk 19:46	Isa 56:7
91	Luk 19:46	Jer 7:11
92	Luk 20:17	Psa 118:22, 23
93	Luk 20:28	Deu 25:5
94	Luk 20:42, 43	Psa 110:1
95	Luk 22:37	Isa 53:12
96	Luk 23:46	Psa 31:5
97	Jhn 1:23	Isa 40:3
98	Jhn 2:17	Psa 69:9
99	Jhn 6:31	Psa 78:24
100	Jhn 6:45	Isa 54:13

101	Jhn 8:17	Deu 19:15
102	Jhn 9:31	Psa 82:6
103	Jhn 12:14, 15	Zec 9:9
104	Jhn 12:38	Isa 53:1
105	Jhn 12:40	Isa 6:9
106	Jhn 13:18	Psa 41:9
107	Jhn 15:25	Psa 69:4
108	Jhn 15:25	Psa 109:3
109	Jhn 15:25	Psa 35:19
110	Jhn 19:24	Psa 22:19
111	Jhn 19:36	Exd 12:46
112	Jhn 19:36	Psa 34:20
113	Jhn 19:37	Zec 12:10
114	Act 1:20	Psa 69:25
115	Act 1:20	Psa 109:8
116	Act 2:17-21	Joe 2:28-32
117	Act 2:25-28	Psa 16:8-10
118	Act 2:31	Psa 16:10
119	Act 2:34	Psa 110:1
120	Act 3:22, 23	Deu 18:15, 18, 19
121	Act 3:25	Gen 22:18
122	Act 4:11	Psa 118:22, 23
123	Act 4:25, 26	Psa 2:1, 2
124	Act 7:3	Gen 12:1
125	Act 7:6, 7	Gen 15:13, 14
126	Act 7:26	Exd 2:13, 14
127	Act 7:32	Exd 3:6
128	Act 7:33, 34	Exd 3:5, 7, 8, 10
129	Act 7:35	Exd 2:14
130	Act 7:37	Deu 18:15
131	Act 7:40	Exd 32:1
132	Act 7:49, 50	Isa 66:1, 2
133	Act 8:32, 33	Isa 53:7, 8
134	Act 13:22	1Sa 13:14
135	Act 13:22	Psa 89:20

136	Act 13:33	Psa 2:7
137	Act 13:34	Psa 55:3
138	Act 13:35	Psa 16:10
139	Act 13:41	Hab 1:5
140	Act 13:47	Isa 49:6
141	Act 23:5	Exd 22:28
142	Act 28:26, 27	Isa 6:9, 10
143	Rom 1:17	Hab 2:4
144	Rom 2:24	Isa 52:5
145	Rom 2:24	Eze 36:20
146	Rom 3:4	Psa 116:11
147	Rom 3:4	Psa 51:4
148	Rom 3:10, 11, 12	Psa 14:1 &c
149	Rom 3:13	Psa 5:9
150	Rom 3:13	Psa 140:3
151	Rom 3:14	Psa 10:7
152	Rom 3:15-18	Isa 59:7, 8
153	Rom 3:18	Psa 36:1
154	Rom 4:3	Gen 15:6
155	Rom 4:7, 8	Psa 32:1, 2
156	Rom 4:11	Gen 17:10
157	Rom 4:17	Gen 17:5
158	Rom 4:18	Gen 15:5
159	Rom 7:7	Exd 20:17
160	Rom 7:7	Deu 5:21
161	Rom 8:36	Psa 44:22
162	Rom 9:7	Gen 21:12
163	Rom 9:9	Gen 18:10
164	Rom 9:12	Gen 25:23
165	Rom 9:13	Mal 1:2, 3
166	Rom 9:15	Exd 33:19
167	Rom 9:17	Exd 9:16
168	Rom 9:25	Hsa 2:23
169	Rom 9:26	Hsa 1:10
170	Rom 9:27, 28	Isa 10:22, 23

171	Rom 9:29	Isa 1:9
172	Rom 9:33	Isa 8:14
173	Rom 9:33	Isa 28:16
174	Rom 10:5	Lev 18:5
175	Rom 10:5	Eze 20:11
176	Rom 10:8	Deu 30:14
177	Rom 10:11	Isa 28:16
178	Rom 10:13	Joe 2:32
179	Rom 10:15	Isa 52:7
180	Rom 10:15	Nah 1:15
181	Rom 10:16	Isa 53:1
182	Rom 10:18	Psa 19:4
183	Rom 10:19	Deu 32:21
184	Rom 10:20, 21	Isa 65:1, 2
185	Rom 11:3	1Ki 19:10, 14
186	Rom 11:4	1Ki 19:18
187	Rom 11:8	Isa 29:10
188	Rom 11:9, 10	Psa 69:22, 23
189	Rom 11:26, 27	Isa 59:20, 21
190	Rom 11:34	Isa 40:13
191	Rom 12:16	Pro 3:7
192	Rom 12:19	Deu 32:35
193	Rom 12:20	Pro 25:21, 22
194	Rom 13:9	Exd 20:13, 17
195	Rom 13:9	Deu 5:16-21
196	Rom 13:9	Lev 19:18
197	Rom 14:11	Isa 45:23
198	Rom 15:3	Psa 69:9
199	Rom 15:9	Psa 18:49
200	Rom 15:10	Deu 32:43
201	Rom 15:11	Psa 117:1
202	Rom 15:12	Isa 11:1, 10
203	Rom 15:21	Isa 52:15
204	1Cr 1:19	Isa 29:14
205	1Cr 1:31	Jer 9:24

206	1Cr 2:9	Isa 64:4
207	1Cr 2:16	Isa 40:13
208	1Cr 3:19	Job 5:13
209	1Cr 3:20	Psa 94:11
210	1Cr 6:16	Gen 2:24
211	1Cr 9:9	Deu 25:4
212	1Cr 10:7	Exd 32:6
213	1Cr 10:20	Deu 32:17
214	1Cr 10:26	Psa 24:1
215	1Cr 14:21	Isa 28:11, 12
216	1Cr 15:25	Psa 110:1
217	1Cr 15:27	Psa 8:6
218	1Cr 15:32	Isa 22:13
219	1Cr 15:45	Gen 2:7
220	1Cr 15:54	Isa 25:8
221	1Cr 15:55	Hsa 13:14
222	2Cr 4:13	Psa 116:10
223	2Cr 5:17	Isa 43:18, 19
224	2Cr 6:2	Isa 49:8
225	2Cr 6:16	Lev 26:11, 12
226	2Cr 6:17, 18	Isa 52:11, 12
227	2Cr 6:17, 18	Jer 31:9
228	2Cr 6:17, 18	2Sa 7:14
229	2Cr 8:15	Exd 16:18
230	2Cr 9:9	Psa 112:9
231	2Cr 10:17	Jer 9:24
232	2Cr 13:1	Deu 19:15
233	Gal 2:6	Deu 10:17
234	Gal 3:8	Gen 12:3
235	Gal 3:10	Deu 27:26
236	Gal 3:11	Hab 2:4
237	Gal 3:12	Lev 18:5
238	Gal 3:13	Deu 21:23
239	Gal 3:16	Gen 22:18
240	Gal 4:27	Isa 54:1

241	Gal 4:30	Gen 21:10
242	Gal 5:14	Lev 19:18
243	Eph 4:8	Psa 68:18
244	Eph 4:25	Zec 8:16
245	Eph 4:26	Psa 4:4
246	Eph 5:31	Gen 2:24
247	Eph 6:2, 3	Exd 20:12
248	Eph 6:2, 3	Deu 5:16
249	1Ti 5:18	Deu 25:4
250	Hbr 1:5	Psa 2:7
251	Hbr 1:5	2Sa 7:14
252	Hbr 1:6	Psa 97:7
253	Hbr 1:7	Psa 104:4
254	Hbr 1:8, 9	Psa 45:6, 7
255	Hbr 1:10, 11, 12	Psa 102:25, 26, 27
256	Hbr 1:13	Psa 110:1
257	Hbr 2:6-8	Psa 8:4-6
258	Hbr 2:12	Psa 22:22
259	Hbr 2:13	Isa 8:18
260	Hbr 2:13	Psa 18:2
261	Hbr 2:13	2Sa 22:2
262	Hbr 3:7-11	Psa 95:7-11
263	Hbr 3:15	Psa 95:7-11
264	Hbr 4:3	Psa 95:11
265	Hbr 4:4	Gen 2:2, 3
266	Hbr 4:7	Psa 95:7, 8
267	Hbr 5:5	Psa 2:7
268	Hbr 5:6	Psa 110:4
269	Hbr 6:14	Gen 22:16, 17
270	Hbr 7:17, 21	Psa 110:4
271	Hbr 8:5	Exd 25:40
272	Hbr 8:8-12	Jer 31:31-34
273	Hbr 9:20	Exd 24:8
274	Hbr 10:5-7	Psa 40:6-8
275	Hbr 10:16, 17	Jer 31:33, 34

276	Hbr 10:30	Deu 32:35, 36
277	Hbr 10:37, 38	Hab 2:3, 4
278	Hbr 11:21	Gen 47:31
279	Hbr 12:5, 6	Pro 3:11, 12
280	Hbr 12:20	Exd 19:12, 13
281	Hbr 12:21	Deu 9:19
282	Hbr 12:26	Hag 2:6
283	Hbr 12:29	Deu 4:24
284	Hbr 13:5	Deu 31:8
285	Hbr 13:5	Jos 1:5
286	Hbr 13:6	Psa 118:6
287	Jam 2:8	Lev 19:18
288	Jam 2:11	Exd 20:13, 14, 15
289	Jam 2:23	Gen 15:6
290	Jam 4:6	Pro 3:34
291	1Pe 1:16	Lev 11:44
292	1Pe 1:24, 25	Isa 40:6
293	1Pe 2:6	Isa 28:16
294	1Pe 2:7	Psa 118:22, 23
295	1Pe 2:9	Exd 19:6
296	1Pe 2:22	Isa 53:9
297	1Pe 2:24	Isa 53:4, 5
298	1Pe 3:10, 11, 12	Psa 34:12-16
299	1Pe 4:8	Pro 10:12
300	2Pe 2:22	Pro 26:11
301	Rev 7:16	Isa 49:10
302	Rev 7:17	Isa 25:8
303	Rev 15:4	Jer 10:6
304	Rev 15:4	Psa 86:9
305	Rev 18:2	Isa 21:9
306	Rev 18:3	Jer 51:7

Total direct quotes = 306

Appendix K: Messianic Prophecies of the Old Testament

	PROPHECY	O.T. REFERENCES	N.T. FULFILLMENT
1	Seed of the woman	Gen. 3:15	Gal. 4:4; Heb 3:14
2	Through Noah's sons	Gen. 9:27	Luke 6:36
3	Seed of Abraham	Gen. 12:3	Matt. 1:1; Gal. 3:8,16
4	Seed of Isaac	Gen. 17:19	Rom. 9:7; Heb. 11:18
5	Blessing to nations	Gen. 18:18	Gal. 3:8
6	Seed of Isaac	Gen. 21:12	Rom. 9:7; Heb. 11:18
7	Blessing to Gentiles	Gen. 22:18	Gal. 3:8,16; Heb. 6:14
8	Blessing to Gentiles	Gen. 26:4	Gal. 3:8,16; Heb. 6:14
9	Bless through Araham	Gen. 28:14	Gal. 3.8,16; Heb. 6:14
10	Of the Tribe of Judah	Gen. 49:10	Rev. 5:5
11	No bone broken	Ex. 12:46	John 19:36
12	Bless to firstborn son	Ex. 13:2	Luke 2:23
13	No bone broken	Num. 9:12	John 19:36
14	Serpent in wilderness	Num. 21:8-9	John 3:14-15
15	A star out of Jacob	Num. 24:17-19	Matt. 2:2; Luke 1:33,78
16	As a prophet	Deut. 18:15,18-19	John 6:14; 7:40
17	Cursed on the tree	Deut. 21:23	Gal. 3:13
18	The throne of David established forever	2 Sam. 7:12-13, 16,25-26 1 Chron. 17:11-14, 23-27 2 Chron 21:7	Matt. 19:28; 21:4; 25:31; Mark 12:37; Luke 1:32 Acts 2:30; 13:23; Rom 1:3; 2 Tim. 2:8; Heb. 1:5-8;
19	A promised Redeemer	Job 19:25-27	John 5:28-29; Gal. 4:4;
20	Declared Son of God	Ps. 2:1-12	Matt. 3:17; Mark 1:11; Heb. 1:5; 5:5; Rev. 2:26-27
21	His resurrection	Ps. 16:8-10	Acts 2:27; 13:35; 26:23
22	Hands and feet pierced	Ps. 22:1-31	Matt. 27:31,35-36

23	Mocked and insulted	Ps. 22:7-8	Matt. 27:39-43,45-49
24	Soldiers cast lots for coat	Ps. 22:18	Mark 15:20,24-25,34
			John 19:15-18,23-24,34
25	Accused by false witnesses	Ps. 27:12	Matt. 26:60-61
26	He commits his spirit	Ps. 31:5	Luke 23:46
27	No bones broken	Ps. 34:20	John 19:36
28	Accused by false witnesses	Ps. 35:11	Matt. 26:59-61; Mark 14:57
29	Hated without reason	Ps. 35:19	John 15:24-25
30	Friends stand afar off	Ps. 38:11	Matt.27:55; Mark 15:40 23:49
31	"I come to do Thy will"	Ps. 40:6-8	Heb. 10:5-9
32	Betrayed by a friend	Ps. 41:9	Matt. 26:14-16,47,50
			Luke 22:19-23; John 13:18-19
33	Known for righteousness	Ps. 45:2,6-7	Heb. 1:8-9
34	His resurection	Ps. 49:15	Mark 16:6
35	Betrayed by a friend	Ps. 55:12-14	John 13:18
36	His ascension	Ps. 68:18	Eph. 4:8
37	Hated without reason	Ps. 69:4	John 15:25
38	Stung by repoaches	Ps. 69:9	John 2:17; Rom. 15:3
39	Given gall and vinegar	Ps. 69:21	Matt.27:34,48; Mark 15:23;
			John 19:29
40	Exalted by God	Ps. 72:1-19	Matt. 2:2; Phil. 2:9-11
41	He speaks in parables	Ps. 78:2	Matt. 13:34-53
42	Seed of David exalted	Ps.9:3-4,19,27-29,	Luke 1:32; Acts 2:30; 13:23
		35-37	2 Tim 2:8
43	Son of Man comes in glory	Ps. 102:16	Luke 21:24,27; Rev. 12:5-10
44	"Thou Remainest"	Ps. 102:24-27	Heb. 1:10-12
45	Prays for his enemies	Ps. 109:4	Luke 23:34
46	Another to succeed Judas	Ps. 109:7-8	Acts 1:16-20
47	A priest like Melchizedek	Ps. 110:1-7	Matt. 22:41-45; 26:64
			16:19; Acts 7:56; Eph. 1:20
			Heb. 1:13; 2:8; 5:6; 6:20
			10:11-13; 12:2
48	The chief corner stone	Ps. 118:22-23	Matt. 21:42; Mark 12:10-11
			John 1:11; Acts 4:11

49	The King comes in the name of the Lord	Ps. 118:26	Matt. 21:9; 23:39; Mark 11:19 19:38; John 12:13
50	David's seek to reigh	Ps. 132:11, 2 Sam. 7:12-13, 16,25-26,29	Matt. 1:1
51	Declared Son of God	Prov. 30:4	Matt. 3:17; Mark 14:61-62 John 3:13; 9:35-38; 11:21 10:6-9; 2 Pet. 1:17
52	Isa. 2:2-4	Luke 24:47	
53	Harts are hardened	Isa. 6:9-10	Matt. 13:14,15; John 12:39
54	Born of a virgin	Isa. 7:14*	Matt. 1:22,23
55	A rock of offense	Isa. 8:14,15	Rom. 9:33; I Pet. 2:8
56	Light out of darkness	Isa. 9:1,2	Matt. 4:14-16; Luke 2:23
57	God with us	Isa. 9:6,7	Matt. 1:21,23; Luke 1:32,33 10:30; 14:19; 2 Cor. 5:19
58	Full of wisdom and power	Isa. 40:3-5	Matt. 3:16; John 3:34
59	Reigning in mercy	Isa. 16:4-5	Luke 1:31-33
60	Peg in a sure place	Isa. 22:21-25	Rev. 3:7
61	Death swallowed victory	Isa. 25:6-12	I Cor: 15:54
62	A stone in Zion	Isa. 28:16	Rom. 9:33; I Pet. 2:6
63	The deaf hear, the blind see	Isa. 29:18-19	Matt. 5:3; 11:5; John 9:39
64	King of kings, Lord/ lords	Isa. 32:1-4	Rev. 19:16; 20:6
65	Son of the Highest	Isa. 33:22	Luke 1:32; I Tim. 1:17; 6:15
66	Healing for the needy	Isa. 35:4-10	Matt. 9:30; 11:5; 12:22 Mark 7:30; John 5:9
67	Make ready the way Lord	Isa. 40:3-5	Matt. 3:3; Mark 1:3
68	The Shepherd dies for sheep	Isa. 40:10-11	John 10:11; Heb. 13:20
69	The meek Servant	Isa. 42:1-16	Matt. 12:17-21; Luke 2:32
70	A light to the Gentiles	Isa. 49:6-12	Acts 13:47; 2 Cor. 6:2
71	Scourged and spat upon	Isa. 50:6	Matt. 26:67; 27:26,30 15:15,19; Luke 22:63-65
72	Rejected by his people	Isa. 52:13-53:12	Matt. 8:17; 27:1-2,12-14,38

73	Suffered vicariously	Isa. 53:4-5	Mark 15:3-4,27-28
74	Silent when accused	Isa. 53:7	John 1:29; 11:49-52
75	Crucified with transgressors	Isa. 53:12	John 12:37-38; Acts 8:28-35
76	Buried with the rich	Isa. 53.9	Acts 10:43; 13:38-39; I Pet. 2:21-25; I John 1:7,9
77	Calling of those not a people	Isa. 55:4,5	John 18:37;Rrom. 9:25-26
78	Deliver out of Zion	Isa. 59:16-20	Rom. 11:26-27
79	Nations walk in the light	Isa. 60:1-3	Luke 2:32
80	Anointed to preach liberty	Isa. 60:1-2	Luke 4:17-19; Acts 10:38
81	Called by a new name	Isa. 62:11	Luke 2:32; Rev. 3:12
82	The King cometh	Isa. 62:11	Matt. 21:5
83	A vesture dipped in blood	Isa. 63:1-3	Rev. 19:13
84	Afflicted with the afflicted	Isa. 63:8-9	Matt. 25:34-40
85	The elect shall inherit	Isa. 65:9	Rom. 11:5,7; Heb. 7:14
86	New heavens/a new earth	Isa. 65:17-25	2 Pet. 3:13; Rev. 21:1
87	The Lord our righteousness	Jer. 23:5,6	John 2:19-21; Rom. 1:3-4 I Pet. 2:5
88	Born a King	Jer. 30:9	John 18:37; Rev. 1:5
89	Massacre of infants	Jer. 31:15	Matt. 2:17-18
90	Conceived by Holy Spirit	Jer. 31:22	Matt. 1:20; Luke 1:35
91	A New Convenant	Jer. 31:31-34	Matt. 26:27-29; Mark 14:22 I Cor. 11:25; Heb. 8:8-12
92	A spiritual house	Jer. 33:15-17	John 2:19-21; Eph. 2:20-21
93	A tree planted by God	Ezek. 17:22-24	Matt. 13:31-32
94	The humble exalted	Ezek. 21: 26-27	Luke 1:52
95	The good Shepherd	Ezek. 34:23-24	John 10:11
96	Stone cut without hands	Dan. 2:34-35	Acts 4:10-12
97	His kingdom triumphant	Dan. 2:44-45	Luke 1:33; I Cor. 15:24
98	An everlasting dominion	Dan. 7:13-14	Matt. 24:30; 25:31; 26:64

99	Kindgom for the saints	Dan. 7:27	Luke 1:33; I Cor. 15:24
100	Time of His birth	Dan. 9:24-27	Matt. 24:15-21; Luke 3:1
101	Israel restored	Hos. 3:5	John 18:37; Rom. 11:25-27
102	Flight into Egypt	Hos. 11:1	Matt. 2:15
103	Promise of the Spirit	Joel 2:28-32	Acts 2:17-21; Rom. 15:13
104	The sun darkened	Amos 8:9	Matt. 24:29; Acts 2:20
105	Restoration of tabernacle	Amos 9:11-12	Acts 15:16-18
106	Israel regathered	Mic. 2:12-13	John 10:14,26
107	The Kingdom established	Mic. 4:1-8	Luke 1:33
108	Born in Bethleham	Mic. 5:1-5	Matt. 2:1; Luke 2:4,10-11
109	Earth filled with knowledge of		
	the glory of he Lord	Hab. 2:14	Rom. 11:26; Rev. 21:23-26
110	The Lamb on the throne	Zech. 2:10-13	Rev. 5:13; 6:9; 21:24
111	A holy priesthood	Zech. 3:8	John 2:19-21; Eph. 2:20-21
112	A heavenly High Priest	Zech. 6:12-13	Heb. 4:4; 8:1-2
113	Triumphal entry	Zech. 9:9-10	Matt. 21:4-5; Mark 11:9-10
			John 12:13-15
114	Sold for pieces of silver	Zech. 11:12-13	Matt. 26:14-15
115	Money buys potter's field	Zech. 11:12-13	Matt. 27:9
116	Piercing of his body	Zech. 12:10	John 19:34,37
117	Shepherd smitten-sheep scattered	Zech. 13:1,6-7	Matt. 26:31; John 16:32
118	Preceded by Forerunner	Mal. 3:1	Mat. 11:10; Mark 1:2
119	Our sins purged	Mal. 3:3	Heb 1:3
120	The light of the world	Mal. 4:2-3	Luke 1:78; John 1:9; 12:46
			Rev. 2:28; 19:11-16; 22:16
121	The coming of Elijah	Mal. 4:5-6	Matt. 11:14; 17:10-12

See discussion of Isaiah 7:14 in Chapter 3, "Bible Issues: Messiah"
Holman Illustrated Bible Dictionary, (Nashville, TN:
Holman Bible Publishers, 2003)
Pages 1112-14

Appendix L: The Books of the Hebrew Bible and the Christian Old Testament

HEBREW BIBLE	**OLD TESTAMENT**

TORAH
Genesis
Exodus
Leviticus
Numbers
Deuteronomy

NEVI'IM (PROPHETS)
FORMER PROPHETS
Joshua
Judges
Samuel (1 & 2)

Kings (1 & 2)

LATER PROPHETS
Isaiah
Jeremiah
Ezekiel
THE TWELVE
Hosea
Joel
Amos
Obadiah
Jonah
Micah
Nahum

PENTATEUCH
Genesis
Exodus
Leviticus
Numbers
Deuteronomy

HISTORIES
Joshua
Judges
Ruth
1 Samuel
2 Samuel
1 Kings
2 Kings
1 Chronicles
2 Chronicles
Ezra
Nehemiah
Esther

POLITICAL/WISDOM
BOOKS
Job
Psalms
Proverbs
Ecclesiastes
song of Solomon

Habakkuk
Zephaniah
Haggi
Zechariah
Malachi

KETUBIM (WRITINGS)
Psalms
Proverbs
Job
(Five Scrolls):
Song of Solomon
Ruth
Lamentations
Ecclesiastes
Esther
Daniel
Ezra-Nehemiah
Chronicles (1 & 2)

There is no
(Apocrypha) in the
Hebrew Bible

PROPHETS
Isaiah
Jeremiah
Lamentations
Ezekiel
Daniel
Hosea
Joel
Amos
Obadiah
Jonah
Micah
Nahum
Habakkuk
Zephaniah
Haggi
Zechariah
Malachi

THE APOCRYPHA
1 & 2 Esdras
Tobit
Judith
Esther (with additions)
Wisdom of Solomon
Ecclesiasticus (Sirach)
Baruch
Letter of Jeremiah
Prayer of Azariah and
    Song of Three
Daniel and Susanna
Daniel, Bel, & Snake
Prayer of Manasseh
1 & 2 Maccabees

Appendix M: The Land of the 12 Tribes of Israel

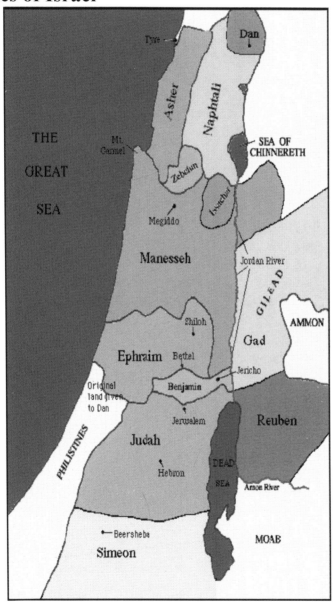

Appendix N: Doublets

1. Creation. Gen 1:1-2:3 (P) and Gen 2:4b-25 (J)
2. Genealogy from Adam. Gen 4:17-26 (J) and 5:1-28 30-32 (Book of Records).
3. The Flood. Gen 6:6:5-8; 7:1-5,7,10,12,16b-20,22-23; 8:2b-3a,6,8-12,13b,20-22 (J) and 6:9-22; 7:8-9,11,13-16a,21,24; 8:1-2a,3b-5,7,13a,14-19;9:1-17 (P).
4. Genealogy from Shem. Gen 10:21-31 (J and P) and 11:10-26 (Book of Records).
5. Abraham's migration. Gen 12:1-4a (J) and 12:4b-5 (P).
6. Wife/sister. Gen 12:10-20 (J) and 20:1-18 (E) and 26:6-14 (J). (Triplet).
7. Abraham and Lot separate. Gen 13:5,7-11a,12b-14 (J) and 13:6,11b-12a (P).
8. The Abrahamic covenant. Gen 15 (J, E, and R) and 17 (P).
9. Hagar and Ishmael. Gen 16:1-2.4-14 (J) and 16:3,15-16 (P) and 21:8-19 (E). (Triplet)
10. Prophecy of Isaac's birth. Gen 17:16-19 (P) and 18:10-14 (J).
11. Naming of Beer-sheba. Gen 21:22-31 (E) and 26:15-33 (J).
12. Jacob, Esau, and the departure to the east. Gen 26:34-35; 27:46; 28:1-9 (P) and 27:1-45; 28:10 (J).
13. Jacob at Beth-El. Gen 28:10,11a,13-16,19 (J) and 28:11b-12,17-18,20-22(E) and 35:9-15 (P). (Triplet)
14. Jacob's twelve sons. Gen 29:32-35; 30:1-24; 35:16-20 (JE) and Gen 35:23-26 (P).
15. Jacob's name changed to Israel. Gen 32:25-33 (E) and 35:9-10 (P).
16. Joseph sold into Egypt, Gen 37:2b, 3b,5-11,19-20,23,25b-27,28b,31-35; 39:1 (J) and 37:3a,4,12-18, 21-22,24,25a,28a,29-30 (E).
17. YHWH commissions Moses. Exod 3:2-4a,5,7-8,19-22; 4:19-20a (J) and 3:1,4b,6,9-18,20b-21a,22-23 (E) and 6:2-2 (P). (Triplet)
18. Moses, Pharaoh, and the plagues. Exod 5:3-6:1; 7:14-18,20b-21,23-29; 8:3b-11a,16-28; 9:1-7,13-34; 10:1-19,21-26,28-29;11:1-8 (E) and 7:6-13,19-20a,22; 8:1-3a,12-15; 9:8-12 (P).
19. The Passover, Exod 12:1-20,28,40-50 (P) and 12:21-27,29-36,37b-39 (E).

20. The Red Sea. Exod 13:21-22; 14:5a,6,9a,10b,13-14,19b,20b,21b,24,27b,30-31 (J) and 14:1-4,8,9b,10a,10c,15-18,21a,21c,22-23,26-27a,28-29 (P).
21. Manna and quail in the wilderness. Exod 16:2-3,6-35a (P) and Num 11:4-34 (E).
22. Water from a rock at Meribah. Exod 17:2-7 (E) and Num 20:2-13 (P).
23. Theophany at Sinai/Horeb. Exod 19:1; 24:15b-18a (P) and 19:2b-9,16b-17,19; 20:18-21 (E) and 19:10-16a,18,20-25 (j). (Triplet)
24. The Ten Commandments. Exod 20:1-17 (R) and 34;p10-28 (J) and Deut 5:6-18 (D). (Triplet)
25. Kid in mother's mild. Exod 23:19 (Covenant Code) and 34:26 (J) and Deut 14:21 (D). (Triplet)
26. Forbidden animals. Leviticus 11 (P) and Deuteronomy 14 (D).
27. Centralization of sacrifice. Leviticus 17 and Deuteronomy12.
28. Holidays. Leviticus 23 (P) and Numbers 28-29 (R) and Deut 16:1-17 (D). (Triplet)
29. The spies. Num 3:1-16,21,25-26,32; 14:1a,2-3,5-10,26-29 (P) and 13:17-20,22-24,27-31,33; 14:1b,4,11-25,39-45 (J).
30. Heresy at Peor. Num 25:1-5 (J) and 25:6-19 (P).
31. Appointment of Joshua. Num 27:12-23 (P) and Deut 31:14-15, 23 (E).

This list is from: Richard Elliott Friedman, *The Bible with Sources Revealed – A New View into the Five Books of Moses*, (New York: Harper Collins Publishers, 2003), Pages 28-30.

About The Author

Jim graduated from Samford University in Birmingham, Alabama, in 1962. He served as an Infantry Officer after graduating from Officer

Candidate School, Ranger School, and Airborne School. Jim served three years of active duty in the U.S. Army, including 13 months with the 2nd Infantry Division in South Korea. After leaving active duty, he joined the 20th Special Forces, Alabama National Guard. Jim received his Masters degree in Social Work from the University of Alabama (1970) as well as a Masters in Public Administration (1971). Three years in Athens, Georgia resulted in a Doctor of Public Administration (1974) from the University of Georgia. This was followed by four years of teaching social welfare administration at the University of Tennessee Graduate School of Social Work.

From 1978 to 2003, Jim worked in various administrative positions in the Florida Department of Health and Rehabilitative Services and the Florida Department of Health in Tallahassee. During his last seven years before retirement, he was the Administrative Officer for Emergency Operations for the Florida Department of Health. One of his primary responsibilities was to write the FEMA Grants for the Department of Health.

Jim married Linda Barron of Troy, Alabama, in 1968. A graduate of Auburn University with a Masters in Human Development from the University of Alabama, she spent most of her working career in early childhood education, and retired as an elementary school assistant principal in 2005. Jim and Linda are active in their home church, First Baptist Church of Tallahassee. Linda is a teacher in the English as a Second Language Ministry to Internationals. Jim and Linda have two adult children, Amy and John.

Amy is an Auburn graduate. Amy and her son Cole (11 in 2015) live in Auburn. Amy is an interior designer and has developed a successful internet business designing and selling personalized party supplies (http://amyspartyideas.com). She is also the Administrative Assistant to the Minister to Singles at Auburn United Methodist Church (2015).

John graduated from Auburn University in Electrical Engineering, the University of South Alabama Medical School and the University of Mississippi Emergency Medicine Residency Program. John served as a flight surgeon with the 185th Aviation Brigade, Balad, Iraq in 2004. John is the inventor of the Abdominal Aortic and Junctional Tourniquet (AAJT) (http://compressionworks.com), which was selected as one of the top ten inventions of the year by *Popular Science* magazine in June 2012 (http://www.popsci.com/technology/article/2013-06/amazing-tourniquet-invention-saves-two-lives). John is currently (2015) an ER Doctor at Princeton Baptist Medical Center in Birmingham. He and his wife Julie have two children, Caleb (16 in 2015) and Katie (14 in 2015).

Made in the USA
Columbia, SC
29 May 2017